Within These Walls

PRAEGER SERIES IN POLITICAL COMMUNICATION

Robert E. Denton, Jr., General Editor

Playing the Game: The Presidential Rhetoric of Ronald Reagan
Mary E. Stuckey

Rhetorical Studies of National Political Debates, 1960–1988
Edited by Robert V. Friedenberg

Political Communication in America, Second Edition
Robert E. Denton, Jr., and Gary C. Woodward

Television Access and Political Power: The Networks, The Presidency, and the "Loyal Opposition"
Joe S. Foote

Listening for a President: A Citizen's Campaign Methodology
Ruth M. Gonchar Brennan and Dan F. Hahn

Attack Politics: Strategy and Defense
Michael Pfau and Henry C. Kenski

Presidential Press Conferences: A Critical Approach
Carolyn Smith

Speak No Evil: The Promotional Heritage of Nuclear Risk Communication
Louis M. Gwin, Jr.

Enacting Political Culture: Rhetorical Transformations of Liberty Weekend 1986
David E. Procter

Within These Walls

A Study of Communication Between Presidents and Their Senior Staffs

Patricia Dennis Witherspoon

Praeger Series in Political Communication

PRAEGER

New York
Westport, Connecticut
London

Library of Congress Cataloging-in-Publication Data

Witherspoon, Patricia D. (Patricia Dennis)
Within these walls : a study of communication between presidents and their senior staffs / Patricia D. Witherspoon.
p. cm.—(Praeger series in political communication)
Includes bibliographical references
(p.) and index.
ISBN 0–275–93394–6 (alk. paper)
1. Presidents—United States—Staff. 2. Communication in politics—United States. I. Title. II. Series.
JK518.W58 1991
353.03'23—dc20 90–7568

British Library Cataloguing in Publication Data is available.

Library of Congress Catalog Card Number: 90–7568
ISBN: 0–275–93394–6

First published in 1991

Praeger Publishers, One Madison Avenue, New York, NY 10010
An imprint of Greenwood Publishing Group, Inc.

Printed in the United States of America

The paper used in this book complies with the Permanent Paper Standard issued by the National Information Standards Organization (Z39.48–1984).

10 9 8 7 6 5 4 3 2 1

Copyright Acknowledgments

For John, Terry and Andy:
Sine te nihil

Contents

Series Foreword

Those of us from the discipline of communication studies have long believed that communication is prior to all other fields of inquiry. In several other forums I have argued that the essence of politics is ''talk'' or human interaction.[1] Such interaction may be formal or informal, verbal or nonverbal, public or private, but always persuasive, forcing us consciously or subconsciously to interpret, to evaluate, and to act. Communication is the vehicle for human action.

From this perspective, it is not surprising that Aristotle recognized the natural kinship of politics and communication in his *Politics* and *Rhetoric*. In the former, he established that humans are ''political beings [who] alone of the animals [are] furnished with the faculty of language.''[2] And in the latter, he begins his systematic analysis of discourse by proclaiming that ''rhetorical study, in its strict sense, is concerned with the modes of persuasion.''[3] Thus, it was recognized over twenty-three hundred years ago that politics and communication go hand in hand because they are essential parts of human nature.

In 1981, Dan Nimmo and Keith Sanders proclaimed that political communication was an emerging field.[4] Although its origin dates back centuries, a ''self-consciously cross-disciplinary'' focus began in the late 1950s. Thousands of books and articles later, colleges and universities offer a variety of graduate and undergraduate courses in the area in such diverse departments as communication, mass communication, journalism, political science, and sociology.[5] In Nimmo and Sanders' early assessment, the ''key areas of inquiry'' included rhetorical analysis, propaganda analysis, attitude change studies, voting studies, government and the news media, functional and systems analyses, technological changes, media technologies, campaign techniques, and research techniques.[6] In a survey of the state of field in 1983 by the same authors and Lynda Kaid, they found additional, more specific areas of concern, such as the presidency, political polls, public opinion, debates, and advertising, to name a few.[7] Since the first study, they also noted a shift away from the rather strict behavioral approach.

In 1990, Dan Nimmo and David Swanson assert that "political communication has developed some identity as a more or less distinct domain of scholarly work."[8] The scope and concerns of the area have further expanded to include critical theories and cultural studies. While there is no precise definition, method, or disciplinary home of the area of inquiry, its primary domain is the role, processes, and effects of communication within the context of politics broadly defined.

In 1985, the editors of *Political Communication Yearbook: 1984* noted that "more things are happening in the study, teaching, and practice of political communication than can be captured within the space limitations of the relatively few publications available."[9] In addition, they argued that the backgrounds of "those involved in the field [are] so varied and pluralist in outlook and approach, . . . it [is] a mistake to adhere slavishly to any set format in shaping the content."[10] And more recently, Nimmo and Swanson have called for "ways of overcoming the unhappy consequences of fragmentation within a framework that respects, encourages, and benefits from diverse scholarly commitments, agendas, and approaches."[11]

In agreement with these assessments of the area and with gentle encouragement, Praeger established the series Praeger Studies in Political Communication. The series is open to all qualitative and quantitative methodologies as well as contemporary and historical studies. The key to characterizing the studies in the series is the focus on communication variables or activities within a political context or dimension.

Within These Walls: A Study of Communication Between Presidents and Their Senior Staffs is the first scholarly study of organizational communication behaviors of U.S. presidents. It demonstrates that a successful president needs to be a good communicator both within the White House and to the general public. The author effectively argues that a president "must understand that communication inside the White House is no less important than that which he directs to press and public." From this study we recognize the importance of a president's inner circle in influencing decision making and the critical role of interpersonal communication.

This book makes several contributions to the study of political communication and the presidency. First, this impressive work extends the notions and theories of organizational communication beyond the executive suites of corporations to the institutional presidency. We see the impact of White House staff organizational design on the flow of information and the structure of communicative relationships. Thus, second, this study extends the concerns of presidential communication beyond public image and presentations. For too long, communication scholars have ignored the dynamics of the more private, interpersonal patterns of presidential communication. Third, Dean Witherspoon identifies critical communication competencies for successful White House interpersonal relationships and communication. Presidents "would do well to remember that the chosen few who literally and figuratively surround a president inside the White House are those to whom he has entrusted much of his future, a future that will depend in large part on the communicative relationship that evolves within its walls." By utilizing new archival material from presidential libraries as well as interviews with former staff members, this work provides new insight into the inner workings of the White House. Finally, this study contributes to the growing literature on presidential management styles. It suggests a model for an effective and efficient White House Staff structure.

I am, without shame or modesty, a fan of the series. The joy of serving as its editor is in participating in the dialogue of the field of political communication and in reading the contributors' works. I invite you to join me.

Robert E. Denton, Jr.

NOTES

1. See, for example, Robert E. Denton, Jr., *The Symbolic Dimensions of The American Presidency* (Prospect Heights, IL: Waveland Press, 1982); Robert E. Denton, Jr., and Gary Woodward, *Political Communication in America* (New York: Praeger, 1985); Robert E. Denton, Jr., and Dan Hahn, *Presidential Communication* (New York: Praeger, 1986); and Robert E. Denton, Jr., *The Primetime Presidency of Ronald Reagan* (New York: Praeger, 1988).

2. Aristotle, *The Politics of Aristotle*, trans. Ernest Barker (New York: Oxford University Press, 1970), p. 5.

3. Aristotle, *Rhetoric*, trans. Rhys Roberts (New York: Modern Library, 1954), p. 22.

4. Dan Nimmo and Keith Sanders, "Introduction: The Emergence of Political Communication as a Field," in *Handbook of Political Communication*, Dan Nimmo and Keith Sanders, eds. (Beverly Hills, CA: Sage, 1981), pp. 11–36.

5. Ibid., p. 15.

6. Ibid., pp. 17–27.

7. Keith Sanders, Lynda Kaid, and Dan Nimmo, eds., *Political Communication Yearbook: 1984* (Carbondale, IL: Southern Illinois University Press, 1985), pp. 283–308.

8. Dan Nimmo and David Swanson, "The Field of Political Communication: Beyond the Voter Persuasion Paradigm," in *New Directions in Political Communication*, David Swanson and Dan Nimmo, eds. (Beverly Hills, CA: Sage, 1990), p. 8.

9. Sanders, Kaid, and Nimmo, *Political Communication Yearbook*, p. xiv.

10. Ibid.

11. Nimmo and Swanson, "The Field of Political Communication," p. 11.

Prologue

Presidential communication consists of more than a chief executive's public speeches and press conferences. It is also the behaviors and processes a president uses to create supportive networks among his personal staff and to facilitate the transmission and use of information to make and execute decisions. Effective presidential communication is not just a chief executive's ability to inform, motivate, and persuade the press and the public. It is also his facility at mobilizing the human resources around him to initiate and implement policies with a view to his personal and presidential agendas.

Journalistic and scholarly attention to, and even emphasis on, the public or rhetorical presidency has obscured the need to evaluate critically a president's communication with his senior staff, his inner circle. The dynamics of interaction among these individuals affects virtually all presidential decisions. The development and implementation of a policy, the preparation of a public speech, the practice for a press conference, and the management of a crisis—indeed, almost anything a president says or does to discharge his responsibilities—are the products of communication with his closest advisers. The dominance of the White House staff over the Cabinet in policy formulation during most of the modern presidencies is a result of this highly interactive atmosphere in the environs of the Oval Office. Moreover, the incidents of abuse and misuse of power among presidential staffs since 1960, most notably the Watergate and Irangate scandals, draw attention to the clout wielded by those who share the president's trust, and often his influence, and demand a critical evaluation of communication between president and senior staff within the walls of the White House. That critical evaluation is the purpose of this book.

Watergate focused press and public attention on those comprising the inner circle around a president, and both Gerald Ford and Jimmy Carter were sensitive to the need for preventing the abuse of structures and processes that might isolate the president from multiple sources of information and divergent opinions. Ronald Reagan paid little attention to the potential problems caused by a "palace guard," but the Iran-Contra scandal raised new questions in the late 1980s about the power of the people surrounding the president. Hence the book's focus in Part II on the post-Watergate presidents.

This study views the White House, specifically the west wing, where the president and his senior aides work, as an information-processing, decision-making environment that depends on a variety of effective organizational communication behaviors. It suggests that the degree to which a president is an effective communicator within the White House affects his success as both an organizational and a public leader.

While Part I generally relies on the memoirs of presidential aides to provide insights on presidential/staff communication between 1933 and 1974, Part II uses information obtained from interviews with members of the post-Watergate presidents' senior staffs. Additionally, archival material from the Gerald Ford and Jimmy Carter presidential libraries is used to offer an "inside look" at organizational structures and systems of information flow in these White Houses. The use of interviews, as well as the Ford and Carter archival materials, makes this study unique among those which have focused on White House organization, and management, and the influence of senior staffs. Additionally, its orientation to communication *within* the White House provides a new perspective on both the study of organizations and of presidents.

Acknowledgments

This study relies to a significant degree on the observations and opinions of individuals who have served in the White House, as president or as a member of a president's senior staff. I am indebted to the following individuals who shared their time and insights with me:

President Gerald R. Ford	Robert McFarlane
Zbigniew Brzezinski	Edwin Meese
Philip Buchen	Ronald Nessen
Richard Cheney	Terrence O'Donnell
George Christian	Joseph (Jody) Powell
James Connor	Donald Rumsfeld
Stuart Eizenstat	Brent Scowcroft
Robert Hartmann	Jack Watson
Hans Mark	Anne Wexler

Additionally, the assistance provided by the directors and archivists of the Gerald R. Ford and Jimmy Carter presidential libraries is greatly appreciated. I am particularly grateful to William Stewart and David Horrocks at the Ford Library and Martin Elzy and David Alsobrook at the Carter Library. A grant from the Gerald Ford Foundation helped support travel expenses incurred during archival research and grants from the University of Texas University Research Institute helped defray travel costs associated with trips to conduct interviews with former White House senior staff.

When one sets out to explore the relationship of concepts in a discipline to a ''new'' or untested subject of inquiry, such as the study of organizational communication in the White House, the insights of one's colleagues are invaluable. For their ideas and suggestions, I am grateful to Fredric Jablin, Larry Browning, Mark Knapp, John Daly, and Kathleen Jamieson. Special thanks are owed W. Charles Redding, for his review of parts of the manuscript and his incisive and helpful comments.

Credit for the preparation of the manuscript is due Deanna Matthews, whose careful competence in word processing, conscientious attention to detail, and cheerful dedication to her work made this endeavor especially rewarding. Manda van Geem, who transcribed interview tapes, handled several of the administrative details during the research phase of the project, and provided unceasing moral support, has my sincerest appreciation. Catherine Canfield, a student in the College of Communication, was extremely helpful working on several technical aspects of the book's production. I also wish to acknowledge the work of Robert Denton, Jr., editor of the Praeger Series in Political Communication, who supported the book from concept to completion, and Alison Bricken, sociology/communications editor at Praeger Publishers, who enthusiastically worked to bring the manuscript to publication.

Finally, there are a few individuals who contributed in special ways to this study:

Robert C. Jeffrey, Dean of the College of Communication at the University of Texas, who supported the project by granting an associate dean time to conduct research and write, and by continually encouraging her efforts; Carolyn Dennis-Willingham, who offered ongoing support during the time the work was "in progress;" Amelia and Ray Dennis, whose political discussions and disagreements throughout the last thirty years fostered my fascination with American presidents and the presidency; John McCormick Witherspoon, whose support, assistance, and patience during the preparation of the book never wavered; and finally, Ernestine Duecker Eckhardt, whose life and memory sustain me still.

PART I

COMMUNICATION IN THE MODERN WHITE HOUSE

Chapter 1

The White House as an Organization

The "White House," as we know it today, obviously did not spring from the head of Zeus as a complete, functioning entity able to handle all presidential assignments at the chief executive's beck and call. According to a "letter" published in the *Portland* (Maine) *Daily Courier* by a political satirist in 1833, the White House staff under President Andrew Jackson was simple in form and function:

> Every day, jest after breakfast, the Gineral (President Jackson) lights his pipe and begins to think purty hard, and I and Major Donaldson begin to open letters for him; and there is more than three bushels every day, and all the while coming. . . . We keep all the Secretaries, and the Vice President, and some District Attorneys, and a good many of our folks . . . moving about; and they tell us jest how the cat jumps. . . . And as I said afore, if it warnt for Congress meetin once a year, we'd put the Government in a one horse wagon, and go jest where we liked.[1]

Despite years of growth in the numbers of White House staff and the specialization of functions into departments, agencies, and councils, a president still relies on a handful of individuals to help him discharge the responsibilities of his office. They are his "inner staff,"[2] his "lengthened shadow."[3] They are a few key individuals (usually between five and ten) with frequent and regular access to the Oval Office who assume the roles of counselor, critic, and confidant.

Since the 1930s political scientists and historians have chronicled the growth and institutionalization of the White House staff, identified more correctly as the Executive Office of the President. This book, however, focuses only on the interactions between a president and his closest advisers—those in personal service to him. It is a study of communication at the apex of presidential government, among individuals on whom a chief executive relies to make sense of the environment in which he finds himself after the campaign cheers and election euphoria have begun to fade. As such, it is a study of organizational communication, and the theoretical contributions from that field applicable to an analysis of presidential communication inside the White House form the basis for the book's perspective.

Throughout these pages we are therefore concerned with how a president organizes, and communicates with, those senior aides who help him acquire and use information to develop and implement the policies of his administration within his environmental context. This discussion begins with the realization that the presidency is a continuum of presidencies; the office is "a living chain of presidents, stretching from George Washington on into the future, each a trustee for those following after."[4] The White House, as an organization, may change personnel and structure every four years and yet remain, in some ways, very much the same as occupants of the Oval Office come and go.

To better understand the communication between president and staff within the walls of the White House, it is beneficial to trace its evolution as an organization from historical and theoretical points of view.

THE EVOLUTION OF THE WHITE HOUSE AS AN ORGANIZATION

Early History

In contrast with their more recent counterparts, U.S. presidents during the early part of the nineteenth century relied on their Cabinets for advice and counsel; there were no White House staffs as they exist today. Until Andrew Jackson entered the White House, chief executives apparently did not have the benefit of discussions, debates, or disagreements with close associates one could deem "advisers." The White House "staff" generally consisted of a young man with impressive writing skills who was paid out of the chief executive's own pocket to prepare correspondence and run errands.[5]

Andrew Jackson, the first "Washington outsider" to become the nation's chief executive, introduced the concept of the "Kitchen Cabinet," an informal group of counsellors who were the forerunners of today's "inner circle."[6] According to Emmet John Hughes, "As if anticipating the needs of most of his successors, Jackson turned to a coterie of personal advisers because he could not find 'the necessary standards of selflessness and candor' in the politicians in his Cabinet."[7] Jackson's innovation did not survive in all subsequent administrations, but the realization that a president needed more administrative help was dawning in Washington. As the number of states in the Union increased, so did the complexity of issues and the resulting paperwork with which the president had to contend. In 1857 Congress acknowledged the need for office help in the White

House by authorizing the expenditure of funds for one personal secretary. Such was the beginning of the White House staff.

Almost immediately these individuals faced some of the same intraorganizational dynamics common to senior staff today. One of Lincoln's biographers, for instance, reveals that protecting the president's time and privacy was as much a staff concern in that president's White House as it has been in more recent administrations. Lincoln's two secretaries, John Hay and John G. Nicolay, attempted to achieve both presidential accessibility to the public and staff protection of his time by organizing the following system. Lincoln "would see people on Monday, Wednesday, and Friday from ten till two, on Tuesday and Thursday from ten till noon, when he was supposed to meet with the Cabinet. His personal secretaries, situated in an adjacent office, were to head off anybody who tried to interrupt him other than during office hours."[8] However, Lincoln, like a number of his successors, had difficulty keeping true to his daily calendar. "If they [the secretaries] told some caller to come back during regular hours, Lincoln would open his door and invite the person in anyway. . . . The trouble was that Lincoln loathed rules and red tape and generally did as he wanted, as though the White House were his Springfield law office."[9]

William Spragen's historical summary of White House staffs from 1789 to 1974 identifies the significant people who assisted the president in each of these administrations. Looking at his work from the perspective of this book, one identifies the following as significant developments in the evolution of the White House staff between 1857 and 1937:

- William McKinley was the first chief executive to name his chief aide "Secretary to the President." This individual, George B. Cortelyou, gained the reputation of organizing his president's schedule more efficiently than had his predecessors. He also "introduced the idea of a White House press spokesman and saw that a White House stenographer made a record of all the President's public appearances."[10]
- According to Ira Smith, a mail clerk in Willard Howard Taft's White House: "Somewhere in Taft's administration the one-big-family atmosphere faded out, and when Woodrow Wilson became President, the times had changed and we were in for a busy office that had little chance for byplay, gossip, or an occasional game of craps in the basement."[11]
- Despite the influence of Colonel Edward M. House on Woodrow Wilson, Joseph P. Tumulty served as the President's secretary and assumed virtually all administrative duties in the office of the president, including oversight of appointments, press and public relations, and the president's time.
- Herbert Hoover's administration introduced the concept of a White House "secretariat." His was comprised of three members: a press secretary, an office manager responsible for correspondence and scheduling, and one additional aide.

Prior to 1937, the degree to which presidential secretaries held the confidence and attention of their bosses obviously varied, depending on the roles they were assigned, the length of time each worked for the president, and the relationship that ultimately developed between them. In that year the White House staff, and the White House as an organization, began to emerge as we know them today—due in part to the imposition of structure and to the imposing character of the president in residence at the time.

As is discussed in more detail in Chapter 2, Franklin Roosevelt's administrative style, not just the needs of the presidency, precipitated changes in the form and function of the White House staff. There was no White House Office prior to 1939, and staff members were borrowed from departments to serve at the pleasure of the president.[12] Obviously neither strong presidents nor jealous Cabinet heads could live productively and in harmony forever under these arrangements. FDR's penchant for informal give-and-take sessions with his most trusted advisers; his delight in fostering competition among them by often assigning each the same task; his insistence on being the center to which information and attention flowed; and his determination to serve as the only source of final decisions in his White House helped prompt a major evolutionary change in the White House as an organization.

The Brownlow Report

In 1937 FDR appointed the President's Committee on Administrative Management to help "the presidency," at a time when he hoped for this "independent" commission's blessing on his administrative style. Chaired by Louis Brownlow, the committee prepared a report that affirmed: "The President needs help. His immediate staff assistance is entirely inadequate. He should be given a small number of executive assistants who would be his direct aides in dealing with the managerial agencies and administrative departments of government."[13] The committee suggested the addition of six administrative aides to the president's office, including a special counsel, an executive clerk, an appointments secretary, and a press secretary, all "possessed of high competence, great physical vigor, and a passion for anonymity."[14] It also recommended the establishment of the Executive Office of the President, with responsibilities for personnel, financial affairs, and planning. Sent to Congress as a reorganization bill in 1937, most of the committee's recommendations became law in 1939. According to Stephen Hess, "The importance of the Brownlow report was in legitimating what Roosevelt had been doing all along. It was a ringing manifesto for presidential supremacy, which had not been an accepted fact before the New Deal."[15] Moreover, the Brownlow report introduced the role of the president as an organizational leader, the director of his specifically chosen group of senior aides. Spragens concludes that the expansion of the White House staff had the effect of institutionalizing it.[16] However, legitimizing its formal structure by designating the number *and* titles of staff members was the first step in creating a White House organization within the modern presidency.

The Brownlow Committee saw the advisability of a "small" number of advisers who would report to the president directly—those who would communicate with him and each other on a daily, or at least on a regular, frequent basis. Since 1939 the number of staff in the Executive Office of the President has grown astronomically. Yet it is those few aides surrounding the president whom Brownlow and his colleagues deemed particularly important: the senior staff whose personal and organizational relationship with the president is the focus of this book.

The Report of the Hoover Commission

Another step along the evolutionary path that helped develop the structure and functions of the White House as an organization was the establishment in 1947 of the Commission on the Organization of the Executive Branch of the Government. The Republican Congress that year probably viewed the establishment of this commission as a means to curb the increasing power of the Executive Branch witnessed during Franklin Roosevelt's terms.[17] Indeed, ''defining and limiting executive functions'' was one of the commission's objectives.[18] Herbert Hoover chaired the work of the commission; other members included Dean Acheson, who served as vice chairman, and Joseph P. Kennedy.

The commission's report was published in 1949, after sixteen months of work, and clearly gave the president more control over the Executive Branch, not less. A number of its recommendations also set the stage for the increase of White House control over the formulation, as well as the execution, of foreign and domestic policy. Perhaps as a reaction to the managerial and communication styles of FDR, discussed in detail in Chapter 2, the commission wrote in its introduction that ''a clear line of authority from top to bottom, and adequate staff aids to the exercise of authority'' did not exist in the Executive Branch.[19] ''Authority is diffused, lines of authority are confused, staff services are insufficient.''[20] Roosevelt, who thrived on a communication network comprised of officials at various hierarchical levels throughout the Executive Branch, would have been amused at this concern. He would have been equally pleased at the commission's subsequent recommendations. These included establishing ''a clear line of control from the President to . . . department and agency heads and from them to their subordinates with correlative responsibility from these officials to the President . . . ,'' and providing ''the President . . . strong staff services . . . which the President . . . should be free to organize at his discretion.''[21]

Political scientists and historians have rightfully emphasized the importance of the Hoover Commission's recommendations as a license used by modern presidents to freely reorganize the Executive Branch, expand their personal staffs, and absorb or create new administrative entities to enhance their power over policy-making. However, little attention has been paid to the importance the Hoover Commission placed on the information needs of the president and its related recommendations. In its discussion of the Executive Office of the President, the commission wrote: ''The need of information for the solution of broad problems and the determination of Government-wide policies has gradually forced the development of better staff services for the President.''[22] In warning that staff services were not intended to duplicate departmental responsibilities, the commission emphasized that staff ''should exist only to give the President the greatest possible information on the activities of the Government as a whole, and to enable him to direct the policies of the departments and agencies.''[23] Indeed, all the major recommendations of the Hoover Commission related to the Executive Office of the President seemed to emanate from an overriding concern that the president have continuous access to information from staff members whose major responsibility should be the acquisition, assessment, and transmission of that information.

The Hoover Commission's report gave a president authority to organize (and reorganize) his staff; appoint heads of White House units, such as the National Security Council, without confirmation by the Senate; and select special advisers and consultants as needed, all for the purpose of providing him information and/or recommendations. Perhaps most important from the perspective of information flow and use in the White House, the commission recommended that funds be provided to the president to employ a staff secretary, one who would ''assist him by clearing information on the major problems on which staff work is . . . done within the President's Office, or by Cabinet or interdepartmental committees.''[24] The Commission's suggestion was based on its observation that no one existed in the White House at the time ''to which the President can look for a current summary of the principal issues with which he may have to deal in the near future; nor is a current summary of the staff work available on problems that have been assigned to his advisers, his staff agencies, or the heads of departments and agencies.''[25] The commission also wrote that a person designated as staff secretary would ''facilitate teamwork'' within the White House, essentially by serving as its locus of information. Since 1949 this individual has served as the conduit and communicator of written information among the president and his staff, but facilitating teamwork has required the efforts of more individuals than the staff secretary.

By the end of Franklin Roosevelt's presidency, the concept of a strong presidency was generally accepted in the country, and with it the affirmation of the president as leader of a powerful and pervasive policy-making organization in Washington: ''the White House.'' The personal office of the president had emerged as both a formal and an informal organization, characterized by an increase in the number of individuals reporting directly to the president, the delineation of task roles and responsibilities among these individuals, and the resulting emergence of communication networks among president and staff, depending on their personalities, aides' designated and assumed roles in the White House, and their individual relationships with the president.

Paul Light has written that the presidency is not comparable with organizations in the private sector because the latter are allowed to age and mature, ''while the Presidency is in constant flux.''[26] He suggests that when organizing the White

House, "each President faces a novel situation. Offices must be staffed, lines of communication established, and working relationships defined. . . ."[27] Within the modern presidency, however, the White House as a formal organization has also aged and matured. Position titles may change and elements of its structure may be modified, as is the case in many organizations, but functional areas, types of organizational roles, and reporting relationships have remained essentially the same throughout several administrations. As in any organization, of course, the informal organization in the White House may change dramatically, depending on each chief executive's personal and presidential needs. All organizations face continual change, and this study suggests that the organization which evolves around each president shares many of the characteristics common to other types of organizations. The establishment of a structure of reporting relationships and the development of organized processes to acquire and use information and make decisions are necessary components of the White House as well as of other organizations. To better understand presidential communication within the walls of the White House, it is instructive to consider several characteristics common to most organizations that the White House shares and that are particularly important to this study.

THE WHITE HOUSE AS AN ORGANIZATION: THEORETICAL CONSIDERATIONS

This study defines the White House as an organization comprised of the president, his senior staff, and the resulting communication networks that have a decisive effect, either facilitative or obstructive, upon information flow and decision making in the Oval Office. Important to the discussion is the realization that the White House, like other organizations, includes a formal structure of titles, delineated roles, assigned office space (of particular importance in the west wing of the White House, where the president works), and specified duties. In the White House some of those duties are mandated by the Constitution and federal statutes, and some by the occupant of the White House at a given time.

Robert McPhee has written that structure "is a defining characteristic of an organization—it is what brings about or makes possible that quality of atmosphere, that sustained, routine purposiveness that distinguishes work in an organization from activities in a group, a mob, a society. . . ."[28] According to McPhee, structure includes "official job titles, descriptions, and objectives for employees . . . ; the official differentiation of divisions, departments, and work units; the book or books of standard operating procedures. . . . Almost on a par with these are derivative descriptions such as the organizational chart, official work-flow diagrams," as well as systems for decision support and management information.[29] Moreover, he suggests, organizations differ in the extent and type of structures they possess, and the consequences of structure vary in organizations.

McPhee emphasizes that studying an organization requires more than an understanding of its formal structure, for "structure alone is not enough—an organization is a collection of people doing work within a formal structure."[30] The importance of structure in this study, for instance, stems from its effects on communication within an organization. Richard Daft and Robert Lengel write:

> Organization structure is the allocation of tasks and responsibilities to individuals and groups within the organization, and the design of systems to ensure effective communication and integration of effort. Organization structure and internal systems facilitate interactions and communications for the coordination and control of organizational activities.[31]

Karl Weick suggests that the substance of organizations is the interdependencies among people.[32] In the White House these interdependencies are created through the communication links the president and his staff forge with one another. On the other hand, lines of authority, titles, and constitutionally mandated duties reflect the power of the White House as the formal organization surrounding the nation's leader. Its structure, which has evolved through presidential preference and legislative mandates, "exerts a strong influence on the characteristics of communication within it."[33] The White House is an adaptive organization that depends on the interrelationships among the structure, functions, and people which coexist within its inner sanctum.

The White House also includes an informal structure that begins to emerge as soon as a president is elected. It consists of the personal and working relationships that evolve, with varying degrees of influence, between president and staff and among staff. These are communication relationships which are fluid and dynamic and will change throughout a chief executive's term. Additionally, they will be affected by the formal structure adopted by the president upon his taking office. For instance, if a designated chief of staff is part of a formal White House structure, the roles of other senior staff will be affected by that formal designation. If there is not a chief of staff, one individual may emerge as first among equals through his own attempts to influence the president on matters of policy or politics, or through a close personal relationship with him, molded as a loyal aide during long months of an election campaign. Similarly, although the Cabinet is part of the formal organization to which a president is accustomed, he may find minimal use, as have several chief executives, for Cabinet leadership of the Executive Branch's agencies and departments. Instead, he may prefer more direct and informal control of the federal bureaucracy through the use of White House aides—those people he sees and speaks with daily and those who are loyal only to him. Both of these examples illustrate Fredric Jablin's observation that "there is an interdependence between formal organizational structure and emergent structure," the informal structure that develops through the interactions of organizational members.[34]

The White House, as defined here, is similar to most contemporary organizations, where, as Peter Monge and Eric Eisenberg emphasize, "both formal and emergent networks [patterns of communication among organizational members] are in constant change. This change . . . is not simply the substitution of people in positions . . . the positions themselves are sometimes altered and the structure significantly changed as a result.''[35] Such was the case, for instance, when Hamilton Jordan was officially named chief of staff in 1979 by Jimmy Carter. Jordan, who essentially had been first among equals among White House aides since Carter's inauguration, now had the ''official'' responsibility for administration of the White House's daily operations.

A number of variables may affect the informal structure that develops in the White House: new tasks, changes in personnel, a president's philosophy about the degree of staff access necessary to meet his informational needs; the proximity of staff offices to the Oval Office and to each other; prior relationships forged among staff members; the degree of an individual's desire to be near the seat of power; and prior relationships between the individuals who become the president and his senior aides. Whatever the reasons for its emergence, the informal structure in the White House, as in most organizations, is that which greatly aids the accomplishment of the work in the organization and that which is continually changing. Reorganization takes place in the White House more than once every four years. As in other organizations, this process is sometimes the result of individuals joining or leaving the organization. Sometimes it is a deliberate strategy because ''management may consciously plan a restructuring of the organization to accomplish a new type of work or to increase productivity.''[36] Such a reorganization took place six weeks into the Ford presidency when Donald Rumsfeld became chief of staff, in practice if not in name, to eliminate the chaos existing in the White House as a result of the president's initial spokes-of-the-wheel organization.

The White House evolved as an organization, as we have seen, out of the chief executive's need for more information and more help in using that information to develop and execute presidential policies. Another characteristic the White House shares with other types of organizations is its use of information to reduce uncertainty and ambiguity—to channel the stream of questions, problems, and issues flowing across the president's desk into coordinated, cogent answers, solutions, and policies. Indeed, as Rebecca Blair et al. emphasize: ''An organization's effectiveness depends on its ability to match its information-processing requirements with the information-processing capacity of its units.''[37] This capacity is not just a measure of the organization's members, but also of its structure—hence the discussions in Chapters 4 and 5 on the ways presidents organize their White Houses and the systems they adopt to acquire and use information. As Richard Daft and Robert Lengel suggest, ''structural design can facilitate the amount of information needed for management coordination and control.''[38]

However, there are factors affecting a president's receipt and use of information in the White House other than his organizational structure and the processes used by senior aides to acquire and send it to him. One such factor is the president's cognitive style, his preferred way of using and evaluating information. According to Alexander L. George, cognitive style includes the "way in which an executive such as the president defines his informational needs for purposes of making decisions," his "preferred ways of acquiring information from those around him," and "his preferences regarding advisers and ways of using them in making his decisions."[39] Richard Nixon's penchant for making decisions in virtual solitude, based on documents prepared by his staff, and Gerald Ford's insistence on staff discussions after reading briefing papers, serve as examples of contrasting cognitive styles. As we shall see in future chapters, cognitive style, which includes the president's preference for written versus orally presented information, affects communication within the White House in a number of ways.

Another factor affecting the president's use of information to reduce ambiguity is the preferred source of that information among those within his staff. Charles O'Reilly et al. state: "Instead of relying on the most accurate sources of information, decision makers, for a variety of reasons, rely on more accessible sources."[40] Cabinet members in several administrations have been aware of this phenomenon, particularly those secretaries of state who watched as national security advisers, with unrestricted access to the time and attention of the chief executive, offered him advice as well as data on foreign policy matters. Evidence also exists to show that organizational leaders judge the validity of the information they receive on the basis of their trust in the source, leading to "the acceptance of a piece of information as 'true' or 'false' depending on how much the recipient trusts the sender."[41] As Irangate illustrated, one of the dangers of an inner circle around a president is "information insularity," where he chooses to receive information only from those closest to him and believes what he hears or reads because they are the sources of that information. Fortunately, in *most* White Houses, information used to make decisions is not usually in the sole possession of one person. According to Phillip Tetlock, "Most important decisions are not . . . the product of isolated information processors; they are the product of intensive interactions among members of groups."[42]

Finally, a factor affecting presidential use of information that is particularly apropos to this study relates to the relative "richness" of that information: the degree to which it is able to communicate clearly in a given time frame. Daft and Lengel define "information richness" as follows: "Communication transactions that can overcome different frames of reference or clarify ambiguous issues to change understanding in a timely manner are considered rich. Communications that require a long time to enable understanding or that cannot overcome different perspectives are lower in richness."[43] Consequently, the "richest" form of information is that provided in face-to-face interactions, where a president can hear the information and see the intensity of opinion in an adviser's nonverbal cues. Impersonal written documents, such as reports and briefing papers, may provide valuable information, but cannot communicate the depth and breadth of emotion (or knowledge) felt and understood by the sender in the preparation of that report. As Daft and Lengel observe: "Memos, reports and other written media can oversimplify complex problems. They do not provide a means to convey personal feelings or feedback. These media do not transmit the subtleties associated with the unpredictable, messy, emotional aspects of organizations."[44] Accordingly, organizational leaders rely on informal, personal media that are "capable of providing richer information . . . about certain problems."[45]

As is seen in more detail in later chapters, Franklin Roosevelt, John Kennedy, Lyndon Johnson, and Gerald Ford were four presidents who thrived on face-to-face interactions with their staffs to acquire, and often challenge, the information they were provided. When discussing political behavior in organizations (including those not associated with U.S. politics or the presidency), Daft and Lengel observe that such behavior occurs "most often at the upper levels of organizations and for decisions high in uncertainty."[46] It is behavior an individual uses to gain a preferred outcome within the organization when uncertainty or disagreement exists, and "involves the utilization of rich media (face-to-face) to reach agreement when diverse goals and reference frames are brought to bear on uncertain problems."[47] Moreover, Daft and Lengel emphasize that "media low in richness cannot be used to resolve political issues because paperwork and reports cannot convey the subtleties of power, obligations, and other intangibles."[48] All the modern presidents, with the exception of Richard Nixon, have seemed to appreciate the informational opportunities afforded them in give-and-take sessions with their staffs, albeit in varying degrees. What became particularly significant in some of these presidencies was the *degree* to which they used "rich" media to gather and utilize information.

In addition to the use of formal and informal structures, and the acquisition of information to reduce ambiguity, the White House shares another characteristic with other types of organizations. Its leader possesses a communication style within the organization as he interacts daily with its members. Robert Norton defines communicator style as the way one communicates, "the signals that are provided to help process, interpret, filter, or understand literal meaning."[49] Individuals do not have one style; they exhibit elements of several over a period of time. However, styles are sufficiently patterned so that one may attribute a given style to an individual. "Every communicative interaction contributes to determining a style profile. As such, norms are constantly shaped, usually reinforced, and ever present as implicit criteria."[50]

Norton identifies several communicator styles:

Dominant—"The person . . . appears to be more confident, enthusiastic, forceful, active, competitive, self-confident, self-assured, conceited, and businesslike. . . . "[51]

Dramatic—An individual "manipulates exaggerations, fantasies, stories, metaphors, rhythm, voice, and other stylistic devices to highlight or understate content," and often does so to minimize anxiety or tension in a group.[52]

Contentious—This style is characteristic of one who is argumentative in a communication encounter, ''closely associated with the dominant style, but potentially entailing negative components.''[53]

Animated—The communicator exhibits frequent and sustained eye contact and the use of many facial expressions and gestures.

Relaxed—This style may communicate multiple messages. ''On one hand it suggests calmness/peace/serenity; on the other, it suggests confidence/comfortableness.''[54]

Open—An individual is ''conversational, expansive, affable, convivial, gregarious . . . unsecretive, somewhat frank, possibly outspoken, definitely extroverted and obviously approachable.''[55] He or she also is prone to disclosing personal information when communicating with others.

Friendly—Not surprisingly, ''the friendly communicator confirms, strokes, and positively recognizes the other.''[56]

Attentive—Simply put, this individual ''makes sure that the other person knows that he or she is being listened to.''[57]

Impression-Leaving—Such persons manifest ''a visible or memorable style of communicating'' through the projection of verbal and/or nonverbal cues.[58]

As one might expect, these style variables may cluster. A person may be dominant, friendly, and animated. Franklin Roosevelt's aides have described his interactions with staff in such a way that we might identify him as dominant, dramatic at times, animated, attentive, and friendly. Ronald Reagan often told jokes or stories at the beginning of meetings, according to former staff members, to relieve tension among the participants. In these settings, Reagan was exhibiting a dramatic communicator style. Lyndon Johnson could be identified as contentious in some meetings with his aides, especially during policy deliberations affecting his conduct of the Vietnam War. However, it is important to remember that no president has only one communicator style; each may exhibit several of the style variables described. Yet *patterns* do emerge, and it is those patterns which are significant in an analysis of communication between a president and his staff.

As is the case in other types of organizations, the White House operates within its own culture, its system of ''beliefs, values, assumptions, and ways of doing things'' that guide the ways individuals work in the organization.[59] This culture is molded by the history of the presidency and the nation as a whole, the political and social values of the president and his staff, and White House traditions—all those elements which make the White House a community of colleagues instead of a loose collection of individuals with no common bond. The meanings and values shared within the culture in turn influence the informal structures created to accomplish the work of the White House. Even the way a president communicates with his staff, at certain times under certain circumstances, may depend in part on the culture within his White House, as well as on his personality and the communication situation. Organizational culture in the White House changes from administration to administration and bears the stamp of each occupant of the Oval Office. At the same time, however, the rich history of the

White House, with its legacy of legends and heroes spanning over 200 years, is the cultural foundation upon which each president embeds the values and expectations that will guide the work and behavior of his staff.

Just as the internal culture of the White House affects its operation as an organization, so does the external environment within which it exists. The socioeconomic and political forces that affected the election of the president become the environmental context in which the president and his staff must conduct the business of the Executive Branch. Jimmy Carter's White House was affected by what he termed the nation's "malaise," and whether it existed throughout the country or only in his mind, the perception affected the work within his White House. Franklin Roosevelt's White House reacted to an economic depression and a world war by creating new structures, organizational roles, and reporting relationships. The Vietnam War, and the deep-seated controversies it engendered, changed the priorities of Lyndon Johnson's White House and directed much of its energies to the waging of that war. The nationalistic, pro-American mood that swept the United States at the beginning of Ronald Reagan's first term bolstered his White House's attempts to develop foreign policies reflecting that mood. On the other hand, changes in the Soviet Union's leadership, and its pronounced attitude toward more positive U.S.–Soviet relations, changed the tone and substance of U.S. policies toward arms control that eventually developed within the Reagan White House. The environment within which an organization exists is comprised of a multitude of influences: public opinion, economic and social conditions, and political forces, to name a few. The ways a president structures and manages his White House, and develops policies within it, are directly related to the environment in which he and his staff find themselves—and perhaps their greatest challenge is that elements within this environment change mercurially.

As is the case in other organizations, the White House evolves through various stages within an organizational life cycle. According to Danny Miller and Peter H. Friesen, five stages comprise an organization's life cycle: birth, growth, maturity, revival or revitalization, and decline.[60] Structure in the birth stage is simple and informal, as is the communicative relationship among organizational members. The White House was in this stage during Franklin Roosevelt's administration, when the president and a few aides comprised the structure of the White House organization. In the growth stage more emphasis is placed on information gathering and processing; the organization expands its numbers and role specializations evolve, requiring increased coordination and the formalization of organizational practices. Such was the case in the White House during the latter part of the Roosevelt administration and in the Truman administration.

In the maturity stage of the organizational life cycle, formalization continues with the addition of sufficient rules, procedures, and organized processes to conduct the work of the organization. Hierarchical layers of administration evolve and the need for communication within the organization between and among levels is critical, based on the organization's high demand for information. The

White House reached maturity, albeit in varying degrees of structure, during the Eisenhower, Kennedy, Johnson, and Nixon presidencies. The revival/revitalization stage in the organizational life cycle depends on the organization's responses to its achieved maturity. In some organizations, adaptation, diversification, and decentralization are needed to renew or revitalize an organization. In the White House, the trauma of the Watergate scandal prompted Gerald Ford to revitalize the organization by restructuring reporting relationships and changing decision-making processes to "open" the Oval Office to opinions and advice from staff and to sources of information outside the organization.

Organizational decline occurs if an organization does not successfully achieve revitalization. Its results include conflict, secrecy, centralization—in other words, a series of seemingly protective measures to keep the organization alive under extremely adverse circumstances. The White House in the latter months of the Nixon administration was an organization in decline—with the wagons of some White House aides circling to keep the president's enemies from penetrating his wall of secrecy and deception. In the last weeks of the administration, the White House was in virtual disintegration—the processes of information flow and decision making were disorganized, key aides had left the White House, others were unsure of reporting relationships. Alexander Haig, as chief of staff, was seemingly the sole source of stability and virtually the only communication link to a president in a state of self-imposed isolation. Richard Nixon's resignation and Gerald Ford's assumption of the presidency began a period of organizational renewal. Since Watergate the White House organization has remained in a state of maturity with revitalization occurring every four or eight years, as needed, when the leader of the organization changes, and each president's White House becomes part of the continuum of administrative organizations.

Within each presidency, the White House evolves through a life cycle. After an inauguration, there are a few weeks or months of infancy as the president appoints a staff, adopts a formal structure, and informal structures emerge. Then there are two to three years of maturation as his goals evolve into legislation and sometimes into implemented programs. Finally, there is organizational decline, as the president shifts his energies and those of his closest advisors to a reelection effort or to considering, if he is a lame duck chief executive, what he will do as a private citizen. If he seeks and attains reelection, the White House may be rejuvenated as an organization in his second term.

The White House today is a mature organization, revitalized or at the very least changed to some degree, when a new president becomes its organizational leader. Some of its functions are now computerized, others are handled much as they were in the 1930s. It is important to remember, however, that presidents and their senior staffs may come and go, but the White House as an organization remains an ongoing component of the Executive Branch in the nation's government, changed in varying degrees by the people who inhabit its rooms and guide its tasks, but relatively stable, if not always creative and innovative, in an ever-changing sociopolitical environment.

The president and his senior staff form an organization within an organizational bureaucracy comprised of agencies, departments, and councils. President Washington and his privately paid secretary comprised the first White House organization—since then it has grown in numbers and in complexity. Franklin Roosevelt's demand for staff assistance as he waged war against a domestic depression and foreign enemies resulted in the expansion of the president's personal staff and his direct control over many of the entities comprising the Executive Branch. Congressional adoption of most of the recommendations from the Brownlow Committee and the Hoover Commission added major operational units, such as the Bureau of the Budget and the National Security Council, to an already busy White House. Each president since Roosevelt has lived with a White House organization that must monitor and lead the larger administrative machine pulsating around it. Nevertheless, each president since Roosevelt has depended on only a few key people to help him in this endeavor.

In the early years of Franklin Roosevelt's presidency, senior aides were generalists handling duties assigned by the president. As the functions of the White House increased in number and complexity, role specialization became necessary—senior aides were hired to handle certain areas of activity in which they evidenced some expertise or at least some interest (e.g., domestic policy, congressional relations, and foreign policy). As FDR came to understand well, to be a "modern" president meant one must be a manager, an administrative as well as a political leader. Under these circumstances, the White House has evolved as a communication-intensive organization, dependent on a constant flow of written information in and out of the Oval Office and on the discussion and debate necessary for policy-making. The citizenry expects the president to possess some degree of facility as a public speaker, but he also must be adept as a communicator within his own organization. At the same time, providing information the president needs, and preventing the isolation he must avoid, depend on a *staff's* ability to communicate effectively with the president and with each other—in a culture that values loyalty, and one hopes, honesty.

During the years between 1933 and 1974, each president adopted organizational structures and information acquisition processes to suit his personality and his political instincts, borrowing or rejecting administrative practices of one or more of his predecessors. Stephen Hess suggests that differences in personnel and organizational structures perhaps reflect "a greater stress on administration in a Republican White House and on policy innovation under Democrats."[61] James Pfiffner states that the two major models used by contemporary presidents to organize their White Houses have been the Roosevelt/Kennedy and Eisenhower models.[62] Eisenhower's system is characterized as a formal organizational structure run by a dominating chief of staff. The Roosevelt-Kennedy model, on the other hand, represents a loosely structured White House with the president accessible to several senior staff. This model is best summarized in a memo written by Clark Clifford to President-Elect Kennedy in November 1960:

> A vigorous President in the Democratic tradition of the Presidency will probably find it best to act as his own chief of staff, and to have no highly visible majordomo standing

> between him and his staff. . . . It is important that all the senior professional persons on the staff should have access to the President, and the staff should consist of no more persons than can conveniently have such access on a day-to-day basis.[63]

As we shall see in the next two chapters, the Democrat and Republican presidents did indeed differ in the ways they organized and communicated with their White House staffs. But the Democrats also differed from each other in significant ways. Harry Truman did not agree with Franklin Roosevelt's managerial style; Lyndon Johnson's ways of communicating with his staff differed significantly from methods used by Kennedy and Truman. Although the modern pre-Watergate Democrat presidents utilized informal, fluid organizational structures, their managerial and communication styles did differ—for such styles are a function not just of party but also of personality.

To understand the role of communication as the White House evolved as an organization, the next two chapters focus on communication between chief executives and their senior staffs from 1933 to 1974. This focus includes an analysis of the organizational structure within each White House; each president's managerial style; the processes he used to acquire information and make decisions; and the communication style(s) he exhibited in daily interactions with his closest advisers. It is appropriate to begin with FDR, who was the creator and leader of the first modern White House organization.

NOTES

1. As quoted in Bradley H. Patterson, Jr., *The Ring of Power: The White House Staff and Its Expanding Role in Government* (New York: Basic Books, 1988), p. 89.
2. Stephen Hess, *Organizing the Presidency*, 2d ed. (Washington, DC: The Brookings Institution, 1988), p. 174.
3. Louis W. Koenig, *The Chief Executive*, rev. ed. (New York: Harcourt, Brace & World, 1968), p. 159.
4. Richard E. Neustadt, "Truman in Action: A Retrospect," in Marc Landy, ed., *Modern Presidents and the Presidency* (Lexington, MA: Lexington Books, 1985), p. 6.
5. William C. Spragens, "White House Staffs, 1789–1974," in Bradley D. Nash, with Milton S. Eisenhower, R. Gordon Hoxie, and William C. Spragens, eds., *Organizing and Staffing the Presidency* (New York: Center for the Study of the Presidency, 1980), p. 7.
6. Ibid., p. 13.
7. Emmet J. Hughes, *The Living Presidency* (Baltimore: Penguin Books, 1974), p. 137.
8. Spragens, "White House Staffs, 1789–1974," p. 20.
9. Ibid.
10. Ibid., p. 22.
11. As quoted in ibid., p. 23.
12. Richard M. Pious, *The American Presidency* (New York: Basic Books, Inc. 1979), p. 243.
13. As quoted in ibid.

14. Hess, *Organizing the Presidency*, pp. 33–34.

15. Ibid., p. 34.

16. Spragens, "White House Staffs, 1789–1974," p. 26.

17. Hess, *Organizing the Presidency*, p. 53.

18. Ibid.

19. *The Hoover Commission Report on Organization of the Executive Branch of the Government* (New York: McGraw-Hill, 1949), p. 3.

20. Ibid.

21. Ibid., p. 7.

22. Ibid., p. 11.

23. Ibid., p. 12.

24. Ibid., pp. 17–18.

25. Ibid., p. 17.

26. Paul C. Light, *The President's Agenda: Domestic Policy Choice from Kennedy to Carter* (Baltimore: Johns Hopkins University Press, 1982), p. 177.

27. Ibid.

28. Robert D. McPhee, "Formal Structures and Organizational Communication," in Robert D. McPhee and Phillip K. Tompkins, eds., *Organizational Communication: Traditional Themes and New Dimensions* (Beverly Hills, CA: Sage, 1985), p. 150.

29. Ibid., p. 149.

30. Ibid., p. 150.

31. Richard L. Daft and Robert H. Lengel, "Organizational Information Requirements, Media Richness and Structural Design," *Management Science*, 32, no. 5, May 1986, p. 559.

32. Karl E. Weick, *The Social Psychology of Organizing*, 2d ed. (Reading, MA: Addison-Wesley, 1979), p. 3.

33. L. W. Porter and K. H. Roberts, "Communication in Organizations," in M. Dunnette, ed., *Handbook of Industrial and Organizational Psychology* (Chicago: Rand McNally, 1976), p. 1570.

34. Fredric M. Jablin, "Formal Organization Structure," in Fredric M. Jablin, Linda L. Putnam, Karlene H. Roberts, and Lyman W. Porter, eds., *Handbook of Organizational Communication* (Beverly Hills, CA: Sage, 1987), p. 413.

35. Peter R. Monge and Eric M. Eisenberg, "Emergent Communication Networks," in Fredric M. Jablin et al., eds., *Handbook of Organizational Communication* (Beverly Hills, CA: Sage, 1987), p. 309.

36. Ibid., p. 311.

37. Rebecca Blair, Karlene H. Roberts, and Paula McKechnie, "Vertical and Network Communication in Organizations," in Robert D. McPhee and Phillip K. Tompkins, eds., *Organizational Communication* (Beverly Hills, CA: Sage, 1985), p. 66.

38. Daft and Lengel, "Organizational Information Requirements," p. 559.

39. Alexander L. George, *Presidential Decisionmaking in Foreign Policy: The Effective Use of Information and Advice* (Boulder, CO: Westview Press, 1980), p. 147.

40. Charles O'Reilly, Jennifer A. Chatman, and John C. Anderson, "Message Flow and Decision Making," in Fredric M. Jablin et al., eds., *Handbook of Organizational Communication* (Beverly Hills, CA: Sage, 1987), p. 616.

41. Ibid.

42. Phillip E. Tetlock, "Accountability: The Neglected Social Context of Judgment

and Choice,'' in Barry N. Staw and Larry L. Cummings, eds., *Research in Organizational Behavior*, vol. 7 (Greenwich, CT: JAI, 1985), p. 298.

43. Daft and Lengel, ''Organizational Information Requirements,'' p. 560.

44. Richard L. Daft and Robert H. Lengel, ''Information Richness: A New Approach to Managerial Behavior and Organization Design,'' in Larry L. Cummings and Barry N. Staw, eds., *Research in Organizational Behavior*, vol. 6 (Greenwich, CT: JAI, 1984), p. 200.

45. Ibid., p. 201.

46. Ibid., p. 226.

47. Ibid.

48. Ibid.

49. Robert Norton, *Communicator Style* (Beverly Hills, CA: Sage, 1983), p. 45.

50. Ibid., p. 50.

51. Ibid., p. 65.

52. Ibid.

53. Ibid., p. 67.

54. Ibid., p. 69.

55. Ibid., p. 70.

56. Ibid., p. 72.

57. Ibid., p. 70.

58. Ibid., p. 69.

59. J. Steven Ott, *The Organizational Culture Perspective* (Chicago: Dorsey Press, 1989), p. 24.

60. Danny Miller and Peter H. Friesen, ''A Longitudinal Study of the Corporate Life Cycle,'' *Management Science*, 10, 1984, pp. 1161–83.

61. Hess, *Organizing the Presidency*, p. 139.

62. James P. Pfiffner, ''White House Staff Versus the Cabinet: Centripetal and Centrifugal Roles,'' *Presidential Studies Quarterly*, 16, no. 4, Fall 1986, p. 668.

63. As quoted in ibid., pp. 668–69.

Chapter 2

Historical Perspectives, FDR to Johnson

FRANKLIN D. ROOSEVELT: THE ADMINISTRATOR AS ARTIST

There was little structure in Franklin Roosevelt's White House. His philosophy of management, and the infant stage of development in which the White House operated, stimulated countless informal networks that accomplished tasks, dissolved, and then reemerged with other participants for other purposes. Roosevelt was the source and nerve center of myriad such networks whose work was conducted through frequent, face-to-face communications between the president and his staff.

FDR saw little need for formal structure in a White House that initially consisted of the president and three secretaries. Stephen Early was the press secretary; Marvin McIntyre scheduled appointments; and Louis Howe was adviser-in-residence, actually living in the family quarters of the White House. Later in the Roosevelt presidency, Colonel Edwin (Pa) Watson took over the responsibility for the president's schedule and McIntyre served as Roosevelt's contact with Congress. After Louis Howe died, Harry Hopkins eventually moved into the family quarters to be the president's trusted adviser during World War II. These individuals and FDR's clerical staff, notably Missy LeHand and Grace Tully, comprised Roosevelt's inner circle prior to September 8, 1939.

On that date, the president signed an executive order providing for the reorganization of the Executive Branch that included the transfer of the Bureau of the Budget from the Treasury Department to the Executive Branch and allowed the president to employ six administrative assistants to help conduct his work. FDR did not appoint a chief of staff; he served as his own—as did his Democratic successors until Jimmy Carter appointed one in mid–1979. However, Roosevelt did tend to select one assistant who could help him with special tasks requiring an expertise in coordinating people and information, such as "behind-the-scenes tasks involved in gathering information, talking to parties concerned in a given dispute, trying to find possible grounds for agreements, and formulating alternative courses of action which he might pursue.''[1] During the war, Harry Hopkins assumed this role, but his power and primacy were derived solely from his relationship with FDR.

Although each of FDR's secretaries was assigned a broadly defined area of responsibility, they were all generalists who worked on tasks assigned by the president as needed. According to Arthur Schlesinger, Roosevelt wanted an inventive government rather than an orderly one, and the functional use of his staff suited his presidential goals as well as his management philosophy.[2] ''The very ambiguity of his scheme of organization—the overlapping jurisdictions and duplicated responsibilities—made flexibility easy. If things started to go bad, he could reshuffle people and functions with speed which would have been impossible in a government of clear-cut assignments and rigid chains of command.''[3] In Louis Koenig's opinion, FDR's fluid organizational structure and his penchant for using staff as generalists ''spurred the flow of information and ideas into his possession and magnified his impact on policy. It released the energies of men from confining bureaucratic routine.''[4]

FDR's approach to guiding his senior staff, including administrative assistants Raymond Moley, Rexford Tugwell, and Thomas Corcoran, was a management style that fostered competition and emphasized his personal involvement in the administration of the White House and the Executive Branch. His style, as is the case with all administrators, was derived in great part from his personality. This gregarious, inquisitive, forceful person demanded to be at the center of all White House activity and not just the activity generated by his inner circle. Roosevelt was in contact with subordinate administrators and their bosses. His span of control extended far beyond the west wing of the White House apparently because of his belief that ''a President's administrative success may well be influenced by the proportion of people whom he is attempting to direct and control with whom he can remain in direct personal contact, either by face-to-face conversation or by the telephone.''[5] He fostered competition among his staff by assigning two or more people the same task, sometimes without their knowledge. This approach did much to keep him in control of the people and processes responsible for policy development and execution in his White House, and provided him a continuous flow of information upon which he based his decisions. One of the principles that apparently guided Roosevelt's approach to administration was his belief that ''Presidents don't act on policies, programs, or personnel in the abstract; they act in the concrete as they meet deadlines set by due dates. . . . ''[6] Consequently he gave few fixed assignments (press relations, appointments, congressional relations), and those who held these responsibilities were generalists who were available to work on ad hoc tasks in accordance with the president's needs at a given moment.

Roosevelt's managerial style was a reflection of his personal and presidential beliefs, values, and skills, including his ''instinct for the basic general issue, his flypaper mastery of detail, his capacity to carry a large variety of problems in his mind, his ability to shift with speed from one problem to another, his appetite for long hours of plain hard work. . . . ''[7] The president may have assigned tasks, but he was not a delegating president as compared with Ronald Reagan or even Dwight Eisenhower, chief executives discussed in later chapters. He was attentive to detail, interested in close supervision of his people and the specific activities in which they were involved on a daily basis. In part his managerial philosophy and his administrative style were responses to what perhaps was a perceived need to guide the White House organization through its embryonic stages. In part it was a reflection of FDR's intense pleasure in being the president. In part it was a function of the relationship he cultivated with those who shared the work of the White House with him.

Roosevelt inspired ''fierce loyalty and warm affection'' among his aides, according to Robert Sherwood, who has written that if one of his senior staff ''could prove possession of these sentiments in abundance,'' he was accepted as a member of the White House ''family.''[8] The president had a personal relationship with his senior aides, unlike several of his successors, in part because he relied on them for companionship as well as for advice and assistance. Since he was confined to a wheelchair, they, along with Mrs. Roosevelt, were his eyes and ears outside the White House, and their reports to him, whether substantive or comprised mostly of gossip, were a mainstay of the president's day.

One of the ways FDR cultivated a close rapport with his staff was of his own creation. It was the ''children's hour,'' his term for cocktail time in the White House. Late in the afternoon or in early evening, when the president summoned them by buzzing the intercoms on their desks, his secretaries and senior aides would convene in the Oval Office, where the president mixed and poured a liquid respite from the day's activities. Grace Tully, the president's secretary who succeeded Marguerite LeHand after the latter's death, wrote in her autobiography that the ''children's hour'' was a time for office and press gossip, and ''served to cement an intangible but deep sense of camaraderie which always existed among those who worked closely and on a personal basis with him.''[9]

Despite this attempt at conviviality, Roosevelt had to deal with other results of his managerial style—the competition he fostered sometimes bred conflict and adversely affected morale among his small staff. Additionally, he apparently was ''adept at cutting down or building up his aides as situations might require,'' and was known to discipline members of the senior staff ''by withholding honors and distinctions, by assigning new authority and programs to someone else.''[10] Consequently, he often engaged in ''hand-holding,'' a process he used to console those who felt slighted by his words or deeds. Tully writes that FDR spent a good deal of his time assuaging the feelings of his aides through this process.

Like many administrators, Roosevelt preferred ''hand-holding'' to ''hand-slapping.'' He loathed disagreeable personal encounters with his aides and found it virtually impossible to fire anyone, which Schlesinger calls ''his best noted and most conspicuous administrative failing.''[11] He often assigned this task to Louis Howe, who also tried to ease friction among the senior aides that was generated by FDR's managerial style. In his account of the relationship between the president and Howe, Alfred Rollins writes: "No one could have managed this [mediation] completely with such a dedicated, ambitious, egotistical, dynamic gang of leaders. But he worked nobly at it."[12] Such was Louis Howe's devotion to Franklin Roosevelt.

No discussion of Roosevelt as administrator and communicator would be complete without acknowledging the roles played by Howe, and then Harry Hopkins, in FDR's presidency. Samuel Rosenman, a valued speechwriter in Roosevelt's White House, has emphasized that the president liked "to have one man with whom he could exchange ideas at any time of day, whose judgment and loyalty he trusted, and whose disinterestedness he knew would make the advice impartial."[13] Howe and Hopkins were the two men he chose to assume that role. Both of these individuals lived in the White House, accessible to the president day and night. Howe was Roosevelt's closest confidant and severest critic. As a reward for his masterful work in shepherding Roosevelt's first successful presidential campaign, he was given the title of secretary to the president, and maintained a special status in the White House as friend, political adviser, and devil's advocate. Indeed, Eleanor Roosevelt once credited Howe with exposing her husband to a "better cross section of people and . . . a greater variety of views" during his years in the White House.[14]

If Howe knew Roosevelt better from pure instinct, Hopkins, beginning in 1940, worked harder than anyone to understand the president and his goals, and to work toward their achievement. FDR had absolute confidence in Hopkins's abilities, assured that he would not represent the president on any matter without explicit instructions. According to Rosenman: "Both Louis and Harry served the President in the same way during their days of greatest influence. They were able to take hundreds of tasks from his shoulders."[15] Both literally worked themselves to death for Roosevelt. Howe died in 1936. Hopkins survived FDR, but was in bad health before the president's death and succumbed to illness in 1946.

Despite the fact that these two individuals, and a handful of others, had the ear of the president day and night from 1933 to 1945, they did not represent a palace guard, a protective shield, around him. Quite to the contrary, they served as the president's antennae, alert to the cacophony of praise and criticism that resounded from Congress, the press, foreign leaders, and various sources of public opinion. There is no question that conflict was created and morale was sometimes adversely affected by the competition that Roosevelt's management style fostered among his White House staff. Yet this style also engendered an obsessive dedication among these same individuals to the successful implementation of the New Deal and the achievement of victory in a world war. In great part this obsession was fed by the president's intense commitment to, and dependence on, daily communication with those who lived and worked with him.

Much has been written about Franklin Roosevelt's prowess as an orator, as a passionate public speaker who moved audiences on ceremonial occasions and during his famous fireside chats. But he was equally masterful as a communicator within the White House, one who thrived on interactions with the White House staff, Cabinet members, agency heads, congressmen, foreign leaders, and a variety of other visitors who streamed through the Oval Office. He did not ignore the formal channels of communication that brought information to him for use in decision making, but he did not prefer them. He was, most assuredly, an "administrator by conversation," preferring to give and receive information and opinions through interpersonal, oral communications rather than through exchanges of memos. According to Wann, "From the time when he woke up in the morning, he spent most of his day-time hours talking to people. It was the regular custom for his secretaries and other immediate personal staff members to go to his bedroom as he was finishing his breakfast in bed to discuss plans for the day's work. . . . "[16]

Visitors to the Oval Office were scheduled at fifteen-minute intervals for approximately two hours before lunch and immediately thereafter. However, FDR's tendency to monopolize a conversation, coupled with the addition of unscheduled discussions with friends and advisers throughout the day, often wreaked havoc with his daily calendar. In addition to frequent, ad hoc conversations during the day with members of his senior staff, there were often chats with off-the-record visitors who used unofficial entrances into the White House. Such individuals included Bernard Baruch, Vincent Astor, and several justices of the Supreme Court.[17] To save the president's time, Grace Tully sometimes urged him to telephone instead of see someone who requested an appointment. However, Roosevelt "preferred to see persons rather than do business in the more impersonal manner of a telephone conversation. He liked to watch facial expressions and he often said they told him more than the words of his visitors."[18] In other words, the president valued the "richness" of the information he received by communicating face-to-face.

FDR used his staff to acquire information in a variety of informal ways. Marguerite LeHand, his first personal secretary, was a trusted and valued staff member, and the president listened to her "as to few others on questions of appointments and even policy."[19] He also used Harry Hopkins as a sounding board, finding in Hopkins someone before whom he could think aloud. Such a person was particularly important to Roosevelt, who preferred to "develop and crystallize his views on a problem most effectively by talking about it at length. . . . "[20]

Roosevelt also scanned his environment for information from other sources, including several daily newspapers, the letters he received from citizens in all walks of life, and oral reports from Mrs. Roosevelt on her visits throughout the country and abroad. She wrote in 1949, "Franklin often used me to get the reflection of other people's thinking because he knew I made it a point to see and talk with a variety of people. . . . I felt that [he] . . . used whatever I brought back to him in the way of observations and information as a check against the many official reports which he received."[21] The president also accepted telephone calls from approximately 100 individuals whose efforts to reach him were not screened by White House secretaries.[22]

Finally, Roosevelt used his special assistants as conduits of information. These individuals kept in contact with administrators in various agencies throughout the Executive Branch and served to improve relationships between them and the White House. Harry Hopkins, for instance, was a communication link between FDR and other administration agencies, particularly the War Department. In this role he also served as a buffer between the president and officials who tried to bring problems to the president that were inappropriate or unnecessary for his review.[23] Occasionally Louis Howe would create his own informal channel of communication to the president without the latter's knowledge. According to Rollins, when FDR failed to accept Howe's ideas on a particular issue, Howe "would plant his ideas with others, hoping to squeeze his boss gently in a ring of advice. Eleanor Roosevelt was one of his favorite agents."[24]

Although preferring to use informal channels of communication to obtain information, FDR certainly did not ignore the formal channels available to him. On most mornings he held a staff meeting that included his three secretaries (initially Watson, Early, and McIntyre), and eventually Rosenman and Hopkins. According to Robert Sherwood, one of the president's speechwriters, these meetings were held to discuss the scheduled work of the day, including appointments and press conferences. Communication was informal and "covered a great deal of ground in a very short time, for all the aides participating knew Roosevelt so well, and he trusted them so fully, that beatings about the bush were unnecessary."[25]

The Roosevelt White House used a formal system to handle the flow of written information into the White House, although it was not nearly as elaborate as the system Dwight Eisenhower would establish upon assuming the presidency. Tully would read the president's mail and, in her words, "letters that appeared most important were decorated with a red tag and these were placed on top of the pile that went to the President's desk. When the letter warranted it, I would attach a sheaf of material from our own files that bore on the subject of the new communication."[26] As has been the case in most, if not all, the White Houses since Roosevelt's time, individuals tried to use the system by urging the secretary to place their letters or memos on the top of the stack.

Despite the formal channels he used to acquire information, Roosevelt created and maintained a complex of informal communication systems "to check and balance information acquired through official channels."[27] He purposefully developed these systems to prevent the insulation from opposing ideas and opinions that has come to haunt several of his successors. Although he was confined to a wheelchair, Roosevelt had no intention of being its prisoner—of enduring an isolation imposed by lack of advice and information from multiple and divergent sources.

If the president sometimes seemed frenetic in his determination to absorb information from the people and papers that flowed into his office, he approached decision making as a deliberate, even slow, process that required considerable reflection and, occasionally, introspection. According to Tully, anyone wishing to commit the president to a course of action by requesting his signature on a piece of paper could expect "long hours and days of thought on the President's part."[28]

FDR was a man who had to see the interrelationships among the component parts of a problem in order to devise a solution—and he insisted on understanding the ramifications of a decision before making it. "Situations had to be permitted to develop, to crystallize, to clarify; the competing forces had to vindicate themselves in the actual pull and tug of conflict; public opinion had to face the question, consider it, pronounce upon it—only then, at the long, frazzled end, would the President's intuitions consolidate and precipitate a result."[29] The reason FDR's decision-making process was protracted can be traced to his preference for gathering information aurally. "What for others might be an interior dialogue had to be externalized for Roosevelt; and it was externalized most conveniently by hearing strong exponents of divergent viewpoints. Listening amiably to all sides, watching the opposing views undergo the test of practice, digesting the evidence, he gradually felt his way toward a conclusion."[30]

But always, always the decision was his to make, for FDR firmly believed that presidents should be decision makers. He would not delegate that responsibility to anyone, even Harry Hopkins. Indeed, he took pride in one of Executive Clerk Rudolph Forster's calculations that he had made "at least thirty-five decisions to each one made by Calvin Coolidge."[31] Most important, Roosevelt was a good example of an organizational leader whose decision-making processes are a function of, a reaction to, a process within, the system he uses to acquire information.

Franklin Roosevelt managed the White House and created policy by using his interpersonal communication skills and by fostering an environment in the White House that cultivated a continual flow of communication between himself and his senior aides. He was a naturally "gregarious man who preferred talking to reading or writing," and was not hesitant to admit that he loved to talk, enjoying the company of those who came to see him from outside the White House and those he selected to surround him within the White House.[32] Supposedly he once told a visitor: "Words are a good enough barrage if you know how to use them."[33] The only exceptions to this rule were the times he "appeared shy and uncomfortable when he broached an unpleasant problem in personal relationships," preferring to postpone disagreeable conversations with friends or aides, or to use Louis Howe as a go-between.[34]

Almost all of Norton's communicator style constructs discussed in Chapter 1 apply to Roosevelt. He was animated, dramatic at times, dominant (to the extent that some Oval Office visitors felt he monopolized their conversations), usually friendly, and generally relaxed. He loved to talk, and to talk a lot, in many, if not most, of his daily encounters. Despite the competition he created among aides, and the administrative inefficiency that might have been created by an overuse of presidential time in the process of discussion, FDR accomplished much of his presidential agenda through his use of communication within the White House. He was just as effective a communicator within the White House as he was an orator speaking to the public from it. Sadly, as the war became the major issue with which he had to deal during the last years of his presidency, his communication relationship with his senior aides changed to some degree. In wartime, aides know less than the commander in chief about what is going on, and "communication scarcely can be free and often is not useful in his business."[35] Richard Neustadt observes that as Roosevelt waged war, "the burden of his choices was severe enough to chain him to his desk, exhaust his energy, cut short his life. The perspective he acquired with that burden on his back was not shared fully, could not be, by even his most intimate assistants."[36] As a result, toward the end, as victory neared, he seemed "a man apart from all his principal associates."[37] Such was the ironic fate of the true "great communicator" of this century.

Several of Roosevelt's biographers quote Harold Smith, his budget director from 1939 to 1945, as saying that the president was an artist in government. If that is so, he did not work in muted tones. His portrait of presidential management and communication was a colorful mosaic, a composite of ideas, impressions, information, and advice, gleaned from almost continuous interactions with his staff and the others he designed to listen to, from the day he took office until the day he died.

HARRY S. TRUMAN: ADMINISTRATION BY COORDINATION

Guiding the White House through its embryonic stages as an organization, Roosevelt had legitimized the president as its chief administrator. Under Harry Truman, the White House as an organization began to mature. The president added staff and further delineated areas of responsibility for those he selected as senior aides. Additionally, new entities such as the National Security Council became part of the White House as a result of the Hoover Commission's recommendations, and responsibilities were added to existing functional areas. (See Chapter 1 for a discussion of the Hoover Commission and its recommendations.)

Truman enacted several changes in the structure of the White House, in part because of its continued evolution as an administrative entity, but mostly because he disagreed vehemently with Roosevelt's lack of order and his management style. In his personal and presidential life Truman valued orderliness and held fast, as much as possible, to a strict daily routine. However, his penchant for order did not reflect an emphasis on formality. At his insistence and to their delight, Truman's working relationship with his staff was informal. He was a true team builder who emphasized coordination and cooperation within the White House.

The president once explained how he organized his staff upon assuming the presidency:

I inherited some excellent men from Roosevelt's staff. But I expanded the staff and set up a personnel office in the White House which relieved me individually of conducting endless interviews. Then I went ahead with my reorganization by setting out for each assistant a certain kind of work to do, and each confines himself to that task. Naturally the executive assistants consult together, just as any other staff would, and in that way it saves me from having to make trivial decisions.[38]

At 10 A.M. every day Truman held a staff meeting with the ten to thirteen people who served as his closest aides, including secretaries for appointments, press relations, and correspondence; an assistant to the president; a special counsel; three administrative assistants; three military aides; and the executive clerk, who had worked in the White House since the McKinley administration. Truman served successfully as his own chief of staff, due in great part to his masterful use of the daily staff meeting, discussed later in this chapter.

Truman's inner circle included the individuals named below.

Dr. John Steelman, a former university professor from Alabama, was given a permanent appointment in December 1946 as "assistant to the president." Although he often referred to himself as *the* assistant to the president, he was not the Sherman Adams or H. R. Haldeman of the Truman administration. Steelman essentially was responsible for the "normal daily flow of White House business."[39] The former head of the Federal Mediation and Conciliation Service, he sometimes served as a mediator within the Executive Branch, resolving disputes between Executive Branch departments and sometimes jurisdictional disputes among Cabinet officers.[40]

Clark Clifford served as special counsel, and as such dealt with major domestic issues. Despite Steelman's title, there was no staff hierarchy in the Truman White House depicted on an organizational chart, and Steelman and Clifford were locked in an ongoing rivalry over who held more power in the president's inner circle. Due in large part to Truman's ability to coordinate and control his staff, and his announced disdain for intrastaff conflict, this rivalry never erupted into open warfare. Power shifted between the two men, depending upon the issue.

Matt Connelly was Truman's appointments secretary, in charge of planning the president's schedule, greeting visitors to the Oval Office, and soothing the feelings of those he determined had no pressing need to see the president. Connelly probably saw the chief executive more in a given day than any other staff member.

Truman's press secretary was Charles G. Ross. Upon his death he was succeeded by Joseph Short. Short also died during the Truman years and was succeeded by Roger Tubby.

William Hassett, the correspondence secretary, was in charge of handling the president's mail.

Charles Murphy was brought to the White House in January 1947 as an administrative assistant "concerned chiefly with helping to put together legislative proposals and, occasionally, shepherding them on Capitol Hill.''[41] Formerly with the Office of Legislative Counsel to the Senate, Murphy succeeded Clark Clifford when the latter left the Truman White House to practice law. Murphy also assumed responsibility for ad hoc problems, including controversies between the Congress and the president or between agencies. As a result, several members of the White House staff worked for Murphy on an ad hoc basis. ''Most of the assistants to the other presidential appointees drifted in and out of Murphy's circle, depending on the projects at hand and the needs of the moment.''[42] Consequently, Murphy depended on a series of emergent networks, forged with ''bright, able, imaginative staff men'' in agencies throughout Washington.[43]

Other administrative aides who served in a variety of capacities, including speechwriter, were George Elzey, David Bell, and David Lloyd. Additionally, the president relied on his military aides, such as Rear Admiral Robert L. Dennison, who undertook special assignments related to defense and foreign affairs. A military aide who would ultimately embarrass the president and leave the White House as part of a conflict-of-interest scandal was Major General Harry H. Vaughn, Truman's friend and companion. Finally, Truman benefited from a number of staff ''loaned'' to the White House by the Bureau of the Budget, at the behest of James E. Webb, who succeeded Harold Smith as budget director. This group of workers was able to help the small presidential staff accomplish its growing number of tasks as Truman faced crucial postwar domestic issues and then began to wage the Korean War.

In 1980 Charles Murphy observed that ''President Truman had his staff organized just about right in terms of achieving a balance between definite, continuing responsibilities and the flexibility to meet special problems, having enough institutionalization but not too much, distributing responsibility among staff members so that they could operate effectively but were not unduly tempted to build their own empires, and keeping the number of staff members who reported directly to him both manageable and diverse.''[44] According to Ken Hechler, a former Truman aide, ''everybody knew precisely what their lines of authority generally were''; it was ''a happy staff and the morale was tremendously high.''[45]

However, Truman's staff was not regarded as a particularly competent one. Most of them lacked the White House experience Truman needed when he suddenly assumed office. Several were former aides from his senatorial staff or friends from Missouri. Historically they have not been compared favorably with Roosevelt's Brain Trust, and some, like Harry Vaughn, fed campaign fodder to the Republicans in 1952 when they used corruption in the Executive Branch as a campaign issue. Obviously an organizational structure, no matter how efficient on paper, works only as well as the people within it. Creating and activating policies and programs are two very different capabilities, especially if one has to work with a Congress controlled by the opposition, as was the case with Truman. To understand what Harry Truman valued in the people he selected as senior staff, it is beneficial to consider the president's relationship with those who saw him daily.

William Hopkins, who served in seven administrations and helped the president coordinate his staff, once described Truman as "a man who was gentle and kind and considerate of his staff," who never uttered "an unkind word to or about any member of his staff."[46] Neustadt remembers: "In the White House office, there was always informality and at least surface friendliness, and generally everyone had a high morale, reflecting the president's own attitudes and personality."[47] Truman's personal qualities included a simplicity, a forthrightness, that endeared him to his staff. According to Charles Murphy, "with his personal staff he was extremely gentle. In fact, he was more lenient at times than he should have been, and that got him into trouble more than once."[48]

Because he was the product of machine politics, one biographer suggests, the president primarily sought loyalty and devotion from the people on whom he depended when he was suddenly thrust into the presidency. He consequently made haphazard, and therefore relatively poor, staff appointments.[49] Nevertheless, careful treatment of his most trusted aides resulted in a staff "that returned his kindness with an extraordinary amount of hard work, voluntary overtime, and wholehearted, single-minded devotion."[50] Ultimately, however, Truman paid a price for surrounding himself with loyal friends who were not necessarily competent advisers. Several aides eventually embarrassed the president, his administration, and the Democratic party through their involvement in scandals: Appointments Secretary Connelly went to prison for fixing a tax case; Harry Vaughn accepted gifts illegally. Throughout his administration, Truman's loyalty to several of his errant staff was longer-lasting than was theirs to him.

What Truman did insist on among his inner circle was the absence of infighting. "His staff and cabinet learned . . . that for their own survival it was essential to keep their quarrels beneath the surface, maintaining at least the appearance of reasonably good relations with one another."[51] Ironically, according to Richard Neustadt, "when power within the staff was relatively polarized and jealously guarded, staff operations probably were at their most effective. Tension drew lines clear and sharp, creating a settled framework for daily operations, with junior staff regularly and informally bridging the staked-out gaps between their seniors."[52] In short, Truman's staff learned what Roosevelt had known: a little rivalry, some competition, may benefit any organization—albeit sometimes at the expense of staff morale. Truman, however, was never purposively responsible for this rivalry and tried very hard, through the management style he utilized, to run an effective White House without the internal competition his predecessor had fostered.

Harry Truman once described his management style in the following manner:

> The duty that you expect a fellow to carry out is specifically outlined, and he is given the authority to carry it out, and if he carries it out in a proper manner, he is backed to

the limit by the President. This doesn't mean that he abdicates any power, because it is also made clear that proper reports will be made to him and that he will be consulted on major decisions. . . .[53]

In other words, Truman emphasized, a president "must have an efficiently organized staff around him and then he must delegate authority."[54] Truman sincerely believed that a chief executive and a White House organization could suffer from a leader who tried to do too much himself—who could not or would not delegate authority to senior staff. As is discussed in later chapters, President Carter was criticized heavily during his tenure in the White House for his perceived inability to delegate tasks and his immersion in administrative detail.

Theoretically President Truman recognized a relationship between structure and efficiency. In practice, however, according to Neustadt, Truman "had more feel for personalities than jurisdictions, and his instinct was to improvise arrangements around problems rather than to work through fixed procedures. In dealing with his staff he set no precise lines of demarcation or of hierarchy; those he did establish he was likely to ignore. . . ."[55] Additionally, as Robert Donovan suggests, Truman was slow to mold his aides into a team and make maximum use of their individual talents, a problem compounded by the mediocrity of the staff during his first term.[56] The president's inability to use his staff effectively, and perhaps their inability to respond adequately to his needs, may have been due to their mutual lack of a clear conception of the president's agenda for the country. Indeed, Truman's initial agenda was to continue FDR's plans for the country. It took him some time to establish his own policy and programmatic goals. After his election to the presidency in 1948, the president was freer to develop his national agenda. David Stowe, one of Truman's administrative assistants, observed years later: "I see the second four years as a period of professionalism, generated by the leadership of the president and molded by his concept of cooperation and coordination."[57]

Truman's managerial style was based on an appreciation of cooperation and coordination with and among those chosen to do his bidding. He realized the value of communication in this endeavor, and relied on structured, yet informal, mechanisms to obtain the information he needed to make decisions.

Harry Truman once told an interviewer that the "ability to get the facts is one of the President's greatest problems. He cannot operate without trusting people."[58] Truman used a variety of formal and informal channels of communication to obtain and share information; perhaps the most significant one, on an ongoing basis, was the morning staff meeting. Through this daily conference he acquired information, communicated his opinions and directives to his staff, and developed a sense of cohesiveness among his team.

Every morning at 10:00 about a dozen individuals, Truman's senior staff, assembled in the Oval Office for approximately thirty minutes. According to William Hopkins, Truman's executive clerk, the president kept one of two files on his desk as a "receptacle for accumulating documents that he wished to hand out to the staff at the morning conference.''[59] The file had tabs for each person attending the meeting and included letters requiring an answer, requests for public appearances, suggested subjects for speeches, and proposals requiring White House staff or Cabinet department study and recommendations. The staff meeting ''was a simple way for the president to turn assignments over to his staff and to help dispose of his mountain of paper work.''[60]

After handing out assignments, the president turned to each member of the group for an update on matters related to his particular area of responsibility. ''Each participant was encouraged to express his views, whether or not the specific matter under discussion was in his specialty. And during all this the president would interject his thoughts, his directives, and his philosophy.''[61] Obviously these short conferences did not lend themselves to in-depth discussions of policy, and they did not substitute for lengthy one-on-one meetings with individual staff members. However,

> The work accomplished in the morning staff meeting was a great timesaver for the president as well as for members of the staff. It gave the staff a feeling of being on the team. It acquainted each member with the type of material and the type of assignments the president was passing along to his fellow staffers. It fostered cohesion and cooperation rather than competition and combativeness.[62]

In short, Truman, who had witnessed the ill effects of competitiveness in Roosevelt's White House, was determined to manage by coordination and avoid being a source of staff conflict. According to Hopkins, the meetings ''helped decrease duplication of effort, the confusion, and the lack of direction that results from working at cross purposes.''[63]

Truman also valued a more structured system of paper flow into the Oval Office than had his predecessor. Two types of folders were brought to the president each day by the executive clerk. One contained documents for signature, such as bills, treaties, and proclamations; the other held reading material, mostly mail. Hopkins recalls:

> These folders were delivered to the president routinely twice a day, in the morning and right after lunch. Customarily he would dispose of the material for signature in my presence, so that it could be processed immediately. This system made it easy to keep track of documents and to answer with dispatch queries from responsible officials in the departments and agencies as to the status of documents in which they had a legitimate interest.[64]

Material in Truman's reading folder ''reappeared the next morning in the form of dictation to his personal secretary or in the material the president distributed from his desk file to the staff at the morning conference. Thus, it was relatively easy to know the status of documents without an elaborate and wasteful system of coordination.''[65] Truman's system of written information flow was more structured than Roosevelt's and less structured than Eisenhower's, who created the staff secretariat. Unbeknownst to the executive clerk, some documents could be taken to the president by individual staff members, as well as Cabinet members and other officials, for his review and possible action. Indeed, Neustadt observed that "there was never any inclusive written record governing disposal of the nonsignature documents transmitted through Hopkins' hands. And, of course, there were still other papers he never saw at any stage and had no notion of, much less any record."[66]

Compared with the paper-tracking systems used in later presidencies, Truman's organization no doubt was lacking; but it was a major improvement over that used by most, if not all, of his predecessors. The maturation of the White House as an organization, which included an increase in the president's personal staff and the development of role specializations, made oversight of written information flow in and out of the White House an appropriate task during and after the Truman years. Such oversight was a different, and more difficult, assignment when the staff had consisted of three or fewer presidential aides.

In addition to the documents he received in the signature and reading folders, Truman requested a number of reports each week dealing with defense and foreign policy matters, including the secretary of state's daily two-page summaries of important diplomatic developments that FDR had received, emergency special reports, bulletins throughout the day on Korea, and a daily report on foreign matters from the secretary of state.[67] After creating the Central Intelligence Agency (CIA), he received CIA reports each morning and a weekly special report from the CIA director. This document was a loose-leaf black book, "a complete roundup of all the military, diplomatic and economic news—a digest of all the cables that have come in during the week, especially the important ones. . . ."[68] Through these reports Truman immersed himself in foreign policy, in part because he was concerned that he had not been fully briefed in this area by Roosevelt when he was vice-president. Supplementing the formal reports were daily meetings with a staff member from the National Security Council, periodic meetings with the Joint Chiefs of Staff, and regularly scheduled meetings, once or twice a week, with the secretaries of state and defense. "It was usually in these meetings that policy questions in the fields of defense and foreign policy were raised and settled. These cabinet officers usually got 'the word' firsthand from the president himself."[69]

Truman had other fixed appointments every week. These included meetings with the Democratic leaders of Congress; the Cabinet (twice a week); the press; the National Security Council; the chairman of the Democratic National Committee; and daily conferences with the executive secretary of the National Security Council.

These meetings, and the system of information flow used by Truman, were his ways of structuring communication within the White House to achieve an efficiency he found lacking in Roosevelt's administration. At the same time, however, Truman was by nature an informal, easygoing individual who knew the worth of informal methods of communicating with those around him. According to Neustadt, "the senior civilians had as much access to the president, day or night, as his outside appointments and their sense of discretion allowed. His door was always open in emergencies, at any hour."[70] Moreover, Matt Connelly, the appointments secretary, "never presumed to deny them access for more than a few hours at a time"; Murphy, Steelman, and Short especially saw the president almost as often as they wished, "usually with relatively little delay."[71] Clark Clifford "always tried to be the last member of the staff to see Truman at the end of each day so that he could give the final word of advice."[72] Truman's penchant for informal communication within the White House also prompted him regularly to visit his staff on their own turf. "Particularly in the mornings between 8:30 and 9:30, the president often bobbed into an office to discuss something that had occurred to him overnight or to give a decision on a matter that had earlier been left for him to study."[73]

Additionally, roundtable drafting sessions for speeches were used in the Truman White House as a means of informal information sharing. As a speech developed under the auspices of one or two drafters, other aides would join the effort to provide information and opinions. For a period of time during these sessions the president would "drop by" to offer his ideas. According to Neustadt:

> This . . . roundtable system served at least two purposes. It focused on policy details in which principals were able informally to exchange views and make recommendations and in which everybody got a chance to gauge the president's feelings, mood, and attitudes toward the subject at hand. . . . There could have been only a very few people on the White House staff who either did not see the president daily, in morning staff meetings, or did not see him two or three times a week in one of these roundtable sessions. This is important because it is so *unlike* the pattern of subsequent administrations.[74]

Accustomed to the informality fostered by the president, the staff took advantage of the White House mess as a place to communicate among themselves. Ken Hechler recalls that "at noontime most of us would eat together and trade ideas back and forth as to what we were doing and what problems we were confronting."[75]

Truman also used the telephone to transact business, particularly to contact his former congressional colleagues and "untangle knots on Capitol Hill."[76] Although his appointments secretary screened his calls as well as his visitors, calls "from the 'great' went through directly," except when the president was in a meeting or conferring in a scheduled appointment.[77] Truman often initiated phone calls from within the Oval Office, eschewing the use of a secretary or the White House operator.

One additional source of information for the president deserves mention: recommendations from an ad hoc group of individuals meeting outside the White House during 1947. Early in that year, several Truman administration officials and representatives from the Democratic National Committee held dinner meetings on Monday nights to discuss actions the president might take on various issues to illustrate his liberal leanings and generate support for his election among Roosevelt partisans. Truman never attended these meetings, but Clark Clifford, his special counsel, did. "The method the group used . . . was liaison through Clifford, allowing him at his discretion to draw upon what was said and proposed at the dinners when counseling with Truman on bills, messages, and speeches. It was by this means that the group hoped to encourage a liberal Truman program."[78] Truman did take some actions consistent with recommendations from the Monday night group, but the extent of their influence is not well known.

By using a relatively structured system of written information flow into the Oval Office, and encouraging a variety of formal and informal meetings between president and staff, Harry Truman sought and used the information crucial to the exercise of his duties. Because he abruptly assumed the presidency following the death of his predecessor, and because Roosevelt communicated with his vice-president only a few times before he died, acquiring sufficient information to make presidential decisions was personally, as well as presidentially, important to Harry Truman.

Just as Truman differed from Roosevelt in his approach to managing the White House, so he differed in his preferred method of decision making. Robert Donovan has compared the two presidents: "Roosevelt's caginess about decisions was foreign to Truman, who itched to make them on the spot, if possible. Roosevelt's creative sense of seeking ideas and strength through deliberately fostered confusion, conflict and personal rivalry in the White House struck Truman as incomprehensible. Truman was straightforward, not devious."[79] Additionally, unlike FDR, Truman used the Cabinet as an advisory body, and the departments participated in decision making in the Truman administration. Roosevelt preferred to make decisions personally, for his own reasons and in his own good time.

In contrast with FDR's penchant for "slow cooking" a decision, that is, letting facts, political ramifications, and public opinion simmer until the time seemed right for presidential action, Truman took pride in quick decisiveness, as is indicated in his description of the decision-making process he used:

> First, get all the facts you can, remembering that you seldom will have *all* the facts. If you do, the decision will be almost automatic. Second, consult your trusted advisers but remember that the secretary of state is going to see the problem in the light of national policy considerations and the secretary of defense from the standpoint of national defense, etc. . . . Third, after gathering the facts and consulting with advisers, go off by yourself, evaluate your advice, and make your decision. Fourth, having made the decision, *never look back*.[80]

William Hopkins remembers the president's decisiveness as follows: "He could make an important decision and get a good night's sleep without rehashing it and being overtaken by doubts. In fact this quality was so well recognized, even by the opposition, that very early in the Eisenhower administration the staff was urged to be decisive."[81]

Despite what appeared to be a quick, even hasty, approach to decision making, Truman refrained from "snap" decisions by using at least two processes. He described one as a procedure whereby he essentially wrote memoranda to himself at least once a week, outlining the facts and people involved in a given issue or problem. The memos were written on five-by-eight pieces of paper, intended only for his review. The president told one interviewer that writing these memoranda helped him "clarify his thinking and serve as notes for further study and decision."[82]

The second process consisted of using expert opinion from governmental officials and private citizens. For example, before deciding to drop the atomic bomb, Truman appointed a civilian committee to study relevant moral, political, and military issues. Additionally, according to Charles Murphy, Truman's decision "to resist aggression in Korea was reached over the course of two days and nights of intensive discussions with the government's top civilian and military leaders. . . ."[83] Regarding one of Truman's more unpopular decisions, Murphy recalls that the "order to relieve General MacArthur of his command was issued only after the president had discussed the matter for days with the secretary of state, the secretary of defense, the Joint Chiefs of Staff, and his special assistant for foreign affairs and had received their unanimous advice that the action was necessary."[84]

During his tenure in the White House, Truman appointed a number of commissions on subjects of critical concern to the country at the time, including higher education, civil rights, migratory labor, immigration and naturalization, health needs, scientific research, and water resources policy. Consequently, the man from Missouri, who was direct in manner and language, was decisive but not rash as he evaluated solutions for the problems he encountered in the Oval Office. He chose from among alternatives after listening to his staff and others selected to give him advice. Having made a decision, he took responsibility for it. Indeed, Truman the decision maker has become synonymous with the quotation that adorned his desk during his years as the chief executive: "The buck stops here."

Few biographies of Truman or discussions of his administration by former aides describe the president's communication style when interacting with his staff, individually or collectively. John Hersey wrote that in staff meetings he usually spoke "in a low, patient, easy voice."[85] He also has been described as a good listener, having trained himself to listen carefully during conversations because much of the knowledge upon which he based decisions was presented orally.[86] Despite Truman's famous tendency to pepper his communication with the press with salty language, there is no indication that he was contentious with his staff in their daily interactions. Although he was not gifted as a public or private orator in the style of Franklin Roosevelt, he was direct, clear, and apparently considerate in his discussions with others, including his senior aides. Consequently, one might describe Truman's communicative style inside the White House as being attentive, open, usually friendly, sometimes dominant but not dominating. Obviously his style varied according to the communication situation in which he found himself, but in general Harry Truman, as a person and as a president, was a calm and steady manager, decision maker, and communicator.

Truman, like Franklin Roosevelt, was an "oral" president who enjoyed and fostered discussion and debate in the White House. However, as a result of his personal sense of orderliness and his concern about the effects of FDR's management style on White House staff, he imposed more structure on interactions with his aides than had Roosevelt. This structure did not make him less accessible to his staff, to a significant degree, or less personable with them. In his mind, it made his White House more efficient than that of his predecessor.

As in Roosevelt's administration, the White House staff served President Truman but did not usurp the functions of the Cabinet, with whom Truman met regularly twice a week. And, as was the case with his predecessor, the structure of the White House organization was a reflection of its leader—informal, communication intensive, with a value placed on both written and oral communication. Most important, Truman and his aides functioned with an emphasis on coordination, symbolized by the morning staff meetings. Truman's White House was a policy-making one; it was not consumed with an overarching interest in administration. NATO, the Truman Doctrine, the Marshall Plan, and Fair Deal domestic programs were significant products of its labor. Compared with Roosevelt's White House, however, it placed more emphasis on formal structure and was more methodical in its deliberations as an organization.

As is discussed in Chapter 3, during the eight years after Truman left office, the White House became a highly structured, hierarchical organization, a reflection of its leader and his penchant for administration. In 1961, when John F. Kennedy and the Democrats assumed the presidency, the Republican emphasis on formal structure and organized systems of information flow was quickly abandoned. And though the young chief executive shared FDR's interest in a policy-oriented, rather than an administrative, presidency, he did not possess several of the organizational leadership traits that characterized FDR.

JOHN F. KENNEDY—THE PRAGMATIST AS ADMINISTRATOR

Despite similarities in upbringing, political philosophy, and commitments to a "personalized" presidency, John Kennedy obviously was not Franklin Roosevelt. He was not the gregarious conversationalist, the incessant inquisitor, the ebullient host in the Oval Office that FDR came to be. Although a symbol of youthful optimism in a New Frontier, Kennedy was a pragmatic politician *and* communicator inside the White House who spoke with his aides in shorthand, thought most meetings a waste of time, and worked with a handful of senior staff to the exclusion of career officials in the Executive Branch. Although JFK valued information from multiple sources, unlike FDR he did not reach deeply into the federal bureaucracy to tap knowledge available to him. He depended on those who saw him daily, who owed their careers to the success of his. Kennedy, like his predecessors, structured and used his staff in ways that suited him best. Unlike the evolving White House organization that FDR had managed in the 1930s and 1940s, by 1961 the organization Kennedy inherited was an island floating atop a sea of federal agencies and departments. While FDR had created the federal entities he needed to supplement his White House organization and implement the programs of the New Deal, Kennedy fell heir to a bureaucracy he generally did not trust.

By the time John Kennedy took office, the nation had experienced eight years of a formally run, highly structured White House and a chief of staff who often spoke, and sometimes acted, on behalf of the president. Eisenhower valued administration as a function necessary for an efficient White House and adopted several of the Hoover Commission's recommendations relating to the structure and operation of the White House as an organization. As will be discussed in Chapter 3, he began using a staff secretariat; deputized Sherman Adams as a powerful chief of staff; and placed great value on role specializations and organized processes of oral and written communication, such as formal meetings and a strictly-adhered-to system of paper flow into the Oval Office. Kennedy thought Eisenhower's emphasis on administration was too confining for policy development, and promptly disbanded the staff and Cabinet secretariats. His staff was one of generalists operating under no imposed hierarchy of reporting relationships. He was his own chief of staff, and his senior aides reported to him directly as the hub of an information-receiving wheel; they were its spokes. Theodore Sorensen remembers that Kennedy "paid little attention to organization charts and chains of command which diluted and distributed his authority."[87] To him, "too much organization stifled debate; it denied him access to a broad scope of information and ideas; and, perhaps more importantly, it undercut his ability to understand the real merits of available options."[88]

According to Sorensen, the failure of the Bay of Pigs invasion "altered Kennedy's entire approach" to how he planned to run his White House.[89] Having depended on career officials who had planned the mission during the last months of the previous administration, Kennedy became suspicious and distrustful of career officers after the failure of the operation. Consequently, he turned for foreign policy guidance to those he had brought with him to the White House. For instance, the National Security Council staff, headed by McGeorge Bundy, became "a little State Department at the White House" and Bundy moved from offices in the Executive Office Building into the White House.[90]

The people closest to President Kennedy in the west wing of the White House were those who had served him while he was a senator or had impressed him with their expertise in various policy areas. The senior staff was comprised of eight individuals. Theodore Sorensen, special counsel, was in charge of domestic issues and speechwriting, and was closer to the president intellectually than any other aide. According to Evelyn Lincoln, the president's personal secretary, "there seemed to be a kind of unspoken communication" between the president and Sorensen that began when Kennedy was a senator.[91] Other than his brother Robert, "there was no one the President trusted or relied upon more."[92] The special assistants to Kennedy were McGeorge Bundy (foreign affairs), Lawrence O'Brien (congressional relations), Pierre Salinger (press relations), and Kenneth O'Donnell (appointments and scheduling). Ralph Dungan and Arthur Schlesinger, Jr., were assistants with varied responsibilities. Dungan was in charge of personnel in addition to other assigned tasks, and Schlesinger was a speechwriter, a liaison with the intellectual community, and sometimes an adviser on Latin American policy. Dave Powers, the president's personal aide, companion, and "official White House greeter," was the first staff member with the president in the morning and the last to see him at night.[93] Nevertheless, it was O'Donnell, according to Pierre Salinger, who had "the greatest responsibility, influence, and accessibility to the President."[94]

JFK's small staff, with "no distinctions in rank connoted by . . . titles and very few differences in title," maximized fluidity of structure, with the emergence of communication networks dependent on a given task or assignment and not on lines on an organizational chart. The purpose of Kennedy's structure was to

> summarize and analyze . . . products and proposals for him, to refine the conflicting views of various agencies, to define the issues which he had to decide, to help place his personal imprint upon them, to make certain that practical political facts were never overlooked, and to enable him to make his decisions on the full range of considerations and constituencies, which no Cabinet member shared.[95]

Describing the fluidity of structure within the Kennedy White House, Sorensen writes: "Our jurisdictions were distinguishable but not exclusive, and each man could and did assist every other. Our assignments and relations evolved with time, as did the President's use of us."[96] As is discussed later in this chapter, the communication that facilitated the accomplishment of assignments was informal, and networks among aides developed on an ad hoc basis. Staff meetings were never held. "Each of us was busy with our separate responsibilities, and each of us met when necessary with whatever staff members had jurisdictions touching our own."[97] Although Kennedy's structure was developed purposively to respond quickly to problems, generate ideas, and evaluate issues, the staff, according to Schlesinger, felt a need for more structure than was provided by Kennedy. The president "had a distressing tendency to take up whatever happened to be on his desk and hand it to whomever happened to be in the room."[98] In response, "the staff on the whole contrived its own clandestine structure, taking care to pass on a presidential directive to the person in whose area it lay."[99]

The weaknesses of Kennedy's structure were reflected in an analysis by Joseph Kraft in December 1962:

> The staff operation, like many other aspects of the Administration, works to put all matters on a pragmatic, case-by-case basis. It does not contribute to the systematic elaboration of coherent programs expressing broad and easily identified public policies. A sense of inner purpose may—no doubt does—exist in the White House. But in part because the operation is so casual, so laconic, so frictionless, the purpose and direction of the Administration . . . have not made themselves felt outside the White House.[100]

These weaknesses in the formal organizational structure of the White House were objects of criticism during the Carter administration as well. (See Chapter 4.) Despite the flaws in Kennedy's White House structure described by Kraft, his organization compensated for some of the problems it generated by using it to facilitate, rather than undermine, staff relationships as well as the flow of information to the president.

John Kennedy valued the people he chose to serve him in the White House and, according to Sorensen, treated them more as colleagues than as employees.[101] Enamored with the idea of a personalized, rather than an institutionalized, presidency, he understood the importance of his personal relationship with his aides. Sorensen describes this relationship as follows: "He was informal without being chummy, hard-driving but easy-mannered, interested in us as people without being patronizing."[102] But Kennedy did impose a psychological distance between himself and his aides; rarely, if ever, were they involved in his social life. Kennedy's intimate friends were found in places other than the White House; but his White House staff was devoted to him and his political principles. "We were appointed for our ability to fulfill the President's needs and talk the President's language. We represented no one but John Kennedy."[103] In turn, the president showed his staff appreciation "not by constant expressions of gratitude—which were in fact rare—but by returning in full the loyalty of his staff. . . . "[104] Additionally, Kennedy spared his aides much of the infighting experienced by their predecessors in FDR's White House by avoiding the temptation to pit staff members against each other. Despite his competitive nature and desire to ferret out the best alternatives as solutions to problems, he apparently had "no taste for ego-baiting and low tolerance for egoism. . . . "[105] According to Pierre Salinger, "JFK insisted on teamwork, not intramural competition. He would not tolerate staff politicking for his favor, and minor White House aides who tried it early in the administration either were transferred to other departments or told to knock it off."[106]

To suggest that Kennedy's men were a close-knit band of happy campers, however, would be erroneous. Sorensen recalls that the staff "was neither as efficient as we pretended nor as harmonious as he [the president] thought. Failure of communication appeared more than once. A degree of envy and occasionally resentment cropped up now and then."[107] Patrick Anderson has written that Kennedy knew his staff "hummed with an undercurrent of jealousy, rivalry, and friction," the result of brilliant, assertive individuals trying to work as a team to accomplish the goals of the president to whom they were individually devoted.[108] They, like their leader, were pragmatists—disciplined, hardworking, task-oriented. Moreover, JFK was accessible to his aides, and apparently no one felt his voice would not be heard, his opinion not considered, by the president. Although there still may have been competition in the Kennedy White House, there was no debilitating conflict due to the traits of the men who served the president and his own managerial style.

Part of the Kennedy staff's ability to walk the fine line between competition and conflict was due, in Patrick Anderson's words, to the president's "exceptional skill in handling men. His ability to cajole, to persuade, to soothe, to inspire, was effortless, virtually invisible. He was, in the best sense of the term, a master manipulator of man."[109] This talent was supplemented by Kennedy's belief in hands-on management, "day-to-day direction and control."[110] Indeed, the president once remarked: "There is a great tendency in government to have papers stay on desks too long. . . . One of the functions of the President is to try to have it move with more speed. Otherwise you can wait while the world collapses."[111] Kennedy's style was to work one-on-one with staff members, giving each one specific duties and holding them individually responsible for completing them.[112] Evelyn Lincoln recalls that "if he wanted something done, he wanted it done immediately. If he selected you to do it, it was because you were on the job and near him at the time. If you proved up to the task, he called on you again. If you were slow on performance, the next time he asked someone else to do it."[113]

Kennedy's managerial style, like that of FDR, included an emphasis on his personal involvement in the work of the White House. Kenneth O'Donnell and Dave Powers recall that "very few small details about the running of the government escaped him. . . . "[114] Louis Koenig wrote: "He put in abundant hours at desk-side conferences and on the telephone, pursuing details well down the line of departmental hierarchy, and took a constant hand in coordination, its weight laid not merely upon top-level endeavor but upon minor affairs as well."[115] Just as one of his Democrat successors, Jimmy Carter, would be criticized for excess attention to administrative detail in the White House, so Kennedy faced concern that he was too immersed in minor matters better delegated to members of his staff. Additionally, his penchant for quick decisiveness was suspect to some who felt that JFK's "swiftness—terse statement, quick strides from one problem to the next—resulted at times in inadequate consideration of alternatives."[116] Kennedy, however, was unconcerned about the way he managed his White House; he was confident in the quality of his staff, their loyalty to him, and his own abilities and priorities. In part this self-assurance, which Jimmy Carter may have lacked, stemmed from an awareness of one of his major presidential strengths: an interest in, and the ability to seek and use, information from people outside the White House.

Although John Kennedy valued a close-knit staff, loyal first and foremost to him, he knew the advantages of receiving information from a variety of external sources. He once said, "I sit in the White House . . . and what I read . . . and

. . . see is the sum total of what I hear and learn. So the more people I can see, or the wider I can expose [my mind] to different ideas, the more effective [I] can be as President.''[117] Accordingly, Sorensen recalls, Kennedy ''refused to take the chance that his subordinates were screening out criticisms, alternatives or information on his or their errors. He made certain that he had the final decision on whom he would see and what he would read.''[118]

The president sought information and ideas through his network of contacts in Congress and the national press, and by soliciting opinions of elder statesmen and the nation's intelligentsia (especially those from Harvard). He was known for inviting people to see him on an unscheduled basis, arranging for Evelyn Lincoln to allow these guests entrance through her door to the Oval Office. This practice was not always popular with other staff members, such as the appointments secretary, who recalls that Kennedy made ''so many closely crowded appointments that Dave [Powers] and I found ourselves piling up so many waiting visitors that we ran out of waiting room space.''[119]

Kennedy also read prodigiously—books, newsmagazines, reports of public polls, and a special reading file comprised of a sample of correspondence from private citizens. Each morning he began the day by perusing several newspapers while eating breakfast, and ''he did not want to talk or be disturbed until he had finished both the papers and his breakfast.''[120] O'Donnell and Powers recall that much of the work in the White House, ''not only appointments but staff assignments in general . . . came out of Kennedy's intensive scanning of the morning newspapers.''[121]

As was the case with his predecessors and his successors, Kennedy was the recipient of both routine and special reports. Written material was placed in a folder each evening for his review at night, and he often read reports and memoranda in the White House residence until midnight.[122] Every Friday he received reports from Cabinet departments on activities in these units during the preceding six days, giving him an overview of major decisions reached, issues under consideration, and potential problems for presidential consideration.[123] Wherever he went, the president took a briefcase ''bulging with whatever he and his staff felt he needed to read by way of mail, magazines, books, briefing memos and assorted dispatches and documents. During absences of forty-eight hours or more, additional materials were flown to him regularly.''[124]

Although he was a conscientious and interested reader of the material sent to him, Kennedy was not a receptacle for all the written material anyone decided to transmit to the Oval Office. His staff were sifters and separators of the information he received. For instance, McGeorge Bundy, Kennedy's National Security Council assistant, sorted through overseas cables each day and took only those he deemed vital for presidential review to Kennedy. After the Bay of Pigs invasion, JFK requested that Attorney General Robert Kennedy and Theodore Sorensen ''keep involved in national security matters by reading reports and attending appropriate meetings.''[125] Sorensen also attended all formal presidential meetings, such as those involving the Cabinet and the National Security

Council, as well as breakfast meetings with legislative leaders and sessions with those responsible for the development of the president's budget and legislative program.[126]

Such delegation was instituted not only to save the president work but also to keep his staff of generalists informed about every aspect of federal activity, "to know everything that was going on, to provide speedy and exact answers to his questions and, most of all, to alert him to potential troubles."[127] Despite the power Kennedy seemed to invest in some members of his staff, he never delegated his authority. "We could not impose our own views, nor assert the President's views, nor speak in the President's voice, without his prior or subsequent approval," Sorensen emphasized.[128] Indeed, Kennedy jokingly once reminded his staff: "I will continue to have some residual functions."[129]

In addition to receiving information from a variety of written sources, Kennedy sought facts and opinions during interactions with his aides and others advisors. However, he was not a conversationalist like Roosevelt, and detested long meetings. According to Stephen Hess, "Kennedy was too restless to sit for long periods, too impatient with long-winded speakers, and too mentally agile to accept repetitious, circuitous cabinet and NSC discussions as a tolerable method of receiving information."[130] If a meeting was absolutely necessary, Arthur Schlesinger, Jr., recalls, Kennedy "preferred a small one with candid discussion among the technicians and professionals who could give him the facts on which decision was to be based."[131] Most of the meetings Kennedy attended were short, "many no more than fifteen minutes, very few running over an hour."[132] According to Sorensen, "He kept his own comments to a minimum and often cut short others . . . who were dealing with generalities or repeating the obvious."[133] The president had a facility for absorbing detail while understanding "the big picture," and when he determined that discussion was no longer fruitful or a decision had been reached, "he would gather up all his papers as a sign that the meeting was over. . . ."[134] While Kennedy rarely used large formal meetings to transact the business of the presidency, he did depend on informal, frequent interactions during the day with individual staff members to conduct his work. Sidney Hyman wrote in October 1963: "At intervals during the day, staff aides . . . will . . . visit the President's office with short oral reports or with a check list of items briefly outlining a development and suggesting a course of action. The President is said to average around 15 'spot decisions' of this sort in a 10-minute meeting."[135]

Unlike Harry Truman, Kennedy thought Cabinet meetings a waste of time, having little interest in suffering pain from his bad back while listening to the views of Cabinet members on issues outside their individual realms of expertise. But he did value the use of small ad hoc task forces "to get at the fact of a major problem, to isolate the issues, to examine possible solutions and consequences, and to make recommendations."[136] Eschewing the large formal meeting, Kennedy felt his informational needs were met by the almost continuous one-on-one interactions he had with senior aides during the day; the short, informal sessions he attended with aides, congressmen, department heads, and others he deemed it appropriate to invite to the White House; the ad hoc task forces that emerged, offered recommendations, and dissolved; and his use of the telephone. According to Lewis Paper, to move the bureaucracy Kennedy "spent a good deal of time on the telephone calling people who had the information he needed. . . ."[137] Sorensen remembers: "He was on the telephone, according to one estimate, more than fifty times in an average day."[138]

Short meetings, terse memos with recommendations for action, and brief interactions with individual staff members throughout his working day—these were John Kennedy's preferred mechanisms for gathering information within the White House, and they supplemented the sources of facts, ideas, and opinions he sought from outside his personal organization. In his memoirs as Kennedy's special counsel, Sorensen writes: "The President's own accessibility, and his insistence on dealing with subordinates as well as chiefs, made certain that he was not denied any relevant counsel or criticism. . . ."[139] Moreover, his preferred sources of information, such as one-on-one conversations and small group discussions, enriched the information he did receive by providing him verbal and nonverbal cues from those who were its originators and transmitters. Kennedy's personalized approach to the presidency, and his pragmatic approach to the administration of the White House as an organization, were well served by the ways he acquired information to make decisions.

John F. Kennedy was not a delegator of decisions. He accepted responsibility for the decision-making process and for the products of that process. According to Koenig, "Kennedy injected himself at any point along the decision-making spectrum from problem-selection to final judgment. Whereas Eisenhower wanted decisions brought to him for approval, Kennedy wants problems brought to him for decision."[140] He fervently believed in relying on his staff and Cabinet members for information and advice but, as O'Donnell and Powers remember, "he wanted to make all of his own decisions and he wanted nobody to speak for him."[141] Although Sorensen has written that staff held considerable discretion in areas where the president's interest or knowledge was limited, no staff member made major decisions for the president. The role of Kennedy aides was to allow the president "more time, facts and judgments with which to make them himself."[142] This philosophy and approach to decision making required more of the president's time as an overseer of the staff's activities, but "he much preferred those burdens to the handicaps of being merely a clerk in his own office, caught up in the routines and recommendations of others."[143]

Just as Kennedy disliked a highly structured White House and formalized systems of information flow, so he had no use for decision making in formal settings. According to Paper, in meetings or discussions with bureaucrats "he would not usually reveal his own thinking—there was too much danger that he would then hear only what others thought he wanted to hear."[144] The process Kennedy did prefer was one of immersing himself in the facts and opinions he received from staff and weighing them against those he sought from outside sources such as journalists, congressmen, and political friends. He was not concerned about differences in opinion among those who worked with and/or for him. In fact, "Kennedy eschewed consensus; he wanted to know a problem's facets and alternative answers, keeping decision for himself in consultation or 'dialogue,' as the administration called it, with advisers."[145] At a point where a decision seemed imminent or was necessary, the president might call a meeting of those most involved with the issue at hand. Although sometimes pretending to make major decisions in large meetings, such as those of the National Security Council, he reached most of these decisions prior to the meetings.[146] According to Sorensen, "He strongly preferred to make all major decisions with far fewer people present, often only the officer to whom he was communicating the decision."[147]

Kennedy's approach to decision making, like his method of managing the White House, was highly personalized and pragmatic. The role of the staff was to present alternatives so that he could make the decision on a given issue, unhampered by formal structures and processes. According to Paper:

> Kennedy believed that Eisenhower's staff operation impeded his effectiveness in making sound decisions. Reliance on formal structures, Kennedy believed, could hamper rather than facilitate a discussion of substantive issues. The paper lineage of responsibilities could perhaps ensure efficiency, but it could not guarantee effectiveness. In Kennedy's eyes, too much organization stifled debate; it denied him access to a broad scope of information and ideas; and, perhaps most importantly, it undercut his ability to understand the real merits of available options.[148]

In his day-to-day work Kennedy also preferred informality in his communications with staff. Anderson suggests that because Kennedy and his senior aides were contemporaries, an "ease of communication" existed between them, "a common style."[149] But if he was informal, he could not be characterized as a gregarious conversationalist among those with whom he interacted daily. Joseph Kraft wrote in December 1962: "Casual terseness marks most of the exchanges between the staff and the President. 'What have you got?' or 'What's up?' is Mr. Kennedy's usual opening phrase. Then, as one aide says, 'You're supposed to tell him—bang, bang, bang.' "[150] Schlesinger later wrote that during daytime working hours in the west wing of the White House, communication between president and staff was a form of oral shorthand. "Kennedy's mind raced ahead of his words; and, by the time he was midway in a thought, he was likely to assume that the drift was evident and, without bothering to complete one sentence, he would begin the next."[151] Schlesinger also characterizes Kennedy as a "superb listener" who would "lean forward, his eyes protruding slightly, concerned with using the occasion not to expound his own thoughts but to drag out of the talker whatever could be of use to him."[152] As a result, Kennedy could hear the opinions and biases of other individuals on a given issue without revealing his own and "without making his visitors conscious that he was holding back."[153]

Compared with Truman, Kennedy was not a patient president or an easy-going communicator. His former aides have written of "moments of irritation" that were occasional but short, during which "his vocabulary was vivid."[154] Salinger has written of the president's "bristling temper" and his "cold sarcasm," accepted by the staff because they knew those episodes would pass and because "we knew he was driving himself harder than he was driving us—despite great and persistent physical pain and personal tragedy."[155] Like Roosevelt, however, at the end of the day he decreased the tempo of his schedule, and he relaxed. Sorensen remembers that around 7:30 in the evening, after his last appointment, the president "was at his reflective best . . . relating some crisis or anecdote of the day, asking me to check into some new problem or suggestion. . . ."[156] Apparently this time period was used by other aides who had been unable to see him during the day, and two or three of his closest advisers would stand around his desk "presenting problems," but in a calmer, quieter environment.[157]

When he was communicating with his staff, it appears that John Kennedy was not the animated, dominant discussant that Franklin Roosevelt was, nor was he always the relaxed and open communicator that Harry Truman seemed to be. He was attentive, sometimes contentious, and relaxed in the sense that he was self-assured, confident in his abilities and his presidential agenda. More reserved than Roosevelt or Truman, he communicated when he had to and in the way he needed to as each situation demanded. He was a pragmatic communicator in the White House, yet assumed the mantle of a passionate orator in his public speeches directed to "a new generation of Americans." Just as it is difficult to assess his accomplishments as a president, it is not easy to evaluate Kennedy as a manager and communicator in the White House because his time there was cut short.

However, two related observations make the structure of, and the relationships within, the Kennedy White House important to this study. In contrast with the inner circles around other modern presidents, Salinger reminds us that "every principal member of JFK's staff who took the oath of office the day after his inauguration was still working for him on the day of his death."[158] Assured of his staff's loyalty and competence, Kennedy consciously conferred great responsibility for domestic and foreign affairs on his senior aides. In so doing, Paper states, the president "gave his stamp of approval to the idea that governmental power can and should be concentrated in the White House rather than in the appropriate executive departments. . . ."[159] As a result, in Paper's opinion, Kennedy "accelerated a trend which culminated in the Watergate scandals under Nixon."[160]

But JFK's personality, and his penchant for seeking information from a vast network of individuals in and outside the White House, were in sharp contrast with Richard Nixon. Kennedy's insistence on personal involvement in operational detail and his interest in information-rich forms of communication with his staff differed significantly from Nixon's approaches to management and communication within his White House. For those who believe that Cabinets should be significant policy-making entities in the modern presidency, John Kennedy's administration left a lot to be desired. Suggesting that the seeds of Watergate were sown in his White House, however, ignores Kennedy's strengths as a hands-on leader, as an astute communicator, within his own organization.

There would be one more Democrat in the White House before the advent of the Nixon administration and its return to a focus on structure, hierarchy, formality, and detachment. After November 22, 1963, the "personalized presidency" would take on new meanings, under the direction of Lyndon B. Johnson.

LYNDON B. JOHNSON—ADMINISTRATION BY DOMINATION

While John Kennedy was knowledgeable about the operational details of his White House, collegial yet detached from his aides, Lyndon Johnson was immersed day and night in the work and the workings of his organization, and viewed his senior aides as companions as well as colleagues. Beginning with the first week of his presidency, Johnson daily used all his energy, and that of those around him, to launch the programs of the Great Society. Later that energy would have to be channeled into managing and coping with the Vietnam War.

With a small staff, an emphasis on a fluid organizational structure, and constant communication with his senior aides, Johnson was a dynamic and dominating organizational leader. He was a devotee of FDR, a master of congressional politics, an individual who eschewed temperance in most forms. By the mid–1960s a number of national problems were reaching varying stages of crisis, such as racial injustice, poverty, and educational needs, as the government became increasingly involved in strife-torn countries in Southeast Asia. Shortly after assuming office, Johnson created a presidential agenda that called for the creation of, and monumental changes in, the nation's domestic programs. He structured and ran his White House to generate the programs and policies he deemed appropriate at this juncture in history.

Like Kennedy, Johnson saw no advantages in a highly structured White House such as that which existed in Eisenhower's administration. Indeed, "hands-on" management took on a new meaning in his White House—the president touched almost every sphere of activity directly. He worked with a small group of aides in an organization known for its loose structure. A new aide once reportedly asked for an organization chart and was told by a career official: "We don't have any organization chart at the White House because we don't have any organization."[161] In response to criticisms about the apparent lack of organization, Cabinet Secretary Horace Busby once remarked that "flow charts aren't necessary among people who understand each other."[162] However, Emmette Redford and Richard McCulley, who perhaps have written the most thorough analysis of Johnson's administration of the presidency, emphasize that LBJ's White House was *not* unstructured. The president designated role specializations, and although he also used the spokes-of-the-wheel structure, with information flowing to him directly from a few aides, some staff members were more equal than others in their interactions with the president. Additionally, "identifiable points of internal coordination and an awareness of individual roles contributed toward orderly operations," especially after the staff became Johnson's own, that is, after the majority of Kennedy's aides had left the White House.[163]

Part of the confusion or disagreement on the part of those who have studied the structure of Johnson's White House stems from the fact that the structure emerged over time: LBJ did not distribute organizational charts on his first day in the Oval Office. Additionally, the way the president assigned tasks and personally directed the work of his aides created such diversity in day-to-day activities that White House operations sometimes seemed chaotic. Hess writes: "The freewheeling staff assignments, the inversion of duties, and the increasing centralization of operations meant that nothing was simple to chart in the Johnson White House."[164]

Although seventeen "principal assistants" to the president were counted in October 1967, there were approximately seven individuals who were senior aides in charge of functional areas throughout the Johnson presidency.[165] These individuals were:

- McGeorge Bundy, succeeded by Walt Rostow—National Security Council special assistant
- Bill Moyers, succeeded by Joseph Califano—assistant in charge of domestic issues and the development of the legislative program
- Lawrence O'Brien, succeeded by "Barefoot" Sanders—congressional liaison
- George Reedy, succeeded by Bill Moyers and then George Christian—press secretary
- Myron Feldman, succeeded by Lee White and then Harry McPherson—special counsel
- Walter Jenkins, succeeded by Jack Valenti, Marvin Watson, and Jim Jones—appointments secretary
- Horace Busby, succeeded by Robert Kintner—Cabinet secretary.

The structure of Johnson's White House evolved around these functional roles and the people who assumed them, for tasks often were assumed and/or assigned based on an individual's capabilities. Redford and McCulley observe that "Johnson allowed and even encouraged the development of role specializations by individual talent, choice, and initiative. While types of functions fashioned personal allocations, men also determined their roles."[166] According to George Christian, the last press secretary to serve in the Johnson White House, the president "frequently hired people and brought them into the White House in senior positions with no clearly defined duties because his method was . . . 'you take whatever you're big enough to take' in the way of responsibilities. . . . If you were man enough to just assume control over something, he didn't object to it—particularly when he thought the person you had to control wasn't all that strong anyway. . . ."[167]

Despite the conflict this process may have caused among staff members, it did enhance flexibility in the structure because aides "constantly worked in a variety of areas of activity. This made collaboration across loose boundary lines imperative."[168] Consequently communication among staff, and between president and staff, became crucial, especially since Johnson served as his own chief of staff. According to Christian, "There was nobody else in the White House who had the authority to tell another senior staff precisely what to do except on order from the President. You never felt that you had to go through somebody to get to him."[169] The only individual who assumed a role with any semblance to that of chief of staff was Walter Jenkins, who became responsible for administration at the beginning of the Johnson presidency.

> Inside the White House, the surest way to get a memo into the "night reading" was to route it through his office. For the outsider, the fastest way to get to see the President was to interest Jenkins. He passed on a number of important presidential letters and documents, and had the authority—or rather simply assumed the authority in an entirely natural way—to instruct that President Johnson's name be signed.[170]

But Jenkins left the White House in disgrace after eleven months in Johnson's service, after being arrested in Washington, D.C., on a morals charge. No aide ever took his place as Johnson's primary assistant for administration.

There is an additional organizational structure during Johnson's term that deserves mention: the Tuesday Cabinet. A group of the president's senior aides met for lunch each Tuesday, beginning in 1965, to deliberate and make decisions on the conduct of the Vietnam War. Those in attendance, in addition to the president, were Secretary of State Dean Rusk, Secretary of Defense Robert McNamara, National Security Council assistant McGeorge Bundy, and Bill Moyers, who joined the group after becoming press secretary. According to Henry Graff, whose book describes this group and its deliberations: "In inviting Moyers the President was meeting the need he felt to have at the table someone not tied bureaucratically to existing policies and with whom he could afterward weight the purport of the sessions."[171] Moyers, McNamara, and Bundy eventually left the White House, in part over their disagreement with U.S. policy in Vietnam. George Christian, Clark Clifford, and Walt Rostow became their respective successors in the White House and in the Tuesday Cabinet. Over time this group would become an important policy-making unit within, and yet external to, the rest of the White House organization.

Lyndon Johnson's White House was a small group of generalists, capable of overseeing functional areas as well as performing assigned tasks outside these areas. This structure maximized flexibility in handling a wide variety of responsibilities, the free flow of communication among staff, and access to the president. However, as Redford and McCulley suggest, such a structure "probably contributed to internal confusions and tensions . . . and placed a heavy burden of oversight and control directly on the president.''[172] Moreover, as was the case in Roosevelt's White House, a small staff is an overworked staff, particularly when it serves an activist president. ''For the presidential purposes inherited from his predecessor or initiated under Johnson's leadership, the staff was minimal and perhaps less than was desirable.''[173] Indeed, the small size of Johnson's staff, the ambitious presidential agenda he established for his White House to accomplish, and the president's own personality were major factors affecting Johnson's relationship with his aides and his managerial style.

Lyndon Johnson was not only accessible to his staff; he was accompanied by at least one or two of them from the time he awakened each morning until he fell asleep at night. Unlike the senior staff in the Kennedy administration, Johnson's aides were his companions as well as his colleagues. According to Jack Valenti, one of his close aides, the president ''gathered his staff about him because he enjoyed being with them, much as a father would be with his family. He relaxed with them, he was comfortable and at ease with them.''[174] He was also defensive about his relationship with them. George Christian remembers that: ''He hated it when they referred to his friends as cronies and somebody else's friends as intellectual stalwarts. He said 'you fellows [staff members] are my cronies. You're the only people I ever really see on a constant basis.' And the truth was that he had a closer relationship . . . with his staff people than he did anybody else.''[175]

Although the relationship between president and staff was informal, it was not always friendly. Included in most of the chronicles of his presidency are stories describing bursts of temper against his close aides. ''He was capable of being very tough on his staff and, to be quite honest, was brutal with them at times.''[176] Patrick Anderson has compared the Johnson White House to Caligula's court, describing the difficulties staff faced when working with the president—a number of aides left the White House during his administration because of the way they were treated. ''Roosevelt, Truman, Eisenhower, Kennedy—each inspired love in the men who served him. Johnson does not. His men feel fascination, sympathy, respect, admiration—but not love.''[177] According to Christian, ''He could be rough, he could terrify, he could explain himself in terms no one could forget.''[178] In their study of the Johnson White House, Redford and McCulley state that ''evidence of confrontation between the president and his top assistants was abundant.''[179] However, although Johnson was famous for punishing his aides by ignoring them, he was known for welcoming them back into the fold by assigning them new tasks or sometimes assuaging their feelings by inviting them to the White House residence for a late evening supper.

Johnson's aides were his friends as well as his subordinates, and he treated them alternately as such, sometimes causing confusion and insecurity among them. Because they were a small staff, they were generally overworked, and the verbal abuse they tolerated did not make for an easy existence in the Johnson White House. On the other hand, LBJ ''could be generous to a fault and exceptionally kind to those around him''—stroking their egos and patting them on the back to apologize, show forgiveness, or express appreciation.''[180] Additionally, he involved his senior aides continuously in the development of policies and programs; staff were integrally involved in the creation of the Great Society. One could assume as much responsibility as he could handle, and the White House teemed with activity and productivity. In short, working for Lyndon Johnson was like being tied to a rocket—it was true excitement but had its risks.

The Vietnam War did create several *major* rifts between this president and several members of his staff. ''As public criticism of his foreign policy mounted, the president became progressively more defensive and intolerant of divergent views within the White House,'' according to Redford and McCulley.[181] He was no longer open to advice from those people who had seemed so personally important to him. ''McPherson . . . became so unhappy with his inability to approach the president forthrightly on the issue that he considered resignation,''[182] but McPherson believed in the president, hoped he knew what he was doing, and decided to stay. Bill Moyers, however, a great influence on Johnson, did leave the White House in conflict with the president's foreign policy. According to Christian, ''Bill Moyers' departure from Johnson's side was the worst thing that could have happened to him. He counseled with him all the time. He was kind of a son to him and when their relationship began to fall apart and Bill had to leave, it was a serious blow to him [Johnson].''[183] By contrast, those aides who helped guide the president's Vietnam strategy were his ''natural friends,'' made so by the work they mutually conducted in meetings of the Tuesday Cabinet.[184] According to Graff, ''By temperament and training his men were not infighters, and they recognized fealty as the shining badge of gentlemen such as they.''[185]

President Johnson managed his White House organization with a hands-on approach unlike that of any other modern chief executive. ''Inheriting a White House already partially established, he directed a multi-centered, semi-hierarchical, flexible system, adapted over time to personal changes and moved by his own unmitigated drive for accomplishment, pervasive and intimate involvement, personal work habits, and desire for unity and loyalty.''[186] As is the case with all organizational leaders, Johnson's management style was affected by his personality and his past. His legislative experience and prowess in congressional political leadership made him ''a master of the art of gaining consensus or compromise on a course of action among those representing conflicting interests and holding different views.''[187]

According to Christian, Johnson had an aptitude for administration. He was policy-oriented, adept at seeing the ''big picture'' in a montage of programs and policies; yet he was attentive to the daily paper flow in and out of the Oval Office. ''Rarely did a letter prepared for his signature wait on his signing table more than one day. No matter how large the stacks were, he would bear down in the late evening and get the job behind him. He read a high proportion of his mail. . . . ''[188] Wanting to be involved in all spheres of White House activity and in exercising complete control over his staff, Johnson became personally involved in the work of his staff. For instance, he might assign a task and then check on the progress of that assignment during the day by repeatedly telephoning an aide. He was, in Hess's words, "the most accessible president since Roosevelt," not just because he wished to be available to his staff—he also was anxious to control them.[189] To LBJ, management meant control as opposed to coordination or facilitation. David Halberstam writes, "if he knew the details he could control the action, he could control subordinates."[190] Because of his attention to detail, he had, in Christian's words, "no tolerance for sloth and very little for blatant mistakes and inefficiency."[191]

As one might expect, the president's management style deemphasized delegation. Christian recalls:

> Where the President was reluctant to delegate was on the things of great sensitivity to him. He delegated very little to the press area. He delegated very little in the foreign policy decision-making except the routine of it. . . . He didn't want things done that he would have to pay a penalty for. He said, "I'm big enough to take the rap if it goes wrong, but I don't want to be surprised." Consequently, he spent an inordinate amount of time just keeping track of everything for his own mental processes and carrying out his business.[192]

The result, according to Hess, of Johnson's perceived need to be involved in all aspects of his presidency was the engagement of his staff in more operational and policy-making matters than had been the case in previous White Houses. A concomitant flow of minutiae into the Oval Office was a by-product of his intense involvement in the ongoing and ad hoc tasks under way within his environs.[193]

To manage the White House with the intensity that Johnson exhibited took considerable physical and mental energy. The president was able to survive, in part, because of his two-shift days. He worked from early morning until early afternoon; ate lunch, exercised and napped for a couple of hours; and then worked from late afternoon until 9 or 10 at night. Additionally, Christian observes, "Johnson diligently conserved his strength by spending part of the day relatively immobile. This entailed a long morning in bed and then a nap in midafternoon. . . . He believed that the time spent before going to the office was his most productive period; he could think, he could read, he could talk, he could decide. His body might be reclining, but his mind was moving like a meteor."[194] One cannot help but recall the routines of Roosevelt and Kennedy, both beginning their days reading in bed. And Johnson, like Roosevelt, conducted business with his aides in his bedroom. His management style was communication-intensive, requiring numerous interactions with staff during each working day as he tried to keep abreast of his work as well as theirs. But, as Redford and McCulley suggest, among the consequences of this management style were "dependence for coordination on the energy and competence of the president personally, strain on personnel, and accompanying danger of lack of adequate analysis and deliberation.''[195] Nevertheless, the president felt compelled to manage, as well as lead, his White House unilaterally. To accomplish this goal he depended on information streaming into his office or his bedroom, day and night, from a multitude of sources.

LBJ's White House has been depicted as one led by a man barking orders left and right, talking on the telephone incessantly, striding through the halls of the White House's west wing asking questions and demanding on-the-spot answers. Johnson was in almost continual motion, but his receipt and use of information were more organized than some accounts would have us believe. This veteran of Capitol Hill knew that information is power, and he desired both. In the White House he possessed ''an insatiable thirst for information—more facts, new facts, instant facts.''[196] Accordingly, in his organization where policy origination was emphasized, senior aides became communication links and information processors to an extent unlike that found in other White Houses. By the time Johnson became president, the White House was a mature organization within a larger bureaucracy, and the White House staff was the link between that bureaucracy and the president.

Unlike Kennedy, Johnson was not distrustful of the rest of the Executive Branch—he just wanted to control it. As a result, the White House staff became the primary channel through which information flowed to the president. Redford and McCulley found in their study that ''the primary role of the staff was communication—upward and outward. And for the president's function of decision making, the key staff role was processing information that flowed to him.''[197] Despite general perceptions of Johnson as an ''oral'' president who, like Roosevelt enjoyed one-on-one interactions with staff and other advisers almost continuously, he received much of his information in written form, in what came to be called his ''night reading.'' A major function of the Johnson staff was to prepare this material for the president each day.

> Memorandums from departments and agencies and from executive office heads, accompanied more often than not by memorandums from White House staff, and a large stack independently generated by the staff accumulated at the end of the day. Staff rushed their memos to completion and then got them to the appointments secretary, the president's personal secretary, the chief usher, or to any other staff member strategically located to place them in the day's stack.[198]

According to Christian, the night reading might include ''eighty or a hundred pieces of reading material—memos, reports, analyses, correspondence, position papers. If he didn't finish this at night, the leftovers stared at him in the morning, and he dutifully resumed his reading.''[199]

Johnson not only read this material; he made comments on it, particularly on those staff memos requiring a response.

> Typically, at the end of the staff memorandum were two blanks for the president's option opposite the words ''Approve'' or ''Disapprove.'' The president often added comments,

rejecting or amplifying the simple, dichotomous options provided him. He occasionally wrote, "See me." The system forced action-oriented memorandums and staff definition of options; it provided for the president also a ready means of prompt instruction of staff on next actions to be taken.[200]

Although the president wanted as much information as possible, the sheer volume of it required some screening and summarization to maximize the use of the president's time. According to Redford and McCulley, the staff's "most crucial function was to pull together information for the president's use, selecting memos that merited presidential attention, organizing and focusing their content, and defining possibilities and perhaps alternatives of decision."[201] Additionally, Johnson attempted to control the bulk of his reading by insisting on relatively short, concise staff memoranda. Christian recalls that "some staff members with few specific assignments were prone to long memos and dissertations of a quality which required many man-hours of labor."[202] Frequently the president would send a memo back to its author if it was too long and unclear, or he would send it to another staff member with an attached note: "Read this and tell me what he's talking about."[203] Johnson also expected clarity in memos from the federal departments. For instance, the State Department was instructed to edit its papers and compose them in "the English language," not only to save the president reading time but also because he believed that government jargon was often used to avoid taking a position or to disguise timidity, a quality, according to William S. White, that annoyed the president more than belligerence.[204]

Johnson was conscientious about paper flow in the White House for several reasons. First, it gave him information—the facts, ideas, and opinions that he wanted. Second, it allowed him to communicate with some people he could not, or chose not to, see during the day. According to Christian, "Some people even preferred to write him memos. He enjoyed their memos. He didn't necessarily enjoy being in a conversation with them."[205] Most important, perhaps, Johnson was determined to create as complete a historical record of his years in the White House as possible. A sophisticated archival system was developed during his presidency, and after memos and papers were no longer necessary for presidential review or action, they were sent to staff responsible for the organization of the Lyndon B. Johnson Presidential Library.

The president also received much of the information he needed orally, particularly through individual conferences, informal chats, and small group meetings. At one point in his presidency he asked Jack Valenti to hold staff meetings, but they "petered out . . . for we soon became so busy doing chores the president had assigned to us, and had no time to spend an hour or so in the morning with each other."[206] Johnson occasionally held a staff meeting, but more often he met with a portion of his staff, and also would suggest to an aide that "meetings be held on some topic or area of work. Variously, the top staff aides would arrange meetings on an occasional or regular basis with those working in their cluster or with all staff members who might collaborate."[207] The president did, however, hold Cabinet meetings with formal agendas and, like Eisenhower, appointed a Cabinet secretary. These meetings, in the main, apparently were more for show than for substance, particularly on issues related to foreign policy.

In addition to the ad hoc interactions he would have with staff members during the day, the president held early morning sessions in his bedroom with at least one or two of his closest aides, such as Moyers, Valenti, Christian and, later in his administration, Larry Temple. As one might expect, the ability to draw "bedroom duty" enhanced an aide's status in the White House. These individuals arrived at approximately 7:30 A.M. "and remained with the president . . . until he was dressed about two hours later. As he flipped through memorandum after memorandum, perhaps completing his night reading, he gave them instructions on action to be taken: set up appointments, make telephone calls, get further information."[208] These oral instructions supplemented the written comments he made on memos and papers that were returned to their authors.

To augment the information Johnson received directly from his staff, he was an avid reader of, and listener to, information available from outside the White House. Every morning he read marked copies of the *Congressional Record*, as well as several morning newspapers. He also watched the morning network television news programs. Indeed, Johnson's Oval Office became famous for its three television sets, often running simultaneously, and its wire service ticker.

The president also spent a good deal of time meeting with representatives of a variety of constituencies, including leaders from business, labor, and the black community. As a creature of Congress, he met frequently with its leaders and worked with them to develop legislative programs using ad hoc task forces. Johnson also sought advice from political friends in Texas, as well as former government officials, including Abe Fortas, Dean Acheson, Omar Bradley, Henry Cabot Lodge, Matthew Ridgway, and Cyrus Vance. Ben Bagdikian wrote in 1965, "Johnson thinks out loud with friends chiefly by telephone, and at all hours of the day and night. But some friends, like Fortas, Clifford [Clark Clifford who would eventually become secretary of defense], . . . and Justice Douglas, go to the White House more or less regularly for private dinners. On occasion the President will drop in on them in their homes."[209]

The president liked his sessions with advisers outside the White House, to "bounce" ideas off them and to get opinions from those independent of him, that is, people other than his own staff. According to Christian, "When military leaders came back from Vietnam he wanted to see them. He wanted to talk to them. He wanted to have as much time as he could with them himself. He didn't want the Joint Chiefs to be filtering stuff."[210] Over time, as mentioned earlier in this chapter, Johnson listened increasingly to his luncheon guests every Tuesday, and that inner circle eventually held more influence over the information he received and the decisions he made about the war in Vietnam.

Another major source of information during the Johnson presidency was the fourteen task forces he appointed to create and mobilize programs of the Great Society. Bill Moyers coordinated the work of these ad hoc groups, comprised mainly of academicians, during the summer of 1964. In the fall of that year these task forces submitted reports that Moyers "parceled . . . out to four other staffers . . . to be boiled down to workable legislative proposals."[211] According to Redford and McCulley, "The task force process reflected central elements of Johnson management: reliance on ad hoc, informal bodies, maintenance of personal control of process, and retention of flexibility through confidentiality."[212]

If he could not have total control over his vast domain, Lyndon Johnson at least tried to keep in constant touch with those within and outside the walls of the White House, who could provide him information and ideas. "From his office and wherever he moved he constantly reached for information or gave directions. He was habituated to grabbing the telephone for instant contact. His direct and feverishly pursued contact with Cabinet and other executives, congressmen, trusted advisors, and numerous other persons supplemented the staff system. . . ."[213] Johnson, like Roosevelt, was essentially a sponge, absorbing as much information as he could read, hear, or see on television. As a result, keeping bad news from him, particularly from Vietnam, was probably impossible. According to Christian, "There was no way to hide anything from him. I'm not saying that couldn't have happened but there was no way to protect him from bad information or discouraging information . . . because he talked to so many people and he watched television and read so much. . . ."[214]

Just as he involved himself directly in the flow of information into and within his White House, so Lyndon Johnson assumed control and responsibility for his decision-making process. Redford and McCulley observe that "His system was centralized in that he did not delegate or allow presidential decisions to pass to others, but decentralized in the access of multiple advisers."[215] Christian corroborates this finding, recalling that Johnson "would study the pros and cons of a subject with something akin to fascination, and if he did not have all of the information he wanted he would call a meeting of everyone connected with the problem and discuss it at length."[216] As was the case with Roosevelt, Johnson used his friends "as sounding boards," revealing his thoughts, absorbing their reactions, in the formulation of a decision. Bagdikian wrote during the Johnson presidency that "The chief function of his friends is to let him talk."[217] Bill Moyers recalls that the president insisted on asking questions until he thought he "pried from you all you know on the subject. Just at the point you think he . . . satisfied himself, he starts hurtling questions around the table like popcorn."[218] Johnson listened to his friends and his aides, but he was not as open to other elements of the federal bureaucracy; "he did not create a system of multiple advocacy in which the viewpoints of elements of the subpresidency were conveyed to him by White House staff acting only as honest brokers."[219] The president certainly was not an organizational isolationist but, as is the case with many organizational leaders, he was more inclined to listen to those closest to him in the organizational structure.

Johnson also wanted his senior aides to recommend decisions, "rather than state a problem."[220] Sometimes he would delay a decision "as he sought further certainty that he had gotten all the information or options he could.''[221] Aides were responsible for providing this information and making staff recommendations in relatively short periods of time to accommodate the president's penchant for action.

> The White House was a center of feverish activity in which ideas for legislation were assembled, numerous programs of immense scope and impact on the welfare of the nation were placed on the agenda, details were worked out and agreements sought or compromises made, and decisions made in rapid succession by the president. Deliberation and contemplation on the effects of proposals were limited by the pace of recommendations.[222]

In other words, ''the White House was a beehive of quick processing of data and ideas to supply options and guidance for one whose decision processes had been shaped for the world of action and who wanted action quickly.''[223] Occasionally the president's decision-making pace would be slowed by an aide, such as Bill Moyers, but changing his mind or disagreeing with him might require making an alternative suggestion or offering a word of caution, since he was known for waiting before changing his mind or acquiescing to an idea other than his own.[224] However, because of its small staff, the White House was not ''a center for thorough analysis of alternatives and results or for unpressured deliberation. Long-run problems in administrative implementation sometimes received scant attention.''[225]

Decisions affecting U.S. actions in Southeast Asia essentially evolved from a process different from that used in domestic policy-making. According to Redford and McCulley, ''Unquestionably, Johnson's position was rigid and his circle of advisers narrowed after major policy decisions on Vietnam were made.''[226] Lewis Paper writes:

> Within a short time Johnson dispensed with most NSC meetings; he did not even care to create the impression of debate and agreement. Most decisions were made in the quiet of the Oval Office when only Johnson and a few advisors were present. This method of decisionmaking enabled Johnson and his advisers to avoid the hard questions which were being raised by their own intelligence briefings and by accounts published in America's newspapers. . . . Thus did Johnson make the most critical decisions concerning the Vietnam War—to bomb North Vietnam and to increase the level of American troops stationed in South Vietnam—without the searching inquiries which so often characterized Franklin D. Roosevelt's method of making decisions.[227]

If it is true that Johnson actively sought information from a multitude of sources, and could not be fooled by those who might have tried to keep information from him, one must assume that he made informed decisions based on what he was told by those he most trusted. The issue is not whether he received adequate information from his inner circle, but how powerful that inner circle became as decision alternatives were discussed, selected, and implemented. Henry Graff observed about a conversation with the president in 1968, shortly before he left office: "I came to the conclusion the last time I saw him—although not on the basis of anything specific he said—that he believed he had been led down a slippery path by men he had relied on too implicitly, and that he would willingly barter anything he owned or deserved for the chance of being able to retrace his steps."[228]

History should not, and most probably will not, condemn Lyndon Johnson's presidency as a failure solely because of its association with the Vietnam War. Its attempts to solve monumental domestic problems, though not all successful, were laudatory, and in some cases relatively lasting. Consequently, in reviewing the ways he made decisions it is important to consider the features of that process as articulated by Redford and McCulley: "deliberateness and even delay of decision in difficult situations, his continuous involvement through stages and frequently in details that other presidents might have left to others, his reach for more information across and beyond regular lines, and his adherence to policy once decision was made."[229]

Lyndon Johnson was a complex man, and depicting his communication style when he was interacting with his aides is a complex endeavor. Numerous biographies and memoirs of his senior staff discuss the president's tongue-lashing of aides, his domineering verbal behavior to punish and/or scare a staff member. Eric Goldman, who left the Johnson White House under less than amicable circumstances, wrote in 1969: "The President could berate his aides in lashing language. Sometimes he did this collectively, as when he exploded at three of them in his office. 'How can you be so goddamn stupid! Why can't I get men with the brains of the Kennedy bunch?' More often, he would turn on a single staff member."[230] On the other hand, Goldman observed, Johnson "would heap praise on a particular aide for a period, much to the discomfiture of the others, then suddenly shift his attitude, giving the man no assignments, rejecting his suggestions *in toto*, scarcely speaking to him. Just as suddenly, the assistant would be lifted from hell and transformed into an angel once again."[231] Doris Kearns, who worked with Johnson as a White House fellow, albeit not a senior aide, has commented on Johnson's treatment of "hold-over" Kennedy aides in the White House, indicating that when speaking to them he "requested rather than ordered; he spoke of his short-comings and shared his doubts. This solicitous manner coming from a President disquieted, shamed, and thereby induced in these men the very cooperation and submission that Johnson was after."[232] With his own handpicked staff, however, "Johnson forbade, insisted, swaggered, and swore. Verbal tirades and fits of temper became an integral part of his image."[233]

From a more detached perspective, Redford and McCulley describe the president's communication with his aides as follows, based on their study of his administration of the presidency: "In Johnson's case, personal qualities could have inhibited some assistants. Johnson's mercurial nature, his moods, his explosiveness, and his castigation of assistants have often been the subject of comment."[234] However, some of the president's former aides interviewed in their study indicate that his "explosions" against staff members have been exaggerated and that those who knew him best understood him and his tendency to praise as well as berate.

In meetings with aides or other advisers, according to Kearns, Johnson developed "an anticipatory feedback system that discouraged views that the President would not receive favorably. . . ."[235] In other words, he sometimes announced his decision on a given matter and then asked individuals seated around the table if they agreed with him. Invariably the response was "Yes, Mr. President." As the Vietnam War wore on, and public criticism of the administration's policies increased, policy decisions became more difficult for the president to make, at least personally and politically. Kearns writes that if Johnson was depressed at meetings of the Tuesday Cabinet, "he would spend hours in rambling talk, turning listlessly from one extraneous subject to another." At such times he reduced the Tuesday lunch to a "stage on which to vent his emotions, a forum for his monologues, holding forth at great length with a diatribe against the critics or calling out in a self-pitying way for understanding of his plight."[236] Such may have been the president's frame of mind as the end of his presidency neared, as his organization essentially evolved into a stage of decline after he announced he would not run for reelection.

In looking at the sum total of the president's days and months in office, however, Johnson cannot be characterized as depressed, for he was proud of his domestic accomplishments and the productivity of his White House organization. Neither was the president always angry at his staff; indeed, much of his time out of the Oval Office was spent with them, either working or relaxing at the residence. According to Christian, Johnson enjoyed joking with his aides and telling stories. "He spent a lot of time telling me stories or joshing me or teasing me about something."[237] The president also enjoyed listening to others, "but at the same time he would 'chip in' because he liked an exchange."[238] Johnson's love of storytelling is indicative of what Henry Graff refers to as his "cowboy style." This style is characterized by "a preference for action rather than the play of mind, a natural taciturnity, an inclination to divide people into 'good guys' and 'bad guys.' . . . The President's language, which was often ribald and scatological, also fitted the stereotype."[239]

Lyndon Johnson, like Franklin Roosevelt, loved to talk. But his moods were more changeable than FDR's and the tenor of his conversations was often unpredictable. Certainly he was dominant, and domineering at times, in his interactions with aides. He could be attentive, although not with the patience of Harry Truman, and relaxed, but perhaps only in early morning or late night sessions with his closest aides. As the evidence indicates, LBJ evoked a "communicator image" of someone who was often verbally overpowering and, with his aides, sometimes abusive. But within him ran a streak of ebullience about his work and his agenda for the country, and a concern for the less fortunate, whose causes he supported in the programs of the Great Society. In short, Johnson felt great compassion for many people he never met, and could deeply hurt those individuals he saw every day. The night before he left the presidency, he gave a party for his staff in the residence, because, as he later wrote, ''we had developed a closeness in our time together.''[240] In his presidential memoirs, that was almost all he said about his White House staff.

Lyndon Johnson's White House organization was small, flexible, and almost totally dependent on the president for its operation. He was intensely involved in both the large and the small issues that found their way to his desk or night reading file, and was equally dedicated to absorbing vast amounts of information from multiple sources. Such was not the case with his successor, who brought an emphasis on detachment and delegation into the White House. Along the way, Richard Nixon made a few mistakes that focused press and public attention on the White House as an organization, and on the importance of communication between a president and his senior staff.

The modern Democrat presidents prior to 1969—Roosevelt, Truman, Kennedy, and Johnson—enjoyed and/or preferred communicating with their staffs in oral and informal interpersonal settings. They also preferred sources that yielded rich information, such as one-on-one and small group meetings and staff memos. They utilized fluid organizational structures and informal management styles that emphasized competition and/or cooperation among their senior aides.

In each case the president's personality determined his organizational structure, approach to management and decision making, and communication style. As the White House evolved as an organization within the federal bureaucracy, beginning with the Franklin Roosevelt years, the president's communication style became important as a cue to his senior staff, helping them determine how the relationship between them would evolve and be sustained. Attention to these relationships, to varying degrees, was a characteristic of these presidents. The Democrats were their own chiefs of staff and kept vigilant eyes, if not complete control, over the people and processes that comprised their White House organizations.

NOTES

1. A. J. Wann, *The President as Chief Administrator: A Study of Franklin D. Roosevelt* (Washington, DC: Public Affairs Press, 1968), p. 39.

2. Arthur M. Schlesinger, Jr., ''The Evolution of the Presidency,'' in Nelson W. Polsby, ed., *The Modern Presidency* (New York: Random House, 1973), p. 30.

3. Ibid., p. 22.

4. Louis W. Koenig, *The Chief Executive* (New York: Harcourt, Brace & World, 1968), p. 166.

5. Wann, *The President as Chief Administrator*, p. 37.

6. Richard E. Neustadt, ''Truman in Action: A Retrospect,'' in Marc Landy, ed., *Modern Presidents and the Presidency* (Lexington, MA: Lexington Books, 1985), p. 192.

7. Schlesinger, ''The Evolution of the Presidency,'' p. 34.

8. Robert E. Sherwood, *Roosevelt and Hopkins, an Intimate History* (New York: Harper & Brothers, 1948), p. 206.

9. Grace Tully, *F.D.R. My Boss* (New York: Charles Scribner's Sons, 1949), p. 72.

10. Koenig, *The Chief Executive*, p. 164.

11. Schlesinger, "The Evolution of the Presidency," p. 29.

12. Alfred B. Rollins, *Roosevelt and Howe* (New York: Alfred A. Knopf, 1962), p. 390.

13. Samuel I. Rosenman, *Working with Roosevelt* (New York: Harper & Brothers, 1952), p. 231.

14. Schlesinger, "The Evolution of the Presidency," p. 11.

15. Rosenman, *Working with Roosevelt*, p. 230.

16. Wann, *The President as Chief Administrator*, p. 33.

17. Tully, *F.D.R. My Boss*, pp. 289–90.

18. Ibid., p. 286.

19. Schlesinger, "The Evolution of the Presidency," p. 12.

20. Wann, *The President as Chief Administrator*, p. 36.

21. Eleanor Roosevelt, *This I Remember* (New York: Harper, 1949), p. 3.

22. Schlesinger, "The Evolution of the Presidency," p. 17.

23. Sherwood, *Roosevelt and Hopkins*, p. 202.

24. Rollins, *Roosevelt and Howe*, p. 454.

25. Sherwood, *Roosevelt and Hopkins*, pp. 206–07.

26. Tully, *F.D.R. My Boss*, p. 80.

27. Schlesinger, "The Evolution of the Presidency," p. 16.

28. Tully, *F.D.R. My Boss*, pp. 81–82.

29. Schlesinger, "The Evolution of the Presidency," p. 20.

30. Ibid., p. 21.

31. Ibid., p. 20.

32. Sherwood, *Roosevelt and Hopkins*, p. 3.

33. Schlesinger, "The Evolution of the Presidency," p. 17.

34. Tully, *F.D.R. My Boss*, p. 73.

35. Richard Neustadt, "Approaches to Staffing the Presidency: Notes on FDR and JFK," in Stanley Bach and George T. Sulzner, eds., *Perspectives on the Presidency* (Lexington, MA: D. C. Heath, 1974), p. 198.

36. Ibid.

37. Ibid., p. 199.

38. Harry S. Truman, quoted in William Hillman, *Mr. President* (London: Hutchinson, 1952), p. 23.

39. Robert J. Donovan, *Conflict and Crisis* (New York: W. W. Norton, 1977), p. 270.

40. Ibid., p. 269.

41. Ibid., p. 271.

42. Richard E. Neustadt in Francis H. Heller, ed., *The Truman White House—The Administration of the Presidency, 1945–1953* (Lawrence: Regents Press of Kansas, 1980), p. 100.

43. Ibid.

44. Charles S. Murphy in Francis H. Heller, ed., *The Truman White House* (Lawrence: Regents Press of Kansas, 1980), p. 126.

45. Ken Hechler, quoted in Heller, *The Truman White House*, p. 141.

46. William J. Hopkins in Francis H. Heller, ed., *The Truman White House* (Lawrence: Regents Press of Kansas, 1980), p. 46.

47. Neustadt, p. 114.

48. Murphy, p. 120.

49. Donovan, *Conflict and Crisis*, p. 24.

50. Murphy, p. 120.

51. Neustadt, p. 114.

52. Ibid.

53. Hillman, *Mr. President*, p. 23.

54. Ibid., p. 22.

55. Richard E. Neustadt, quoted in Patrick Anderson, *The Presidents' Men: White House Assistants of Franklin D. Roosevelt, Harry S. Truman, Dwight D. Eisenhower, John F. Kennedy and Lyndon B. Johnson* (Garden City, NY: Doubleday, 1968), p. 91.

56. Donovan, *Conflict and Crisis*, p. 23.

57. David H. Stowe, quoted in Francis H. Heller, ed., *The Truman White House*, p. 143.

58. Hillman, *Mr. President*, p. 25.

59. Hopkins in Heller, *The Truman White House*, p. 44.

60. Ibid.

61. Ibid.

62. Ibid.

63. Ibid., pp. 44–45.

64. Ibid., p. 45.

65. Ibid.

66. Neustadt in Heller, *The Truman White House*, pp. 113–14.

67. Harry S. Truman, *Memoirs by Harry S. Truman*, vol. 1, *Years of Decisions* (Garden City, NY: Doubleday, 1955), p. 14.

68. Hillman, *Mr. President*, p. 22.

69. Neustadt in Heller, *The Truman White House*, p. 123.

70. Ibid., p. 116.

71. Ibid.

72. Donovan, *Conflict and Crisis*, p. 270.

73. Neustadt in Heller, *The Truman White House*, p. 117.

74. Ibid., p. 151.

75. Ken Hechler in Francis H. Heller, ed., *The Truman White House* (Lawrence: Regents Press of Kansas, 1980), p. 141.

76. Donovan, *Conflict and Crisis*, p. 271.

77. Neustadt in Heller, *The Truman White House*, p. 104.

78. Donovan, *Conflict and Crisis*, p. 272.

79. Ibid., p. 21.

80. Robert L. Dennison in Francis H. Heller, ed., *The Truman White House* (Lawrence: Regents Press of Kansas, 1980), pp. 138–39.

81. Hopkins in Heller, *The Truman White House*, p. 46.

82. Hillman, *Mr. President*, p. 91.

83. Murphy in Heller, *The Truman White House*, p. 127.

84. Ibid.

85. John Hersey, "Ten O'Clock Meeting," in Nelson W. Polsby, ed., *The Modern Presidency* (New York: Random House, 1973), p. 59.

86. Ibid., p. 64.
87. Theodore C. Sorensen, *Kennedy* (New York: Harper & Row, 1965), p. 281.
88. Lewis J. Paper, *The Promise and the Performance: The Leadership of John F. Kennedy* (New York: Crown, 1975), p. 146.
89. Sorensen, *Kennedy*, p. 630.
90. Stephen Hess, *Organizing the Presidency*, 2d ed. (Washington, DC: The Brookings Institution, 1988), p. 81.
91. Evelyn Lincoln, *My Twelve Years with John F. Kennedy* (New York: David McKay, 1965), p. 248.
92. Ibid.
93. Pierre Salinger, *With Kennedy* (Garden City, NY: Doubleday, 1966), pp. 71–72.
94. Ibid., p. 64.
95. Sorensen, *Kennedy*, p. 258.
96. Ibid., p. 262.
97. Ibid.
98. Arthur M. Schlesinger, Jr., *A Thousand Days* (Greenwich, CT: Fawcett, 1965), p. 631.
99. Ibid.
100. Joseph Kraft, "Kennedy's Working Staff," in Nelson W. Polsby, ed., *The Modern Presidency* (New York: Random House, 1973), p. 157.
101. Sorensen, *Kennedy*, p. 374.
102. Ibid., p. 373.
103. Ibid., p. 260.
104. Ibid.
105. Richard Neustadt, "Approaches to Staffing the Presidency," in Stanley Bach and George T. Sulzner, eds., *Perspectives on the Presidency* (Lexington, MA: D. C. Heath, 1974), p. 201.
106. Salinger, *With Kennedy*, p. 74.
107. Sorensen, *Kennedy*, p. 260.
108. Patrick Anderson, *The Presidents' Men* (Garden City, NY: Doubleday, 1968), p. 200.
109. Ibid.
110. Schlesinger, *A Thousand Days*, p. 627.
111. Sorensen, *Kennedy*, p. 282.
112. Salinger, *With Kennedy*, p. 73.
113. Lincoln, *My Twelve Years with John F. Kennedy*, p. 5.
114. Kenneth P. O'Donnell and David F. Powers with Joe McCarthy, *"Johnny, We Hardly Knew Ye": Memories of John Fitzgerald Kennedy* (Boston: Little, Brown, 1972), p. 258.
115. Koenig, *The Chief Executive*, p. 171.
116. Ibid., p. 175.
117. Sorensen, *Kennedy*, p. 372.
118. Ibid.
119. O'Donnell and Powers, *"Johnny, We Hardly Knew Ye,"* p. 118.
120. Lincoln, *My Twelve Years with John F. Kennedy*, p. 6.
121. O'Donnell and Powers, *"Johnny, We Hardly Knew Ye,"* p. 257.
122. Sorensen, *Kennedy*, p. 373.

123. Sidney Hyman, "How Mr. Kennedy Gets the Answers," in Nelson W. Polsby, ed., *The Modern Presidency* (New York: Random House, 1973), p. 159.
124. Sorensen, *Kennedy*, p. 376.
125. Paper, *The Promise and the Performance*, p. 156.
126. Sorensen, *Kennedy*, p. 263.
127. Schlesinger, *A Thousand Days*, p. 631.
128. Ibid., p. 258.
129. Ibid.
130. Hess, *Organizing the Presidency*, p. 80.
131. Schlesinger, *A Thousand Days*, p. 632.
132. Sorensen, *Kennedy*, p. 372.
133. Ibid.
134. Ibid.
135. Hyman, "How Mr. Kennedy Gets the Answers," p. 159.
136. Ibid., pp. 158–59.
137. Paper, *The Promise and the Performance*, p. 166.
138. Sorensen, *Kennedy*, p. 371.
139. Ibid., p. 282.
140. Koenig, *The Chief Executive*, p. 172.
141. O'Donnell and Powers, *"Johnny, We Hardly Knew Ye,"* p. 253.
142. Sorensen, *Kennedy*, p. 259.
143. Ibid.
144. Paper, *The Promise and the Performance*, p. 165.
145. Koenig, *The Chief Executive*, p. 172.
146. Sorensen, *Kennedy*, p. 284.
147. Ibid.
148. Paper, *The Promise and the Performance*, p. 146.
149. Anderson, *The Presidents' Men*, p. 196.
150. Kraft, "Kennedy's Working Staff," p. 151.
151. Schlesinger, *A Thousand Days*, p. 631.
152. Ibid., p. 617.
153. Ibid.
154. Ibid., p. 618.
155. Salinger, *With Kennedy*, p. 63.
156. Sorensen, *Kennedy*, p. 374.
157. Ibid., p. 375.
158. Salinger, *With Kennedy*, p. 80.
159. Paper, *The Promise and the Performance*, p. 157.
160. Ibid.
161. James P. Pfiffner, "White House Staff Versus the Cabinet: Centripetal and Centrifugal Roles," *Presidential Studies Quarterly* 16, no. 4, Fall 1986, p. 669.
162. Charles Roberts, *LBJ's Inner Circle* (New York: Delacorte Press, 1965), pp. 40–41.
163. Emmette S. Redford and Richard T. McCulley, *White House Operations: The Johnson Presidency* (Austin: University of Texas Press, 1986), p. 183.
164. Hess, *Organizing the Presidency*, pp. 97–98.
165. Redford and McCulley, *White House Operations*, p. 42.
166. Ibid., p. 57.

167. George Christian, interview with the author, August 1, 1989.
168. Redford and McCulley, *White House Operations*, p. 65.
169. Christian, interview with author.
170. Eric F. Goldman, *The Tragedy of Lyndon Johnson* (New York: Alfred A. Knopf, 1969), p. 105.
171. Henry F. Graff, *The Tuesday Cabinet: Deliberation and Decision on Peace and War Under Lyndon B. Johnson* (Englewood Cliffs, NJ: Prentice-Hall, 1970), p. 4.
172. Redford and McCulley, *White House Operations*, pp. 198–99.
173. Ibid., p. 182.
174. Jack Valenti, *A Very Human President* (New York: W. W. Norton, 1975), p. 97.
175. Christian, interview with author.
176. Valenti, *A Very Human President*, p. 97.
177. Anderson, *The Presidents' Men*, p. 305.
178. George Christian, *The President Steps Down: A Personal Memoir of the Transfer of Power* (New York: Macmillan, 1970), p. 10.
179. Redford and McCulley, *White House Operations*, p. 72.
180. George Christian, *The President Steps Down*, p. 10.
181. Redford and McCulley, *White House Operations*, p. 73.
182. Ibid.
183. Christian, interview with author.
184. Graff, *The Tuesday Cabinet*, p. 24.
185. Ibid., pp. 24–25.
186. Redford and McCulley, *White House Operations*, p. 49.
187. Ibid., p. 50.
188. Christian, *The President Steps Down*, pp. 18–19.
189. Hess, *Organizing the Presidency*, p. 91.
190. David Halberstam, *The Best and the Brightest* (New York: Random House, 1969), p. 432.
191. Christian, *The President Steps Down*, pp. 9–10.
192. Christian, interview with author.
193. Hess, *Organizing the Presidency*, p. 103.
194. Christian, *The President Steps Down*, p. 9.
195. Redford and McCulley, *White House Operations*, p. 49.
196. Ibid., p. 67.
197. Ibid., p. 66.
198. Ibid.
199. Christian, *The President Steps Down*, pp. 7–8.
200. Redford and McCulley, *White House Operations*, p. 66.
201. Ibid., p. 182.
202. Christian, *The President Steps Down*, p. 18.
203. Ibid.
204. William S. White, *The Professional Lyndon B. Johnson* (Boston: Houghton Mifflin, 1964), p. 254.
205. Christian, interview with author.
206. Valenti, *A Very Human President*, p. 78.
207. Redford and McCulley, *White House Operations*, p. 62.
208. Ibid., p. 67.

209. Ben H. Bagdikian, "The 'Inner, Inner Circle' Around Johnson," in Nelson W. Polsby, ed., *The Modern Presidency* (New York: Random House, 1973), p. 183.
210. Christian, interview with author.
211. Roberts, *LBJ's Inner Circle*, p. 61.
212. Redford and McCulley, *White House Operations*, p. 78.
213. Ibid., p. 69.
214. Christian, interview with author.
215. Redford and McCulley, *White House Operations*, p. 199.
216. Christian, *The President Steps Down*, p. 18.
217. Bagdikian, "The 'Inner, Inner Circle,' " p. 184.
218. Bill Moyers, quoted in Redford and McCulley, *White House Operations*, p. 70.
219. Ibid., p. 199.
220. Christian, interview with author.
221. Redford and McCulley, *White House Operations*, p. 70.
222. Ibid., p. 184.
223. Ibid., p. 75.
224. Roberts, *LBJ's Inner Circle*, p. 63.
225. Redford and McCulley, *White House Operations*, p. 185.
226. Ibid., p. 71.
227. Paper, *The Promise and the Performance*, p. 116.
228. Graff, *The Tuesday Cabinet*, p. 16.
229. Redford and McCulley, *White House Operations*, p. 20.
230. Goldman, *The Tragedy of Lyndon Johnson*, p. 102.
231. Ibid.
232. Doris Kearns, *Lyndon Johnson and the American Dream* (New York: Harper & Row, 1976), p. 175.
233. Ibid., p. 176.
234. Redford and McCulley, *White House Operations*, p. 74.
235. Kearns, *Lyndon Johnson and the American Dream*, p. 322.
236. Ibid.
237. Christian, interview with author.
238. Ibid.
239. Graff, *The Tuesday Cabinet*, p. 16.
240. Lyndon Baines Johnson, *The Vantage Point: Perspectives of the Presidency 1963–1969* (New York: Holt, Rinehart and Winston, 1971), p. 560.

Chapter 3

The Eisenhower–Nixon Legacy

Dwight Eisenhower and Richard Nixon do not share this chapter because their personalities or their presidencies were similar. What they did have in common was an interest in (in Eisenhower's case a devotion to) order unlike that seen in any previous modern presidency. Eisenhower developed a formal, hierarchial structure within his White House that Nixon adapted to suit his presidency. Eisenhower also cultivated the use of informal communication networks to supplement formal structure in the White House and give him access to information he otherwise might not have received. And he controlled the structure he imposed and the people it comprised by direct and continuous attention to administration. This Nixon did not do—and his inability or unwillingness to manage his White House, his detachment from its work and many of its people, ultimately contributed to the demise of his presidency.

The revisionist histories of Dwight Eisenhower's presidency, most notably the works of Fred Greenstein and Phillip Henderson, convincingly illustrate the strengths of that president as an organizational leader. His administration was not a success in public policy-making, in part because he served in the White House during years the Democrats dominated Congress. Nevertheless, he seemed to leave to John F. Kennedy and Lyndon Johnson the emerging domestic and foreign problems of the 1950s. Eisenhower's presidency was not effective if one measures effectiveness by the development of long-term solutions to major problems. But his White House was efficient; it aided his efforts to achieve the presidential goals he established and attained—peace and prosperity.

As will be discussed in Chapter 7, it is not necessarily impossible to adopt a personal approach to the conduct of the presidency and concurrently utilize formal organizational structures and systems of information flow. To date, however, the modern presidents have found it difficult, in some cases impossible, to find a balance between structure and flexibility, delegation and detachment. Dwight Eisenhower, however, serves as an excellent example of a president who valued the merits of formal structure while using a variety of informal communication networks to delegate work and yet remain in control of his White House.

DWIGHT EISENHOWER: LEADERSHIP THROUGH INITIATION OF STRUCTURE

Fred Greenstein persuasively argues that Dwight Eisenhower was not a grandfatherly caretaker of the presidency during the 1950s, but a "hands-on" organizational leader who was more politically astute than most of his contemporaries and many of his biographers realized. According to Greenstein, Ike's personal makeup was a set of dichotomies that included "a reassuringly benign-seeming public self and a private one with a well-developed capacity for tough-minded political realism"[1] Throughout his life, as military leader, federal bureaucrat, university president, and the nation's chief executive, Eisenhower learned to establish space between his public self and his private self. As a result, suggests Greenstein, the president was "well suited to carry out the organizational procedures necessary to rationalize the official routines of public leadership while maintaining a capacity to develop flexible unofficial means for adapting organizational leadership to the complexities and idiosyncrasies" of those he led.[2] In short, although known for his penchant for administration, Eisenhower appreciated the informal, emergent structures, including communication networks outside the White House, that supplemented the formal and hierarchical organizational structure he established to serve him.

As he began his first term, Eisenhower was confident that he could drastically improve the White House as a decision-making organization. He wrote in the first volume of his presidential memoirs:

> I had been in frequent contact in the executive office of the White House, and I had certain ideas about the system, or lack of system under which it operated. With my training in problems involving organization it was inconceivable to me that the work of the White House could not be better systemized than had been the case in the years I observed it.[3]

According to Eisenhower, organization "makes more efficient the gathering and analysis of facts, and the arranging of the findings of experts in logical fashion."[4] Throughout his presidency this chief executive valued the power of formal structure to enhance efficiency and was responsible for several administrative innovations in the White House that some of his successors eventually adopted.

Eisenhower fully appreciated the significant roles assumed by a president's personal staff and believed both during and after his presidency "that the careful development . . . of a personal staff, able to assure effective and unobtrusive performance of . . . duties on his [the president's] behalf, is one of the most important things he can do in the interest of efficient government.''[5] His senior staff and their respective organizational roles initially included:

Sherman Adams—assistant to the president (chief of staff)

James C. Hagerty—press secretary

Major General Wilton B. Persons—head of the Congressional Relations Office

Thomas E. Stephens—initially special counsel and then appointments secretary. (Stephens was succeeded as special counsel by Bernard Shanley, and then Gerald D. Morgan and David Kendall. This office concentrated on legal and legislative matters, giving up the speechwriting responsibilities that had been part of the special counsel's office during the administrations of Franklin Roosevelt and Harry Truman.)

According to Sherman Adams, he and Eisenhower agreed ''that the complex and wide-ranging variety of work in the White House could be handled most efficiently by a small group of versatile trouble shooters, who could move with knowledge and assurance into any problem that happened to be pressing the President at the moment. . . .''[6] Moreover, Eisenhower firmly believed in the use of his Cabinet members to develop and execute policy. In his opinion there was no need for a large cadre of specialists within the White House.

There *was* a need, in Eisenhower's opinion, for more attention to order than his predecessors had shown, for efficient administration facilitated by the development of formal structures. In developing such a structure for his White House, Eisenhower benefited from an advisory council comprised of Nelson Rockefeller, Milton Eisenhower (his brother), and Dr. Arthur S. Flemming. This group became the Advisory Committee on Government Organization and held its discussions informally until it became official after Eisenhower was inaugurated. Essentially its plan called for a line of command from the president to an assistant to the president and then to the other members of the White House staff who were nominally under the supervision of the assistant to the president.''[7] The president did establish the position of assistant to the president or chief of staff, as well as special sssistant to the National Security Council. Additionally, he created staff and Cabinet secretariats to improve the processes of information acquisition and use, and policy execution within the Executive Branch.

Until the publication of more recent studies of Eisenhower's administration, specifically those written by Fred Greenstein and Phillip Henderson, Eisenhower's penchant for structure was viewed by journalists and biographers as the knee-jerk reaction to civilian administration by a former military commander. However, Henderson convincingly argues that the chief of staff concept and the idea for systematized processes of information flow in the White House—the secretariats—did not originate in the president's military background but in a number of major reorganization plans developed prior to 1937, as well as in the Hoover Commission report, which Eisenhower studied.[8]

Having observed White House operations in several presidencies, and having served as an assistant in one of the Executive Branch departments, Eisenhower was convinced that a chief of staff in the White House could improve its functioning. Consequently he selected former New Hampshire governor Sherman Adams to reside "at the top of the staff," coordinate White House operations, and keep the president informed "of appropriate developments on a daily basis."[9] According to Eisenhower, Adams "did not lay down rigid rules to restrict the staff members in their access to me; they worked flexibly, with a voluntary cooperation based on mutual friendship and respect."[10]

To some congressmen, members of the press, and even federal officials in the Eisenhower administration, Sherman Adams was the H. R. Haldeman of his time. In his memoirs, however, he attempts to clarify his role in the Eisenhower White House.

> He never gave me, nor did I ever seek, a delegation of presidential power and authority, as so many capital correspondents and politicians have assumed.
>
> Eisenhower simply expected me to manage a staff that would boil down, simplify and expedite the urgent business that had to be brought to his personal attention and to keep as much work of secondary importance as possible off his desk. Any power or authority that I exercised while carrying out this appointed task was solely on a de facto basis and, except when I was acting on an explicit directive from the President, my duties and responsibilities were implied rather than stated.[11]

Eisenhower used Adams as a deputy, and the assistant to the president spent a "superhuman amount of time" acting in this capacity.[12] According to Greenstein:

> It involved not only long hours spent in his own office but also being present at a large number of Eisenhower's meetings, including regularly scheduled ones, such as cabinet and Legislative Leadership meetings, as well as ad hoc presidential conferences. By spending so much time in Eisenhower's presence, and by being filled in by whatever aide was assigned to make a summary of a meeting he had missed, Adams was able to keep abreast of Eisenhower's views. He also was at liberty to enter the Oval Office for a decision without knocking, when he deemed it necessary.[13]

In addition to these responsibilities, Eisenhower expected Adams to handle a variety of personnel problems with Cabinet members, Republican leaders, and the president's advisers outside government.[14] In short, Adams was a receptacle and disseminator of information, a decision maker, a crisis manager, and a point of access for those outside the White House. As a result, "he found little time to be a staff coordinator," and Ike ultimately reassigned that task to a staff secretary.[15]

In its 1949 report, the Hoover Commission had recommended the establishment of a staff secretariat within the White House. Eisenhower, already concerned about the lack of structure in the process that guided paper flow into the Oval Office, took that recommendation to heart. In his administration the secretariat "kept track of all pending presidential business and ensured the proper clearances on all papers that reached the Oval Office.''[16] In Eisenhower's opinion, the staff secretary was responsible for ensuring that a document intended for presidential action was complete. He wrote in his memoirs: ''If coordination with other pertinent agencies was required, he would see to it that the matter was brought to their attention.''[17] The first staff secretary, Brigadier General Paul T. Carroll, died after serving in the White House for a year and a half; he was succeeded by Colonel (later Brigadier General) Andrew J. Goodpaster.

Upon assuming the presidency, Eisenhower established the Congressional Liaison Office and appointed a special assistant to the National Security Council. According to Adams, ''It was plain that the President needed a liaison officer who had the executive mandate to organize and tighten up the Council's activities from the planning stage right through to getting action on every policy decision.''[18] The first such assistant was Robert Cutler, who was succeeded by Dillon Anderson, then William Jackson, and finally Gordon Gray. Beginning with the Eisenhower administration, the National Security Council assistant represented the addition of another functional area in the White House and became an important member of the president's senior staff.

Although Eisenhower was committed to the creation of an adequate complement of senior staff to assist the president in the exercise of his constitutional duties, he had witnessed conflict between White House senior staff and Cabinet members in previous presidencies, and sought to remedy that problem in his administration in at least two ways. First, as Henderson emphasizes, the president ''would not tolerate the development of a situation in which members of the White House staff sought to interpose themselves between the President and his department heads. Nor would Eisenhower countenance the practice . . . of allowing members of the . . . staff to sit at the Cabinet table during Cabinet meetings.''[19] Second, the chief executive established a Cabinet secretariat. Its role was to ensure that ''departments with business on the agenda prepared background papers explaining their proposal in advance of the meetings and circulated the papers and agenda to all members in time for them to arrive briefed at the Friday meeting.''[20] Additionally, the secretariat organized a meeting of the executive assistants to Cabinet secretaries after each Cabinet session, ''to initiate implementation of the proposals and . . . review the cabinet discussion.''[21]

One of the noteworthy accomplishments of the Eisenhower administration was its development of these organizational innovations designed to facilitate the administration of the White House and the presidency. The president's focus on formal structures and his desire to delegate administrative responsibilities gave him, in Hess's words, ''considerable freedom of action by giving his subordinates considerable latitude to act.''[22] As he began to conduct the business of the presidency, the formal structures he created became the shield behind which Eisenhower would guide his presidency with ''a hidden hand.''[23] According to Goodpaster, Eisenhower ''was . . . the most skillful man when it came to organizing . . . with the deepest understanding of the role of organization, of how to use staff, of subordination and decentralization . . . of anyone I've ever known or known of.''[24] That understanding was evident in his relationships with his senior staff and in the management style he exhibited.

According to Stephen Ambrose, one of Eisenhower's biographers, being one of the president's friends ''counted for nothing'' when he selected his Cabinet and White House staff.[25] Most of his senior aides had worked on his presidential campaign—he respected their abilities and appreciated their dedication to his work, but he did not require their personal friendship. Such was even the case with Sherman Adams. Speaking of their relationship, Eisenhower wrote: ''We never built up between us the easy informality I had enjoyed with such men as Bedell Smith and Alfred Gruenther, who served with me in the Army in somewhat similar positions. Nevertheless, I liked, trusted, and highly respected . . . Adams and admired his powers of concentration and judgment.''[26] The two saw each other frequently during the day, but their relationship was based on the business of operating the presidency. In Eisenhower's words, ''On the many occasions during our White House years when I called him on the telephone to ask a question, he never added a word to his 'yes' or 'no' if such an answer sufficed. It never occurred to him to say 'Hello' when advised by his secretary that I wanted him on the phone or to add a 'Good-bye' at the end of the call. For Sherman Adams this was neither bad manners nor pretense; he was busy.''[27]

In addition to Adams, Eisenhower had a close professional relationship with James Hagerty, John Foster Dulles, and Allen Dulles, the few aides allowed to awaken the president in times of crisis. Although the congeniality and camaraderie that marked the presidential–staff relationships in the White Houses of Franklin Roosevelt and Harry Truman were not as visible in the Eisenhower administration, neither were staff relationships marred with internecine conflict.

Perhaps, as Greenstein and Henderson emphasize, Ike's penchant for formal structure was not rooted in his military background. However, it is quite possible that his skill in organizing and motivating his staff was due in part to his military experience—and to his work as a football coach prior to World War II. According to Richard Immerman, Eisenhower knew how to evaluate people and mold them into a team; as a coach his ''emphasis was always on coordinated effort as opposed to individual performances, and he preached that victory was the collective responsibility of all the participants.''[28] It is therefore not surprising that at a pre-inauguration Cabinet meeting, held in New York on January 12, 1953, he told his department heads and key aides to practice ''spontaneous mutual coordination'' by discussing their common interests at small dinner meetings.[29] ''He regularly put people together in ad hoc or standing groups, seeking reports from them, encouraging them to develop the personal ties necessary for successful cooperation. . . . ''[30]

According to Greenstein, Eisenhower's experience in commanding large organizations and in managing the headquarters of such organizations ''sensitized him to 'personnel psychology.' ''[31] During his lifetime he became adept at matching people with positions, based on his perceptions of their aptitudes, and his method of delegating responsibilities in the White House depended on the qualities he observed in his subordinates.[32] Most of his predecessors and several of his successors had no similar organizational experience, as is evident when one studies their managerial styles.

As an administrator Eisenhower was adamantly opposed to dealing with operational details. Indeed, in his memoirs he wrote: "Whenever I had to make a decision that properly belonged to a subordinate I admonished him at once, but if he failed again it was time to begin looking for a replacement."[33] Similarly, he granted appointments only to those individuals who had, in his opinion, important governmental business to discuss at the presidential level. Adams, or other aides he chose, were responsible for dealing with people and paper judged to be routine by the president. As a result, Adams, not Eisenhower, became the object of anger when administrative decisions and actions were unpopular with one or more individuals. Adams was the president's buffer against that anger—Eisenhower's general popularity was left intact.

Although Ike delegated authority to handle routine matters to his chief of staff, all major policy decisions were made by the president, in consultation with his key aides.[34] As the manager of the White House organization, he encouraged staff "to think of themselves as part of a collective enterprise rather than as individual entrepreneurs."[35] He exhibited concern both with the quality of the organization's product, its decisions and policies, *and* the maintenance of group satisfaction among his aides. Accordingly, Eisenhower's style of management reflected these dual concerns—he delegated tasks and responsibilities willingly, but he did not abdicate his responsibility as a decision maker on matters requiring presidential attention.

The president was usually at his desk at 8 A.M. during the work week, but indicated in his memoirs that only on rare occasions was he not reading by 7 A.M.[36] Each morning he perused the major New York and Washington newspapers. Additionally, he would read 50 to 100 letters from the average 3,000 received daily in the White House.[37] The president also received the latest military, CIA, and State Department intelligence reports in written form each morning. Every week he was sent a one-page "fact sheet" prepared by the Executive Branch liaison, the office responsible for coordinating speeches for those with policy-making roles in the administration. These fact sheets were short summaries of controversial issues, major objectives, and accomplishments of the administration.[38] As Eisenhower began his work in the Oval Office, Sherman Adams met with the appointments secretary, reviewing the president's daily schedule. Adams would then speak with Ann Whitman, Eisenhower's personal secretary, who "often revealed the Eisenhower mood, which was of great help in smoothing out the arrangements for the day's activities."[39]

The most important documents the president saw were briefing papers, whose passage into the Oval Office was controlled by the staff secretariat. Each document included a synopsis, "to provide a brief summary of the problem at hand, the recommended course of action, a discussion of implementation, and the necessary lateral clearance and concurrences.''[40] According to Sherman Adams, ''Eisenhower was not much of a reader. He was impatient with the endless paperwork of the Presidency and always tried to get his staff to digest long documents into one-page summaries, which was sometimes next to impossible.''[41] Had Eisenhower not also depended on formal meetings and informal interpersonal discussions to provide him information, the richness of that information would have been sorely lacking. However, like FDR, he preferred to receive information through conversations. Adams has written:

> He seldom exchanged written memoranda with me or with the Cabinet members or his staff. He preferred to get his information from talking with people who knew the issues involved in the matter he was considering. He listened intently, keeping the conversation brief and to the point with no wandering digressions, and he interrupted now and then with a quick and penetrating question that brought the whole discussion into clearer focus.[42]

Consequently, although Sherman Adams may have been the gatekeeper to the Oval Office, Eisenhower adopted ways of avoiding ''information insularity.''

In Stephen Hess's opinion, the president's preference for listening rather than reading ''accounted for the heightened role of the cabinet and the National Security Council.''[43] Eisenhower chaired 329 of 366 NSC meetings during his two terms, thereby showing his support for the use of this forum for information-sharing.[44] Some of the meetings lasted two and a half hours or more, with the president encouraging the NSC members to feel free to share their opinions and even their opposition to his positions on issues.[45]

Eisenhower also insisted on other regularly scheduled meetings to provide him insights and ideas on matters of public policy. These included a daily, early-morning briefing on national security matters, a Monday morning meeting with congressional leaders, and Friday Cabinet meetings. Additionally, the president met at least one hour each week with the chairman of the Joint Chiefs and with the secretary of defense.[46] He also appointed groups of individuals, including persons outside of government, to gather and present information to him. These advisory committees included:

- The Quantico Panel, chaired by Nelson Rockefeller, which explored recommendations for arms control that were submitted to the July 1955 Geneva Summit Conference
- The Gaither Committee, headed by the chairmen of the boards of the Ford Foundation and the RAND Corporation, which studied national security issues and made recommendations to the National Security Council
- The ''Seven Wise Men,'' who represented different walks of life and served as National Security Council consultants. These individuals included the president of Cornell University, the head of Pacific Gas and Electric, and a scientist who had worked on the Manhattan Project.[47]

Eisenhower not only preferred to receive information orally, he also preferred to obtain it face-to-face. According to Adams:

Eisenhower disliked the telephone. The only person in the government who spoke to him frequently on the telephone was Dulles, who consulted the President constantly on foreign policy matters that required an immediate decision. It was understood that other Cabinet officers and agency directors with questions for the President would come to his office rather than call him on the telephone.[48]

Referring to White House telephone logs, however, Greenstein found that Eisenhower sometimes placed up to a dozen calls a day through which he "sought information, gave instructions, rallied support, and made policy decisions."[49] In short, the president did not rely solely on his chief of staff for information and certainly not for advice. This is not to suggest that Adams was not a powerful person in the Eisenhower White House. Indeed, he was, but his power lay in the way the president used his talents, not in Adams's usurpation of authority. In a little-quoted passage from his memoirs Adams explains:

Eisenhower did ask me to sit in on all of his important meetings and, when I could, on office appointments with government officials and with visitors where important decisions were to be discussed. He did not invite me to his meetings specifically to make any comments, although I was always free to do so if I had anything to say. . . . Eisenhower merely wanted me to hear everything that was going on so that I would become as familiar as possible with his attitude on most of the passing problems. I was then to use this knowledge in making decisions for him in the matters that he left for me to resolve.[50]

Greenstein emphasizes Eisenhower's interest in seeking information from a variety of individuals other than Adams, reflecting the president's understanding of the dangers of isolation behind Oval Office doors.

Even with Adams serving him . . . Eisenhower drew for advice on many White House aides, other administration members, and friends and acquaintances for what appears to have been as rich—if not as palpably contrived—a flow of face-to-face conversation, questioning, and thinking out loud as occurred under Roosevelt. By the same token the key aides freely exchanged tactical and substantive ideas with each other and not only at Adams' behest.[51]

As is mentioned in Chapter 1, formal and informal structures are interdependent in organizations, and Dwight Eisenhower understood this element of organizational theory. He therefore supplemented the information he received through the formal structures he created in the White House with ideas and opinions obtained through informal, emergent networks. During his first months in office, for instance, the president invited all members of Congress to the White House for breakfast or lunch, and then extended similar invitations to the nation's governors.[52] Frequently he would ask his personal secretary to find friends or colleagues who might be available in the early evening to discuss his presidential agenda for an hour or so.[53] During this time of day, after he had returned to the residence, "Eisenhower often sat around informally with members of his Cabinet and staff, or with influential members of Congress such as William Knowland, Lyndon Johnson, Everett Dirksen, Sam Rayburn . . . or with close friends who had some advice to give.''[54] The president also was known for his ''stag dinners,'' to which he would invite prominent businessmen, Executive Branch officials, party leaders, celebrities, members of the clergy, academics, and labor leaders. These men would join Eisenhower in the mansion for drinks, dinner, and ultimately, discussion. According to Greenstein, ''Although the tone was easygoing, Eisenhower would consistently direct the conversation to discussion of immediate and long-run problems about which he wanted information, insight, and advice.''[55]

The president also requested ideas from close staff members to whom he turned during his years in office. His press secretary, James Hagerty, conversed with him extensively when they traveled together for public appearances and was of great value to Eisenhower because he had numerous sources of off-the-record information.[56] The president kept abreast of changes in the organization and techniques of the armed forces by talking with his personal military aides when they escorted him to and from the Oval Office or on out-of-town trips.[57] Additionally, he valued the opinions of his personal secretary, Ann Whitman, who sometimes suggested appointments with people she thought he would enjoy meeting. He also trusted Whitman to relay information to designated members of his staff and, occasionally, ''to don headphones in her office and listen in on many of his telephone conversations and make notes for the record.''[58]

However, the opinions Ike valued the most were from his brother, Milton. President of Penn State and then Johns Hopkins University during the Eisenhower presidency, Milton served three days a week as a presidential aide. He met with his brother in unscheduled appointments and also sent him advisory messages. In Greenstein's opinion, ''Milton Eisenhower was at least as important to his brother as Robert Kennedy was to John F. Kennedy.''[59] Whether in Washington, Camp David, or Colorado, Eisenhower thrived on a vast network of friends and advisers who offered him a wide array of information on a variety of topics. As a result, he received ''at least as diverse a flow of information and advice as any of the other modern presidents.''[60]

In 1958 Sherman Adams resigned as assistant to the president following allegations of influence-peddling in exchange for gifts. Although he denied wrongdoing at the time and later in his memoirs, he resigned under political pressure two months before the mid-term elections, leaving the administration under considerable press and congressional attack. Eisenhower expressed his confidence in Adams at the time and in his own memoirs. But he did accept the resignation. This president, unlike some of his predecessors and successors, knew when to distance himself from a member of his inner circle.

Eisenhower, Adams, and historians have argued about the influence Adams wielded in the president's White House, and the degree of access to the chief executive he allowed other individuals. According to Adams, ''Any allegations that I or any other member of the White House staff used presumptuous or arbitrary tactics to keep high-ranking executives or legislators from seeing Eisenhower are completely false.''[61] However, after his resignation and the appointment of Wilton Persons as his successor, procedures governing presidential access did change. Instead of singularly approving all appointments on the president's schedule and reviewing all documents sent into the Oval Office, Persons encouraged the president to discuss matters with several interested parties present, and believed he facilitated access to the president and provided Eisenhower with information that Adams would not have transmitted.[62]

There is no overwhelming evidence to indicate that Dwight Eisenhower made better, more informed decisions after Sherman Adams left the White House. Indeed, speaking in general about the president's aides during his eight years in office, Patrick Anderson has suggested that the senior staff was ''loyal and efficient . . . but the group as a whole seems to have rarely performed the most important service a staff can give a President: being a source of ideas, of imagination, of stimulation.''[63] Part of this fault lies not in Eisenhower's staff but in his structure—the organizational fluidity that characterized the Democrat White Houses, despite the president's call for mutual cooperation, does not emerge as a significant force in the Eisenhower administration. As his organization's leader, Eisenhower organized and orchestrated the channels and sources of information he used in making decisions, and he alone controlled the decision-making process.

Years after leaving the presidency Ike responded to those historians and journalists who had described him as a detached decision maker:

> Some writers have said that I conducted the Presidency largely through staff decisions. This, of course, is nonsense. Naturally, I consulted constantly with my staff, and I valued their opinions. But staff work doesn't mean that you take a vote of your subordinates and then abide by that majority opinion. On important matters, in the end, you alone must decide.[64]

In an oral history interview in 1967 the president described the process he used to make decisions:

> I know of only one way in which you can be sure that you have done your best to make a wise decision. That is to get all of the people who have a partial and definable responsibility in this particular field, whatever it may be. Get them with different viewpoints in front of you, and listen to them debate.
>
> I do not believe in bringing them in one at a time, and therefore being more impressed with the most recent one you hear. . . . You must get courageous men, men of strong views, and let them debate and argue with each other.
>
> You listen, and you see if there is anything that has been brought up, any idea that changes your own view or enriches your view or adds to it. Then you start studying. Sometimes a case becomes so simple that you can make a decision right then. Or you may go back and wait two or three days, if time is not of the essence. But you make it.[65]

Eisenhower's use of the Cabinet, the National Security Council, and the formal and informal groups that gathered information was purposively designed to assist him in this preferred decision-making process. Although he may have delegated authority within the White House to handle routine administrative matters and operational details, he retained control over all major decisions. His best and most recent biographers agree that his decision-making process was neither detached nor uninformed. According to Henderson, "Clearly, Eisenhower's decision-making style was not passive or disinterested, as some of the scholarship on his Presidency has suggested. Rather, it was deliberate, contemplative, and well-informed—at times boldly detached from the counsel of administration insiders, but always mindful of the importance of free and open debate in arriving at sound decisions."[66]

In an earlier analysis of the Eisenhower administration, Ambrose emphasized that the president "tried to hear all sides before deciding, to expose himself to every point of view, which required a great deal of reading, listening intently to oral presentations, and asking penetrating questions."[67] From 1953 to 1956, Ambrose reveals, Eisenhower "turned increasingly to small private meetings in the Oval Office when making his decisions."[68] The larger, more formal meetings, he suggests, were pro forma gatherings. "He used them to explain what he was going to do, and to get support for it, not to discuss what to do."[69] In working with the National Security Council, for instance, Eisenhower summoned small groups of policymakers into the Oval Office for informal discussions after the formal NSC meetings. In the smaller gatherings he would actually make his operational decisions.[70]

As was mentioned earlier in this chapter, Eisenhower preferred to obtain information by listening, by discussing with key advisers and close confidants the issues and problems requiring presidential action. He, perhaps more than any other modern president, was a chief executive who understood the importance of formal structure in the White House *and* the necessity of preventing its interference with the free flow of information important in the decision-making process. One of the individuals within his administration wrote in 1962:

> With people he knew well and trusted, Eisenhower liked to think out loud. He would sometimes make what would seem to be completely outlandish and politically naive remarks, just to test them, perhaps even believing in some of them momentarily. He was very bold, imaginative and uninhibited in suggesting and discussing new and completely unconventional approaches to problems. Yet he probably was one of the most deliberate and careful Presidents the country had ever had.[71]

When he wrote this passage in *Six Crises*, Richard Nixon seemed to value the behavior he observed in the president he served. By 1972 he appeared to have forgotten much of what he might have learned about information flow and decision-making from his presidential mentor. He also had forgotten, or never accepted, Eisenhower's decision-making criterion. As described by Greenstein, the criterion was explicit and simple: "A decision must be in the long-term public interest *and* must be acceptable domestically so that congressional support can be assured."[72]

Dwight Eisenhower delegated some, but abdicated none, of his responsibilities as an organizational leader. To discharge them he relied on an open but structured process of information flow among, and with, his staff. An appreciation for leader–staff communication was part of his personal makeup, and the result of both his experiences as a military leader *and* his observations of how other presidents had used, and in his mind abused, their senior aides.

One of the prominent elements of Eisenhower's communication style within the White House was his aptitude for listening. His "concentration was intense: his excess energy spilled over as he would doodle, finger his glasses, swivel in his chair, and look at other speakers with piercing bright blue eyes that innumerable observers sensed as windows to an inner dynamism."[73] He also had the ability to quickly adapt his powers of concentration to different subjects as guests or staff members entered his office for discussions.

Walter Bedell Smith described the personal qualities that enhanced Eisenhower's ability to communicate with his staff:

> His personality is such that it impresses itself immediately upon senior subordinates as completely frank, completely honest, very human and very considerate. . . . He has great patience, and he disdains no advice regardless of source. One of his most successful methods in dealing with individuals is to assume that he himself is lacking in detailed knowledge and liable to make an error and is seeking advice. This is by no means a pose, because he actually values the recommendations and suggestions he receives.[74]

Indeed, shortly after assuming the presidency Eisenhower observed: "My job here . . . is not to create friction, not to accentuate differences, but to bring people together so we can actually achieve progress."[75] In attempting to accomplish this goal, he valued information-rich forms of communication—small group meetings and individual consultations.

This chief executive's abilities to organize and manage structure and cogently discuss information from a variety of sources were not reflected in his public communications. His speeches generally were regarded as uninspired and vague, not reflecting an analytical, incisive mind. Yet his communication with staff inside the White House reflected preciseness, a "clear incisiveness" and a "keen analytic mind."[76] During Cabinet meetings or in discussions with his senior aides, Greenstein writes, "Eisenhower's comments impressed his colleagues not simply because they were made with intensity, but also because they reflected his extensive personal knowledge of governmental affairs."[77]

Like Johnson, Eisenhower had a temper that sometimes exploded during his interactions with staff. But he did not bear grudges, and his outbursts resembled "summer thunderstorms followed by balmy good humor."[78] Moreover, he did not enjoy angry confrontations, so common in the realm of politics, and worked to control his emotions because he deeply felt that "a leader's *duty* is to keep his impulses in check and act rationally."[79] Responding to a *Life* editorial that his presidential leadership had been too gentle, the president wrote: " 'In war and peace I've had no respect for the desk-pounder and have despised the loud and slick talker.' "[80]

Eisenhower is an example of a president whose public communications did not reflect his personal presidential strengths, which lay mostly in the organization and administration of his presidency. Inside the White House he was open, attentive, and expressive; he was a much better interpersonal communicator than he was a public speaker. Greenstein, who has done much to refocus attention on the strengths of Eisenhower as president, argues that the 1950s "were so static and politically uneventful that his approach of subordinating the visible side of political leadership could work then . . . but the approach would have no applicability to the tumultuous years which followed."[81] As historians rewrite their analyses of Eisenhower, these observations may be reinforced. However, even though the president did have to work with a Democratic Congress, one wonders if Eisenhower maximized his organizational talents to address the domestic and foreign problems that began emerging during his administration. John Kennedy and Lyndon Johnson inherited myriad such problems that seemed to explode in their presidencies partly due to a previous lack of presidential attention. As a result, it is fair to ask if Eisenhower might have made better use of the organizational innovations he initiated. Rightly or wrongly, they were not perceived as structures that enhanced policy development, and Kennedy eliminated most of them, in favor of a less formal structure that supposedly facilitated a more creative organizational environment within the White House.

Dwight Eisenhower left the presidency in January 1961; the Republicans returned, with Richard Nixon, in January 1969. Nixon was to adopt some of Eisenhower's organizational changes, including the use of a chief of staff. But as managers and communicators, the two men were very different indeed.

RICHARD NIXON—ADMINISTRATION IN ISOLATION

Analyzing the organizational structure Richard Nixon used in the management of his White House, and the communication behaviors he exhibited when interacting with senior aides, is a complex task because Nixon's private and presidential personalities were complex. As his presidency aged, and as the Watergate scandal took increasing amounts of presidential and staff time and attention, major changes took place in the way he structured the White House, received information, made decisions, and communicated with his senior staff.

Before Nixon took office, he determined to utilize several of Dwight Eisenhower's organizational innovations in structuring the operational functions of the White House. Accordingly, his eventual chief of staff, H. R. Haldeman, consulted with General Goodpaster about developing a "modification of some of the Eisenhower staff structure approaches and most particularly the concept of a staff secretariat.''[82] Out of those discussions, according to Haldeman, ''it became clear that someone had to be the broker within the operation, both for external Cabinet-level type relationships and the internal White House staff relationships. My role evolved out of that.''[83] Haldeman also spoke with Eisenhower, who suggested that Haldeman could be of greatest service to Nixon by protecting him from administrative trivia and urging him to concentrate on only a few major issues.[84]

Nixon's initial staff appointees, like Haldeman, were mostly former campaign loyalists and in general were younger than Kennedy's chief aides. However, unlike many of their predecessors, most had no political or governmental experience in Washington.[85] Initially the president's key assistants headed eight separate functional areas. These areas, and the staff members who oversaw their operations, were:

- Personal services—H. R. Haldeman
- Press relations—two staffs, headed by Ronald Zeigler and Herbert Klein
- Domestic policy—two staffs, reporting to Arthur Burns and Daniel P. Moynihan
- National security—Henry Kissinger
- Congressional relations—Bryce Harlow
- Political operations—Harry Dent and John Sears
- Personnel—Peter Flanigan and Harry Flemming
- Speechwriting—James Keogh.[86]

By 1970, John Ehrlichman had evolved as the president's principal adviser on domestic issues, in part because the opposing political philosophies of Burns and Moynihan prompted almost continuous infighting between them and subsequent requests for presidential intercession in their quarrels. The rest of Nixon's inner circle emerged as Haldeman, assistant to the president or chief of staff; Kissinger; and George Shultz, who was in charge of economic policy. Interested in adapting some of Eisenhower's ideas on organizational structure for his own use, Nixon apparently wanted a formally structured staff operation in the White House at the beginning of his administration, with close, cooperative ties to Cabinet officers. However, according to Hess, ''he quickly rejected a collegial use of the cabinet, and, lacking Eisenhower's skill in the art of using staff, his methods turned out to be more a perversion than an extension of the Eisenhower system.''[87] As Kissinger has written: ''There can be little doubt that the so-called Nixon team never existed except in the White House, and even there it later disintegrated under stress.''[88]

Just as Sherman Adams was a dominant force in the Eisenhower administration, so Haldeman evolved as the most pervasive force within his president's White House. Nixon recalls that the role Haldeman was asked to play was administrative, not substantive, from a policy-making perspective.

He would examine the paperwork to ensure that opposing views were included and then bring the material to me for my decision; he would be a funnel rather than a filter. His intelligence and his capacity for detaching his personal prejudices from the examination of issues made him the ideal man for the job. He would also be the gatekeeper of the Oval Office. This would place him in the unenviable position of having to say no to a lot of people who felt they needed to see me personally and often, but I knew that his strong ego would be able to handle the jealousy and unpopularity such a role inevitably engenders.[89]

According to Haldeman, Nixon's original senior staff structure was to include five generalists with no assigned areas of responsibility. As time passed and the president assessed his administrative needs, Haldeman evolved as a general assistant while others assumed responsibility for policy areas.[90] As he describes the responsibilities of his organizational role: "I knew at all times what the President was doing, what his current priorities were, what he was expecting others to accomplish. I had no independent schedule of my own. I operated totally at the President's beck and call, working my own projects in between his demands."[91] Additionally, Haldeman recalls, "I reviewed all paperwork before it went to the President and most of what came from him for action."[92] All appointments with Nixon were cleared through Haldeman, who allowed the chief executive sufficient time in his daily schedule to meet with individuals and to consider decisions. To maximize use of the president's time, Haldeman was responsible for preparing Nixon for each meeting by collecting and presenting appropriate background information.[93]

Despite Haldeman's reputation in the press as part of the "palace guard" that eventually encircled Nixon, and his role in the Watergate cover-up that prompted his forced resignation, he has continued to defend the structure that Nixon initially established in his White House. At a conference in 1986 he emphasized:

We set up a tight ship . . . but it was not set up on the basis that people reported to me and I reported to the president. There were a number of assistants . . . who reported to the president, and a number of agency heads reported directly to the president. Actually way too many people.[94]

Haldeman explained that the structure of the Nixon White House was not designed to prevent access to the president but to organize it, to give individuals with reasons to see the president "the time they needed . . . at the time they needed it. The system channeled and balanced and assured that opposing views would be coming in, avoiding the possibility of someone dominating the president on one issue from one direction and thereby filibustering out the opposing view."[95] According to Haldeman, the "system" was abandoned when the president and his senior staff became embroiled in the cover-up of the Watergate break-in. "The fault is not that we had a bad system at all. . . . it's that we didn't use the system when we needed it the most."[96]

As the Nixon administration entered its second and third years, power dissipated within the Cabinet departments and became concentrated within t House. Additionally, as Richard Nathan has written, the president be creasingly interested in opportunities "to achieve policy aims through istrative action as opposed to legislative change."[97] This interest was due to Nixon's desire for more control over the policy development process as well as his problematic relationship with Congress. According to Nathan: "The President's men—trusted lieutenants, tied closely to Richard Nixon and without national reputation of their own—were . . . placed in direct charge of the major program bureaucracies of domestic government for the second term."[98] Consequently, Nixon's initially strong Cabinet model of government, adapted from the Eisenhower model, was replaced. Additionally, to circumvent the federal bureaucracy that he, like Kennedy, did not trust, Nixon implemented a reorganization proposal developed by his Advisory Council on Executive Organization. This committee became known as the Ash Council, named after its chairman, industrialist Roy Ash. Under its plan a Domestic Council was established, a counterpart to the National Security Council, and the Bureau of the Budget became the Office of Management and Budget. John Ehrlichman took charge of the Domestic Council and, with administrative units in the White House now primarily responsible for all domestic, foreign, and economic policy, Nixon essentially had created a counterbureaucracy in the federal government under his direct control.

To add to his "counterbureaucracy," Nixon appointed special administrative units to deal with specific problems, such as the Council on Environmental Quality, the Council for Urban Affairs, and the Office of Telecommunications Policy. One result of adding these formal structures to those already existing in the White House was that the president's staff became increasingly involved in administrative details and "decisions were delayed or never made."[99] Moreover, the increase in administrative units created a burgeoning White House staff—too many for the senior staff to manage adequately. When the White House staff increases in size, as Hess observes, "the standard complaint is that it exceeds the span of a president's control, and aides go into business for themselves."[100] But senior staff in the Nixon White House faced an additional problematic result of this trend. "New people moved in who did not know the president intuitively and were likely to accept presidential directives too literally."[101]

In the meantime, the White House organization "became too compartmentalized, with each office or council operating in isolation."[102] In short, the structure was out of administrative control. Ehrlichman recalled at a 1987 symposium, "Anybody that takes a cross section of the Nixon administration White House and says it is this kind of creature will be right for a certain amount of time. But things changed, and as we got into trouble, things changed very rapidly."[103] In 1971 Nixon attempted to restructure the Cabinet, suggesting its departments be reduced to eight, including four consolidated ones. Seen by some as another attempt to increase White House control over the federal departments, support for this reorganization proposal never was sufficient in Congress to approve the necessary legislation; by 1973 the Nixon White House was immersed in problems related to the Watergate scandal and the idea was dropped.

Nixon's administrative problems in part were due to constant changes in his organizational philosophy about the role of the White House in policy development. At the beginning of his presidency he announced complete support for a Cabinet-centered administration. Yet almost from the beginning of his term he delegated policy-making power to members of his White House staff. After the 1972 election he attempted to resurrect Cabinet government by putting loyal aides in charge of the departments; then he suggested a restructuring of the Cabinet that some department heads felt was a ploy for increasing the power of his senior staff. Gradually the structure around him weakened, as his aides became entangled in the Watergate controversy. In the spring of 1973 he asked for the resignations of Haldeman and Ehrlichman, who had become the most powerful aides in the White House. For a little more than a year his White House slowly sank into organizational decline, and eventually disintegration.

Nixon's problems within the White House were related to his management style as well as to his organizational structure. To understand that style it is first important to understand the complex relationship he had with his senior aides. It was professionally intimate but personally distant—a reflection of the president's complex personal makeup. Former aides Raymond Price, William Safire, and H. R. Haldeman have written, using different metaphors, of Nixon's dark and light sides. Price concludes that Nixon's administration was a combination of personalities that reflected the president's contradictory nature. Although eventually he would rely on only a handful of intimate advisers, particularly Ehrlichman and Haldeman, Nixon's initial staff appointments included experienced professionals, young and inexperienced loyalists, and "old hands from past Nixon incarnations."[104] The latter included such individuals as Arthur Burns, Robert Finch, Bryce Harlow, Maurice Stans, and Rose Mary Woods. According to Price:

> These old hands, his associates over the years, had seen him in all of his moods. They were not moths attracted to the flame of the presidency. They were mostly people of independent stature, and uniformly people of high public purpose. They saw their loyalty to Richard Nixon as an extension of their concern for the country's welfare. They were natural, instinctive allies of the light side rather than the dark side, and they believed in him because over the years they had seen that he, too, was an instinctive ally of the light side.[105]

Ironically, as Haldeman writes in his memoirs, Nixon "shunted long-time personal friends as far away as possible during his Administration," regarding individuals like Finch "as people, which meant he would have had trouble dealing with them on an official basis."[106] Those who gained the most frequent entry to the Oval Office were those who proved their loyalty to Nixon, "measured by the most unquestioning opposition to forces and people that were thought to be against their president.''[107] Nixon's ''true'' friends did not always fit this mold.

Haldeman and Ehrlichman were identified as the president's closest advisers, although in their memoirs both discuss the difference between their professional and personal intimacy with him. According to Ehrlichman, ''Haldeman once wrote that Nixon never could remember how many children the Haldemans had, or their names. In my case it was *my* name.''[108] Similarly, Haldeman emphasizes that he never was one of the president's social friends. ''Only once, in my entire relationship with him over many years, were my wife and I invited to an informal personal dinner at his home, and that was in 1962.''[109] Even Alexander Butterfield, who brought papers into the Oval Office several times a day for Nixon's review and/or signature, reported that Nixon called him by name only after he had worked in the White House for several months.[110]

Haldeman was perceived by the public, the press, and his fellow aides as the president's alter ego, such that ''by 1968 it was hard to tell where Richard Nixon left off and H. R. Haldeman began.''[111] Ehrlichman, perhaps writing out of jealousy, perhaps from detached observation, suggests that Nixon ''grew totally dependent on the Nixon-Haldeman relationship. Virtually nothing Nixon did was done without Haldeman's knowledge. That is not to say that Haldeman approved everything Nixon said or did; but it was essential that he know, and have a chance to object, before it happened.''[112] Although not disputing this observation, Haldeman writes in his memoirs that Nixon did not see him as a human being but as a machine, a robot.[113] In his account of the firing of Haldeman and Ehrlichman, however, Nixon describes the sadness he felt after they left his White House. ''They had been my closest aides. They were my friends.''[114] The passage of time, of course, alters memories and one's ability to describe them adequately.

Nixon's lack of personal intimacy with his aides is reflected in Ehrlichman's observation that the president could not easily forge personal relationships. ''He was a fellow who at the time I knew him . . . was very weak in family relationships and in friendships. He had no strong friendships based on an exchange of interests and views and mutual confidence. His personal relationships, as with Bebe Rebozo and one or two others, were almost unilateral, not reciprocal.''[115] It is not surprising, therefore, that Nixon based his interpersonal interactions on *professional* intimacy and personal loyalty. Describing the first appointment to his White House staff, the selection of Rose Mary Woods as his personal secretary, the president writes: ''Rose had been part of my political life since 1951. She combined professional skill with unexcelled personal charm. And she had total dedication.''[116] Moreover, according to Henry Kissinger, fierce and uncompromising loyalty existed among Nixon's advisers long before he entered the White House. After his 1962 gubernatorial defeat in California, Nixon's aides ''shared his sense of isolation and resentment. The Nixon team drew the wagons around itself from the beginning; it was besieged in mind long before it was besieged in fact.''[117]

During his years as president, Nixon was a wary politician, an introverted personality, and as a result "possessed a congenital distaste for dealing with all but a few select aides, those with whom he felt at ease."[118] As his presidency wore on, their numbers dwindled rapidly. Considering the nature of his relationships with senior aides, the strategy he used to manage his staff is not surprising.

Unlike Eisenhower, Nixon had no significant managerial experience prior to assuming the presidency—other than, perhaps, organizing his congressional and vice presidential staffs. According to Nathan, "His notion of management in 1969 seemed to be that it was a profession or science, that expert managers from the business world could greatly improve the performance and efficiency of the government, but that this was not an area of direct presidential responsibility and action."[119] Instead, Nixon managed through intermediaries, especially Haldeman, and felt no particular need to emphasize teamwork. Kissinger recalls a get-acquainted session for Cabinet members in December 1968:

> It was a harbinger that briefings outlining the problems facing the new Administration were given not by the Cabinet officer . . . but by Presidential Assistants. . . . Whether these able, astute, strong men could have formed a cohesive team under any leadership will never be known; their complex chief chose to manipulate them as disparate advisers while he undertook his solitary journey with a system of policymaking that centralized power in the White House.[120]

Moreover, since Nixon assigned tasks to specific advisers rather than cultivating his initial notion of working with them as a group of generalists, conflicts were bound to develop. Unlike Roosevelt, who purposively generated this conflict but also took pains to manage it and mend the feelings of those senior aides involved, Nixon had no interest in personally managing his staff. Hess states, "For a president to choose a system of staff conflict, he must be prepared to assume a major role in making assignments, mediating disputes, and unruffling feathers. This Nixon was unwilling to do."[121]

Haldeman, who as chief of staff under Nixon was the manager of that staff, has characterized the differing management styles he and Nixon used.

> I would come straight on at a problem or person, hammering culprits over the head verbally. Nixon would attack the same problem or person by coming in at the side, often through subordinates, when the victim wasn't looking, and trying to strike the blow unseen. Interestingly, Nixon never worried about his own deviousness; instead he was concerned that his Chief of Staff was *too* direct."[122]

Haldeman has freely admitted his role as a gatekeeper, even a human barrier, to other people in the Nixon White House. He assumed this role essentially for two reasons:

> Nixon wanted . . . officials to submit their problems in writing or to deal with someone on the staff better able to handle their concerns than the President *before* they were granted

precious Presidential time. The other reason for the wall was my secret. I soon realized that *this* President had to be protected from himself. Time and again I would receive petty vindictive orders.[123]

Thus, the organizational environment Richard Nixon created by using Haldeman to manage the White House, and even at times to manage the president himself, was conducive to the growth of isolation around the Oval Office. The formal, hierarchical reporting structure he imposed at the beginning of his presidency and increasingly relied on as the Watergate scandal evolved also fostered this isolation, especially since Nixon, unlike Eisenhower, did not supplement formal structure with informal communication networks. Kissinger provides an insightful description of the president's use of staff and its results.

Nixon tended to work in spurts. During periods when he withdrew he counted on his assistants to carry on the day-to-day decisions; during spasms of extreme activity he relied on his assistants to screen his more impetuous commands. They were needed to prevent the face-to-face confrontations he so disliked and dreaded. And they were to protect Nixon against impulsive orders or the tendency to agree with the visitors he did receive. Haldeman's staff system did not "isolate" the President as was often alleged; Nixon insisted on isolating himself; it was the only way in which he could marshall [*sic*] his psychological resources and his instructions could be given systematic review.[124]

Richard Nixon, unlike his predecessors, did not manage his White House. As a result, the ways he created and sought sources of information both in and outside the White House became critically important in the process of policy development within his administration.

On September 18, 1968, Nixon spoke to a national radio audience during his campaign for the presidency. He emphasized the need for an "open" administration in the White House.

It's time we once again had an open administration—open to ideas *from* the people, and open in its communications *with* the people—an administration of open doors, open eyes, and open minds. We should bring dissenters into policy discussions, not freeze them out; we should invite constructive criticism, not only because the critics have a right to be heard, but also because they often have something worth hearing.[125]

Despite this emphasis on openness in Nixon's campaign communication, his communication within the White House reflected little, if any, interest in seeking information from a variety of diverse sources. The written information that came to him was screened by a White House aide, and most of his interpersonal discussions were with those comprising his inner circle.

In their report of an interview with Alexander Butterfield, individuals representing the Senate committee investigating the Watergate scandal reported that Butterfield, as deputy assistant to the president, "totally controlled" the flow of paper going to the president and "weeded out memos" he did not think the president had to see.[126] Another of Butterfield's roles was to meet daily with the president to review his schedule for the following day. According to the investigators' report, each of the president's meetings required a briefing paper that included "talking points."[127] The person preparing the paper would most likely attend the meeting and then would be responsible for preparing a memorandum for the president "which would include the subject, tone of the meeting and any commitments made."[128] If only White House staff were involved in one of these meetings, a follow-up memo might not be prepared unless, in the case of discussions deemed significant by Nixon, the president instructed its preparation.

Even information originating from outside the White House was "prepared" for the president by his aides. Every morning he received a daily news summary compiled by Patrick Buchanan, and used it to supplement information supplied by the federal departments and agencies.[129] This summary, sometimes fifty pages in length, was designed more to monitor the bureaucracy he distrusted than to provide him information to assist in decision making. According to Hess, Nixon's written comments in the summary's margins were transcribed and became a "formal channel of command between president and staff."[130]

Unlike Eisenhower, Nixon preferred to obtain information by reading rather than by listening. He writes in his presidential memoirs, "I knew that I could absorb far more material by reading it than by talking about it, and I have invariably found that staff members will present problems more concisely and incisively in writing than they will in meetings."[131] While he may have gained conciseness and clarity in the information he received, he most likely lost the richness of that information by forsaking the benefit of seeing and hearing the depth and breadth of an aide's knowledge and opinions on an issue. As a result he failed to use an innovative policy-making mechanism to its full advantage–the deliberations of working groups that John Ehrlichman organized to initiate domestic policy-making.

Ehrlichman assigned issues and problems to these groups, which were comprised of a member of his staff, an assistant from the Office of Management and Budget, officials from the Cabinet departments or federal agencies who were experts on the subject at hand, and representatives from the private sector, business, and academia. Ehrlichman describes their process as follows:

> These working groups, chaired by one of my people, would meet and attempt to draft either a position paper or an option paper depending on what the President was going to be called to do. Once they got it in some kind of form, it would be sent to the Cabinet members involved. It would be passed around the White House if there were people in the White House who had areas of responsibility involved. Eventually it would come to me as a final product and I would hand it to the President for his weekend reading. He might carry two or three of these away on a weekend, fairly thick documents with a covering memo of anywhere from half a page to ten pages. The covering memo always ended with a summary of what we thought his options were.[132]

Unlike Eisenhower, who used such documents as the basis of both formal and informal meetings with Cabinet members and with staff, Nixon generally chose not to interact with the authors of the works he read. Similarly, in the process of developing foreign policy, he preferred to read information of potential use to him. In Haldeman's words, "he read the things that Henry [Kissinger] told him to read."[133]

With Nixon's propensity for receiving information in written form, it is not surprising that he used memos to communicate to his staff. As a result, such communications were "information poor." According to Hess, "memos, when they are not supplemented by an opportunity to probe the president's intent, can take on the stark, absolutist quality of a command. Communication was still a two-way process in the White House at the end of 1969, but through Haldeman, and in writing, the process screened out subtleties."[134] The chief of staff was also chief of internal communications. He met with Nixon every day at 9 A.M. for approximately thirty minutes, reviewing the day's activities and planning trips. After these sessions "Haldeman would leave the President . . . to go to his own office and translate his jottings of Presidential will . . . into dictated, crisp, one-paragraph memos."[135] Lawrence Higby, Haldeman's assistant, would then distribute the memos to the intended staff members. Even messages to Cabinet secretaries came from Ehrlichman or Haldeman, not the president, causing some, if not considerable, consternation among them.

Early in the Nixon administration Ehrlichman was quoted as saying that the reason for the president's reluctance to speak with a variety of individuals from outside the White House was that he did not like to discuss a complex subject in only fifteen minutes.[136] The president rationalized that his staff could meet with many of the individuals seeking access to the Oval Office because they had more time to spend with these persons. At a 1987 conference, however, Ehrlichman stated that Nixon just did not like to talk with those outside his close-knit cadre of senior aides—even Cabinet members and congressmen.[137] He describes the president's Tuesday morning meetings with the Republican leadership as follows: "Our dynamic legislative leaders drank coffee and occasionally took notes, but they rarely were given a chance to say anything. Nixon deliberately scheduled the sessions early in the morning because he knew the Members were not often called upon to emerge into the early-morning light."[138] Between 1969 and 1972, according to a study by Bill Timmons of the White House staff, presidential contact with congressmen, an important source of information and ideas for previous presidents, declined dramatically.[139] The president held 125 meetings with senators in 1969, but only 23 in 1972. He met with members of the House of Representatives 87 times in 1969, but held only 30 such meetings in 1972. He had 204 telephone conversations with federal legislators in 1969, but only 61 in 1972.

As time passed, and the president spent less and less of his time in meetings with congressmen, Cabinet officials, and even several members of his staff, "more of the business of the presidency," according to Hess, "was conducted in writing, and the function of the gatekeeper became more important."[140] As he began his second term, and as he became immersed in the troubles that the Watergate break-in was creating for his administration, Nixon saw fewer and fewer individuals—even old friends and advisers like John Connally and Melvin Laird. The president never told these outside advisers about the extent of his involvement in the Watergate cover-up, and as a result their advice was of little use. Hess writes that "Soon he stopped seeing them altogether. After Haldeman and Ehrlichman left, Nixon had even fewer direct contacts with even fewer people. At the end he limited those with whom he regularly met to Alexander Haig and Ron Ziegler."[141] An irony of this created isolation is that, throughout his presidency, Nixon used private investigators within the federal bureaucracy because "he felt he needed information that he did not trust the usual mechanisms of the permanent government or his political party to supply."[142]

The flow of information in Richard Nixon's White House perhaps was less a stream than a trickle—and a carefully screened trickle at that. He declined to cultivate, much less use, the diverse sources of information available to him as the chief executive. He depended on Haldeman to collect and present sufficient information with which decisions could be made. He was, in a sense, an organizational isolate through his own choice. And yet his work was exceedingly important to him; he put a premium on quiet times in his Old Executive Office Building enclave where he could think and plan, where he could consider policy alternatives, where he could make decisions . . . alone.

Richard Nixon writes in his presidential memoirs that "the key to a successful presidency is in the decision-making process."[143] He believed in delegating some decision-making authority, believing that "the matters brought before a President for decisions should be only those that cannot or should not be made at a lower level on the White House staff, or by the Cabinet member responsible for them."[144] And yet, despite his stated belief in the importance of the decision-making process, his process was woefully lacking—it included the input of very few individuals. Richard Cheney recalls:

> Nixon was not one who liked extensive policy debates with large numbers of people. He liked to work off paper. He liked to consult with one or two individuals but never with a group. Most of the group meetings in which I participated with Nixon . . . were almost like a public meeting. It was not a place where you'd seriously discuss policy.[145]

Additionally, Kissinger recalls, Nixon "abhorred confronting colleagues with whom he disagreed and he could not bring himself to face a disapproving friend."[146] Consequently, decisions were not reached in a structure or environment conducive to a free flow of discussion.

The one person Nixon seemed to consult regularly and frequently before making a decision was H. R. Haldeman, whose influence was "truly enormous, albeit more passive than active, more custodial than creative, and more private than public.''[147] Haldeman acknowledged his role in the decision-making process at a 1987 conference:

The objective people who served with me at the time will tell you that we did achieve that objective of an honest broker relationship, getting both sides or all sides of adversarial positions presented, weighed, and considered properly, and a decision made on the basis of consideration of all aspects and varying views rather than the development of a policy intentionally starting from a preconceived viewpoint to arrive at a preconceived destination.[148]

Additionally, in his account of the Nixon presidency he wrote:

I had adopted the invariable practice . . . of expressing my views as strongly and effectively as possible during the time the decision was being formulated in Nixon's mind. I also made sure all other viewpoints were at least as strongly represented. If it was something in which I was directly concerned or on which I felt strongly, I would fight hard for my position. But, without exception, once the decision was finally made . . . I then made every possible effort to see that it was carried out as effectively as possible.''[149]

Because he was the most pervasive, and most trusted, source of information upon which Nixon depended, Haldeman's organizational role was especially significant. His performance in that role has been controversial in both press and scholarly assessments of the Nixon White House, particularly during the months in which the Watergate cover-up evolved. In his memoirs he maintains that he did provide the president with information representing different sides of an issue, thereby compensating for the president's dependency on him as an information source. Ehrlichman observes that Haldeman's role ''was to argue (gently) the opposite of the President's thesis, raising factual issues and suggesting further inquiry if it appeared necessary.''[150]

Once he possessed the information he needed to make a decision, Nixon was a deliberative decision maker. According to Ehrlichman, ''Richard Nixon was like a cow. He would chew his cud over and over on a subject and turn it over and chew it some more, and turn it over and chew it some more.''[151] Using another metaphor to describe the president's consideration of alternatives, Ehrlichman recalls: ''He would turn the same rock over a dozen times and then leave it and then come back to it two weeks later and turn it over another dozen times.''[152] Most of the time this cud-chewing and rock-turning was done in the presence of Haldeman or, in his absence, Ehrlichman, and Haldeman therefore became an important participant in Nixon's decision-making process. Kissinger confirms that, wherever possible, the president made decisions ''in solitude on the basis of memoranda or with a few very intimate aides.''[153] Since so much of the conduct of the Nixon presidency was in isolation or semi-solitude, the manner in which the president communicated with his aides becomes particularly significant.

The portrait painted of Richard Nixon as a communicator inside the White

House by his aides illustrates at least two sides of the many referred to earlier in this chapter. On the one hand, he was uncomfortable during interpersonal interactions, avoiding meetings with individuals other than his closest aides. On the other hand, he apparently greatly valued a process of thinking out loud with one or two of his senior staff, usually Haldeman. Discussing Nixon's avoidance of small group meetings, Ehrlichman observed: "He didn't want meetings around the Cabinet table with passionate advocates pounding away at each other and at him and he cross-examining them. He was not comfortable with face-to-face contact."[154] According to Haldeman, the president had a "bewildering combination of a great grace and amazing awkwardness in dealing with people face-to-face on a personal basis."[155] In informal settings, he was apparently unable to relax with persons other than his family.[156]

The result of Nixon's unwillingness, or inability, to communicate comfortably in interpersonal settings sometimes created political problems for him. Comparing his persuasive ability with that of Lyndon Johnson, Haldeman writes: "Johnson could envelop a Congressman in charm, make him come out doing what Johnson wanted and at the same time lay in a very tough threat of what would happen if the Congressman *didn't* do it. Nixon tried the same approach, but the charm wasn't there—and the threat would be left hanging bald, bare, and glaring."[157] He was awkward when speaking informally with governmental officials, corporate leaders, or other individuals with whom he might socialize.[158] According to Haldeman, Nixon "hated to see people who needed either to be personally persuaded or forced to take action. He preferred to pass that job to others."[159]

Another characteristic of Nixon as an interpersonal communicator was his tendency to change his communication style, depending on the individual to whom he was speaking at the time.

> He tended to avoid controversy by presenting an aspect of himself which he probably subconsciously calculated would be acceptable to the person that he was dealing with. He could switch around and present the opposite aspect to another person. There were people on the staff with whom he was very profane because he thought that was where he made contacts with them. There were other people with whom he would never use a swear word.[160]

As a communicator, Richard Nixon kept both physical and psychosocial distance from those with whom presidents interact the most: congressmen, party leaders, Cabinet officials, and even members of the White House staff. The major exception to this behavior was his propensity for thinking about a problem or issue out loud with a senior staff member present, not to participate in a discussion but to listen. Ehrlichman cites this behavior as one disadvantage of presidential access; one had to listen to "countless hours of rambling and rumination."[161] He recalls that "Someone had to sit with Richard Nixon to listen. Usually it was Haldeman; sometimes it was Henry Kissinger, George Shultz,

Daniel Patrick Moynihan or I, and later it became Ron Ziegler by default.''[162] When Ehrlichman substituted for Haldeman in these sessions, he has written, ''I grew to appreciate how Nixon-Haldeman truly worked. I was expected to sit with the President as he leaned back in his chair, feet up, toying with his wristwatch and talking up and down a subject.''[163]

Just as he was almost a manager in absentia in his own White House, so Richard Nixon was generally an uncommunicative president, except with one or two aides. His communication style was not open, friendly, or relaxed. According to Haldeman, he had a terrible temper and ''with one of us who worked closely with him, he could really blow.''[164] Indeed, Nixon seemed almost dysfunctional as an interpersonal communicator. He grew more so as the Watergate scandal focused increasing attention on the misuse or abuse of power in his White House. In time the web of deception created by the president and his senior aides would entangle his administration in congressional inquiries, press and public outcries, and judicial proceedings. Ultimately it would squeeze the potency out of the Nixon White House as a policy-making entity and disable the president as a political and public leader.

Unlike Eisenhower, Richard Nixon did not develop informal networks to enhance his management of the formal White House structure or his communication with those most involved in its daily functions. His was not a personal, but a private, presidency—and his detachment from, and distrust of, many of his own staff and most of the federal bureaucracy began long before the break-in at the Watergate complex. This is not to say there were not presidential accomplishments during the Nixon administration. There were, especially in the field of foreign policy. But the interdependence of formal and informal structure, cemented by presidential attention to communication within the White House, was absent. Among the modern presidencies prior to 1974, his was therefore an anomaly.

In March 1974, prior to Nixon's resignation from the presidency, the National Academy of Public Administration issued a report on Watergate's implications for responsible government. Part of that report states:

> The U.S. government [under Nixon] would be run like a corporation—or at least a popular view of the corporate model—with all powers concentrated at the top and exercised through appointees in the President's office and loyal followers placed in crucial positions in the various agencies of the Executive Branch. . . . No one can guess how close the American government would be to this closed hierarchial model had not Watergate exposures halted the advance towards it—at least temporarily.[165]

As was seen in Chapter 2, the concentration of policy-making power in the White House did not begin in the Nixon administration. However, unlike Eisenhower, Kennedy, and Johnson, Richard Nixon exercised little if any constant control over those exercising that power—power assumed and wielded in his name. The Watergate cover-up became a scandal because it was based on the abuse of unsupervised power in a White House that also involved the misconduct of a president, not just his chief of staff. During and after Watergate, press and public attention focused on the importance of presidential–staff interactions and the role of senior staff as they affect the conduct of the president and the presidency.

The Eisenhower–Nixon legacy is the attention to structure and process that subsequent administrations have, to varying degrees, borrowed. It is also the centralization of power in one or two individual that, left *unchecked* in Nixon's White House, contributed to the demise of the White House as an organization and to distrust of the presidency as a branch of government. Such power evoked concern about the potential dangers of the White House as an organization, if it is peopled by a powerful staff acting at the behest of a president who insulates himself from information and ideas outside the organization he has created. That concern, and presidential perceptions of public interest in the organization and management of the White House, prompted the post-Watergate presidents to create, at least initially, organizational structures different from those used within the Eisenhower and Nixon presidencies.

In August 1974, the White House, which had developed into a mature organization during the Eisenhower years, experienced organizational decline and, immediately before Nixon's resignation, virtual disintegration. However, as is the case with other organizations, the White House was rejuvenated by a new leader who made some changes in its structure and systems of information flow, and who, more importantly, took an interest in the management of the organization.

In Part II presidents are analyzed as social architects (the creators of structure), as decision makers, and as intraorganizational communicators. The focus is on Gerald Ford, Jimmy Carter, and Ronald Reagan, who, in varying degrees and in different ways, reacted to the effects of the Watergate scandal on the White House as an organization.

NOTES

1. Fred I. Greenstein, *The Hidden-Hand Presidency; Eisenhower as Leader* (New York: Basic Books, 1982), p. 54.
2. Ibid.
3. Dwight D. Eisenhower, *The White House Years: Mandate for Change 1953–1956* (Garden City, NY: Doubleday, 1963), p. 87.
4. Ibid., p. 114.
5. Ibid., p. 88.
6. Sherman Adams, *Firsthand Report* (New York: Harper & Brothers, 1961), p. 54.
7. Ibid., pp. 52–53.
8. Phillip G. Henderson, *Managing the Presidency* (Boulder, CO: Westview Press, 1988), p. 18.
9. Eisenhower, *Mandate for Change*, p. 118.

10. Ibid.
11. Adams, *Firsthand Report*, p. 50.
12. Greenstein, *The Hidden-Hand Presidency*, pp. 142–43.
13. Ibid.
14. Adams, *Firsthand Report*, p. 76.
15. Greenstein, *The Hidden-Hand Presidency*, p. 141.
16. Stephen Hess, *Organizing the Presidency*, 2d ed. (Washington, DC: The Brookings Institution, 1988), p. 66.
17. Eisenhower, *Mandate for Change*, p. 117.
18. Adams, *Firsthand Report*, p. 8.
19. Henderson, *Managing the Presidency*, p. 64.
20. Greenstein, *The Hidden-Hand Presidency*, p. 114.
21. Ibid.
22. Hess, *Organizing the Presidency*, p. 61.
23. See Greenstein, *The Hidden-Hand Presidency*.
24. Andrew J. Goodpaster in Samuel Kernell and Samuel Popkin, *Chief of Staff* (Berkeley: University of California Press, 1986), p. 67.
25. Stephen E. Ambrose, *Eisenhower* vol. 2, *The President* (New York: Simon and Schuster, 1983), p. 20.
26. Dwight D. Eisenhower, *The White House Years: Waging Peace 1956–1961* (Garden City, NY: Doubleday, 1965), p. 311.
27. Ibid.
28. Richard H. Immerman, "Eisenhower and Dulles: Who Made the Decisions?" *Political Psychology*, 1, no. 2, Autumn 1979, p. 29.
29. Greenstein, *The Hidden-Hand Presidency*, p. 108.
30. Ibid., p. 246.
31. Ibid., p. 236.
32. Ibid., pp. 236–37.
33. As quoted in Patrick Anderson, *The Presidents' Men: White House Assistants of Franklin D. Roosevelt, Harry S. Truman, Dwight D. Eisenhower, John F. Kennedy and Lyndon B. Johnson* (Garden City, NY: Doubleday, 1968), pp. 137–38.
34. Henderson, *Managing the Presidency*, p. 176.
35. Greenstein, *The Hidden-Hand Presidency*, p. 115.
36. Eisenhower, *Mandate for Change*, p. 266.
37. Charles J. V. Murphy, "Eisenhower's White House," in Nelson W. Polsby, ed., *The Modern Presidency* (New York: Random House, 1973), p. 92.
38. Henderson, *Managing the Presidency*, p. 27.
39. Adams, *Firsthand Report*, p. 71.
40. Ibid., p. 26.
41. Ibid., pp. 72–73.
42. Ibid., p. 73.
43. Hess, *Organizing the Presidency*, p. 60.
44. Ibid., p. 68.
45. Murphy, "Eisenhower's White House," p. 96.
46. Ibid., p. 93.
47. Henderson, *Managing the Presidency*, p. 118.
48. Adams, *Firsthand Report*, p. 73.
49. Greenstein, *The Hidden-Hand Presidency*, p. 147.

50. Adams, *Firsthand Report*, p. 75.
51. Greenstein, *The Hidden-Hand Presidency*, p. 148.
52. Murphy, "Eisenhower's White House," p. 93.
53. Eisenhower, *Mandate for Change*, p. 270.
54. Adams, *Firsthand Report*, p. 86.
55. Greenstein, *The Hidden-Hand Presidency*, p. 150.
56. Ibid., p. 148.
57. Eisenhower, *Mandate for Change*, pp. 262–63.
58. Robert J. Donovan, *Confidential Secretary: Ann Whitman's Twenty Years with Eisenhower and Rockefeller* (New York: E. P. Dutton, 1988), p. 68.
59. Greenstein, *The Hidden-Hand Presidency*, p. 149.
60. Ibid., p. 150.
61. Adams, *Firsthand Report*, p. 51.
62. Greenstein, *The Hidden-Hand Presidency*, p. 148.
63. Anderson, *The Presidents' Men*, p. 147.
64. Henderson, *Managing the Presidency*, p. 32.
65. Eisenhower, quoted in ibid., p. 95.
66. Ibid., p. 118.
67. Ambrose, *Eisenhower*, p. 27.
68. Ibid., pp. 344–45.
69. Ibid.
70. Greenstein, *The Hidden-Hand Presidency*, p. 134.
71. Richard M. Nixon, *Six Crises* (New York: Doubleday, 1962), p. 169.
72. Greenstein, *The Hidden-Hand Presidency*, p. 25.
73. Ibid., p. 40.
74. Walter Bedell Smith, letter to General Maxwell Taylor, February 1, 1956, quoted in ibid., p. 34.
75. Adams, *Firsthand Report*, p. 462.
76. Greenstein, *The Hidden-Hand Presidency*, p. 18.
77. Ibid., p. 33.
78. Ibid., p. 43.
79. Ibid., p. 45.
80. Eisenhower, quoted in ibid., p. 240.
81. Ibid., p. 231.
82. H. R. Haldeman, quoted in Kenneth W. Thompson, ed., *The Nixon Presidency* (New York: University Press of America, 1987), p. 77.
83. Ibid.
84. Theodore H. White, *Breach of Faith: The Fall of Richard Nixon* (New York: Atheneum, 1975), p. 108.
85. Hess, *Organizing the Presidency*, p. 111.
86. Ibid., p. 110.
87. Ibid., p. 73.
88. Henry Kissinger, *White House Years* (Boston: Little, Brown, 1979), p. 25.
89. Richard M. Nixon, *The Memoirs of Richard Nixon* (New York: Grosset & Dunlap, 1978), p. 337.
90. H. R. Haldeman, with Joseph DiMona, *The Ends of Power* (New York: New York Times Books, 1978), p. 51.
91. Ibid.

92. Ibid., p. 52.

93. Ibid., p. 51.

94. H. R. Haldeman in Samuel Kernell and Samuel Popkin, *Chief of Staff* (Berkeley: University of California Press, 1986), p. 65.

95. Ibid., p. 65–66.

96. Ibid., p. 67.

97. Richard P. Nathan, *The Plot That Failed: Nixon and the Administrative Presidency* (New York: John Wiley & Sons, 1975), p. 7.

98. Ibid., p. 8.

99. Ibid., pp. 52–53.

100. Hess, *Organizing the Presidency*, pp. 118–19.

101. Ibid., p. 119.

102. Ibid., p. 117.

103. John Ehrlichman in Kenneth W. Thompson, ed., *The Nixon Presidency*, (New York: University Press of America, 1987), p. 126.

104. Raymond Price, *With Nixon* (New York: Viking Press, 1977), p. 31.

105. Ibid.

106. Haldeman, *The Ends of Power*, p. 74.

107. Hess, *Organizing the Presidency*, p. 120.

108. John Ehrlichman, *Witness to Power: The Nixon Years* (New York: Simon and Schuster, 1982), p. 77.

109. Haldeman, *The Ends of Power*, p. 65.

110. Dom Bonafede, "White House Staffing: The Nixon–Ford Era," in Thomas E. Cronin and Rexford G. Tugwell, eds., *The Presidency Reappraised*, 2d ed. (New York: Praeger, 1977), p. 158.

111. Ehrlichman, *Witness to Power*, p. 78.

112. Ibid.

113. Haldeman, *The Ends of Power*, p. 74.

114. Nixon, *Memoirs*, p. 848.

115. Ehrlichman in Thompson, *The Nixon Presidency*, p. 139.

116. Nixon, *Memoirs*, p. 337.

117. Kissinger, *White House Years*, p. 20.

118. Bonafede, "White House Staffing, p. 158.

119. Nathan, *The Plot That Failed*, p. 38.

120. Kissinger, *White House Years*, p. 38.

121. Hess, *Organizing the Presidency*, p. 116.

122. Haldeman, *The Ends of Power*, p. 56.

123. Ibid., p. 58.

124. Kissinger, *White House Years*, pp. 47–48.

125. Richard M. Nixon, quoted in Lewis J. Paper, *The Promise and the Performance: The Leadership of John F. Kennedy* (New York: Crown, 1975), p. 118.

126. Interview with Alexander Butterfield, July 13, 1973, folder: "Photocopies of Related Items in Erwin Committee Records," box 1, papers of Alexander Butterfield, Gerald R. Ford Library, pp. 7–8.

127. Ibid., p. 9.

128. Ibid.

129. Hess, *Organizing the Presidency*, p. 112.

130. Ibid., pp. 112–13.

131. Nixon, *Memoirs*, p. 338.
132. Ehrlichman in Thompson, *The Nixon Presidency*, p. 127.
133. Haldeman in Thompson, *The Nixon Presidency*, p. 90.
134. Hess, *Organizing the Presidency*, p. 119.
135. White, *Breach of Faith*, pp. 115–16.
136. John Pierson, "The Nixon Style: President Seeks Order in His Decision-Making, but Events Intrude," in Nelson Polsby, ed., *The Modern Presidency* (New York: Random House, 1973), p. 206.
137. Ehrlichman in Thompson, *The Nixon Presidency*, pp. 132–33.
138. Ehrlichman, *Witness to Power*, p. 204.
139. Ibid., p. 203.
140. Hess, *Organizing the Presidency*, p. 118.
141. Ibid., p. 130.
142. Ibid., p. 113.
143. Nixon, *Memoirs*, p. 337.
144. Ibid.
145. Richard Cheney, quoted in R. Gordon Hoxie, "Staffing the Ford and Carter Presidencies," in Bradley D. Nash et al., *Organizing and Staffing the Presidency* (New York: Center for the Study of the Presidency, 1980), p. 53.
146. Kissinger, *White House Years*, p. 45.
147. Bonafede, "White House Staffing," p. 162.
148. Haldeman quoted in Kenneth W. Thompson, ed., *The Nixon Presidency* (New York: University Press of America, 1987), p. 78.
149. Haldeman, *The Ends of Power*, p. 288.
150. Ehrlichman, *Witness to Power*, p. 80.
151. Ehrlichman in Thompson, *The Nixon Presidency*, p. 128.
152. Ibid.
153. Kissinger, *White House Years*, p. 45.
154. Ehrlichman in Thompson, *The Nixon Presidency*, p. 127.
155. Haldeman, *The Ends of Power*, p. 70.
156. Ibid.
157. Ibid., p. 71.
158. Ibid.
159. Ibid.
160. Ehrlichman in Thompson, *The Nixon Presidency*, pp. 139–40.
161. Ehrlichman, *Witness to Power*, p. 79.
162. Ibid.
163. Ibid., p. 80.
164. Haldeman, *The Ends of Power*, p. 74.
165. National Academy of Public Administration, "Watergate: Its Implications for Responsible Government," Summary, March 1974, quoted in Nathan, *The Plot That Failed*, p. 89.

PART II

COMMUNICATION IN THE POST-WATERGATE WHITE HOUSES

Chapter 4

The President as Social Architect: Organizational Structure in the White House, 1974–1988

''Watergate'' focused public and press attention on the importance of the White House staff in the conduct of the presidency, and the potential that a chief executive's inner circle has for facilitating the abuse or misuse of power. These effects of Watergate on one president provided a lesson two chief executives resolved not to forget—and one failed to remember—as they organized their White House staffs.

To establish organizational roles in the White House, such as chief of staff and staff secretary, to create reporting relationships and other formal and informal communication networks among staff and between president and staff, and to weave a social system comprised of channels of information flow to make and execute decisions, presidents adopt formal organizational structures at the beginning of their terms. Such structures may create, as well as alleviate, interpersonal conflicts and their resultant effects on the organization's internal environment. As a result, each president is a social architect, designing the organizational framework of his White House to fit his personal preferences and his policy-making needs, through which he may plan and pursue his organization's goals.

Stephen Hess suggests that it is a president's style—''his work habits, the way he likes to receive information, the sort of people he prefers to have around him, the manner in which he makes up his mind''—which determines how a White House is organized.[1] However, the formal structure he selects also depends on his perceptions of the successes and failures of the structure adopted by his predecessor(s). Concerned about Richard Nixon's pyramidal structure, for instance, Gerald Ford adopted a ''spokes of the wheel'' arrangement through which nine senior aides reported directly to the president. He wrote in his memoirs, ''Initially, when I became President, I did not want to have a powerful chief of staff. Wilson had had his Colonel House, Eisenhower his Sherman Adams, Nixon his Haldeman, and I was aware of the trouble those top assistants had caused my predecessors. I was determined to be my own chief of staff.''[2]

Formal structure in any organization serves a variety of purposes. According to Robert McPhee, formal structure clarifies who is in control and who is being controlled within an organization. It assists in decision making by defining who is responsible for providing information and/or making certain decisions. Additionally, the structure is itself a form of communication, informing organizational members about their job titles and their place on the organizational chart, which in turn tells them indirectly about their role and status in the organization.[3]

In addition to the imposition of formal structure, organizations are continually defining roles and responsibilities through the process of structuration, ''the production and reproduction of social systems via the application of generative rules and resources.''[4] Patricia Riley explains, ''the systems of deeply layered structures explain the 'framework' of the organization, while people creating and recreating structures form the patterns of interaction. The importance of individuals in structuration needs to be underscored, since they are the carriers and creators of the rules and resources—structures.''[5] As will be seen throughout this chapter, the key aides of Gerald Ford and Jimmy Carter spent much time and effort using procedures, policies, and a series of scheduled meetings to create organizational structure out of chaos and/or to eliminate ambiguous and ineffective management systems.

As the social architects of their White Houses, the post-Watergate presidents were responsible for the formal organizational structures they chose to establish and the ongoing attempts at structuration generally conducted by their senior aides. As is the case in other types of organizations, not every president, as an organizational leader, initially chooses the most appropriate or most effective organizational structure with which to manage the White House. The result may be a change in formal structure, continuous attempts at structuration throughout his presidency, or both. Even if the formal structure he chooses seems to work, as did Reagan's triumvirate in his first term, the dynamic nature of the organization is such that key staff will still find it necessary to supplement formal structure with constant attempts at organizing the work of the White House. The purpose of this chapter is to look at how the post-Watergate presidents functioned as social architects and to assess the strengths and weaknesses of the structures they imposed and that evolved during their presidencies—structures that affected, and were affected by, the communication that took place between each chief executive and his senior staff.

The White House is a centralized organization, whether the president resides at the top of an organizational pyramid or at the hub of a wheel, receiving information from staff members who serve as its spokes. In centralized organizations, as Jerald Hage et al. suggest, if participation in decision making decreases among individuals at lower levels in the hierarchy, inhibitions on communication in an organization may result.[6] Such was the case in the Nixon administration during the Watergate cover-up. Nixon solicited information from only a few of his top aides, those closest to him in the organization's structure, and over time communication between the president and many of his staff decreased.

Gerald Ford and Jimmy Carter considered, and in varying degrees reacted to, the increasing centralization of the organizational structure used in the Nixon White House during its last months. The structure, programs, and policies of Gerald Ford's administration, indeed its very credibility, were affected by the shadow of the Watergate White House. As Nixon's successor, Ford realized the need to adopt an organizational structure that would increase the access of people and the flow of written information to his Oval Office and restore some measure of trust in the White House as a decision-making environment. Ronald Reagan, on the other hand, reacted to perceived problems in Jimmy Carter's organizational structure. He saw the advantages of a chief of staff, an ordered system of reporting relationships to the president, and the need for people in his structure who understood the external environment in which the White House sits, the politicized city of Washington, D.C.

FORMAL AND EMERGENT STRUCTURE IN GERALD FORD'S WHITE HOUSE

Since he was mindful of problems created by the lack of staff participation in decisions concerning the Watergate cover-up, one of Gerald Ford's first decisions as the social architect of his White House was to increase the number of people with access to the president, to increase his span of control. His response to criticisms of the Nixon White House was evidence of Jay Galbraith's assertion that an organization adjusts to environmental pressures by changing the information-processing capacity of its structure.[7] Ford worked to enlarge this capacity by increasing the number of individuals with direct access to the Oval Office. According to James Connor, who became Ford's Cabinet and staff secretary, the president's organizational structure was purposively not designed like Roosevelt's system of "finding different people, giving them responsibilities . . . which would overlap, letting them compete, letting them build up their cases, and then letting the President make the decision."[8] It was a system patterned somewhat after Eisenhower's in order "to get a control over the government."[9] Not surprisingly, Ford has said he initially preferred the Johnson White House structure to that of Nixon, with several people reporting directly to the president, but then saw the worth of a coordinator for his schedule and paperwork.[10] During the first few weeks of his administration, however, he paid an organizational, if not a political, price for his attempts to increase the number of individuals with direct and unrestricted access to the Oval Office.

In the first month and a half of the Ford administration "there was a great deal of disorder in the Oval Office in the way papers and appointments were being handled. People were taking . . . papers into the president that had not been staffed by appropriate staffing authorities."[11] Although some ambiguity and disorder is inherent in any executive transition, in Ford's case the rapid departure of his predecessor exacerbated his organizational problems. Additionally, members of his vice presidential staff continued to seek unrestricted and informal access to him when they became members of his presidential staff. Despite this early experience with chaos in the Oval Office, Ford initially insisted on a more "open" structure for staff access and information flow as a reaction to negative perceptions of Nixon's inner circle. Richard Cheney, who became the president's second "staff coordinator," observes that the "notion was abroad in the land that Bob Haldeman and the structure inside the Nixon White House somehow contributed to Watergate or made it worse. So he [Ford] tried to run what he called the 'spokes of the wheel' concept and that didn't really work because nobody was in charge."[12] This structure consisted of nine aides reporting directly to Ford as the hub of an information-receiving wheel.

By early October 1974, the structure was phased out when Donald Rumsfeld entered the White House as assistant to the president in title but chief of staff in practice. Ford had realized the spokes-of-the-wheel concept allowed unrestricted access to too many people and required too much of his time. Accordingly, he employed Rumsfeld to develop and oversee an organized system of people and information flow into the Oval Office. "Don . . . and I agreed that you had to funnel more through the Chief of Staff—not that that automatically precluded people from seeing me, but it better utilized my time."[13] Ford's perception of this organization role was one of "scheduling appointments, coordinating paper flow, following up on decisions . . . and giving me status reports on projects and policy development."[14] In his memoirs Ford relates the conversation that prompted his decision to appoint Rumsfeld as a staff coordinator with the title of assistant to the president. Rumsfeld told the president that he (Ford) did not have the time to personally supervise the administration of the White House organization. "I know you don't want a Haldeman-type chief of staff, but someone has to fill that role, and unless I can have that authority, I won't be able to serve you effectively."[15] According to Ford; "I concluded he was right. Everyone wanted a portion of my time . . . and the 'spokes of the wheel' structure wasn't working well."[16]

By adding Rumsfeld to his staff in this role, the president changed the formal structure of his White House, as well as the emerging structure of role relationships surrounding him. According to notes taken by Jack W. Hushen, assistant to press secretary Ron Nessen, at the first senior staff meeting chaired by Rumsfeld, the president described his new senior aide as the chief coordinator of the White House. "The responsibility is on you to work through Don. But in significant matters, my door is open. But make sure that Don is cognizant of what is happening. We want an open door administration but I'm damn sick and tired of a ship that has such leaky seams."[17] From this point on, Rumsfeld was chief of staff in practice if not in name—placed at the head of the organization's formal structure by Ford, but creating his place as first among equals through a variety of structurational processes he used to guide task accomplishment in the White House.

Using a grid of all White House staff members and Cabinet officials, Rumsfeld and Ford decided whose input was needed on a given policy paper or a proposed speech. This responsibility eventually was undertaken by the staff secretary under Rumsfeld's (and later Cheney's) supervision. According to Cheney, who came into the White House as Rumsfeld's deputy, "by December [1974] we had . . . reorganized the place. We were really, without ever formally announcing it, back to a model that was very close to the Haldeman model."[18] The restructuring curtailed unrestricted access to the president; senior staff were each given standing appointments with the president, of varying frequency and length. However, some of the senior staff also had "peek in" privileges. These individuals could "peek in" to the Oval Office during the day and, seeing no one with the president, enter without an appointment.[19]

On December 18, 1974, the White House issued a press release announcing its formal structure, which, it indicated, had been evolving since August 9, the day Ford took office. The formal structure included the following components:

- Four Cabinet-rank advisers with staff responsibilities
- Nine key staff officers reporting directly to the president
- Seven other assistants and special assistants working "directly with the president"
- Deputies for each key staff member, authorized to act on behalf of that staff member.[20]

Those individuals identified as having oversight over functional areas in the White House, that is, those who were named as part of the formal structure, included:

John O. Marsh—counselor to the president in charge of congressional relations and the office of public liaison

Henry Kissinger—National Security Council adviser and, simultaneously for over a year, secretary of state

Ronald Nessen—press secretary

Philip Buchen—White House counsel

Ken Cole, and then James Cannon—assistant to the president for domestic affairs and executive director of the Domestic Council

Robert T. Hartmann—counselor to the president and director of the Editorial Office

L. William Seidman—assistant to the president for economic affairs and executive director of the Economic Policy Board

Roy Ash, and then James T. Lynn—assistant to the president for management and budget and director of the Office of Management and Budget

Donald H. Rumsfeld—assistant to the president, White House operations.

These individuals were Ford's favorite few in the development and implementation of presidential policies.

As will be discussed later in this chapter, Rumsfeld was insistent that deputies be included in the organization's formal structure, and that these individuals have access to the president if their superiors were unavailable for meetings or the completion of important, or emergency, tasks. The press release reads: "Thus, no one individual will be 'indispensable' and this approach should help to alleviate the excessively long hours which can prevent White House staff members from leading reasonably balanced lives."[21] A reference to the importance of emergent structures in the Ford White House is reflected in the last paragraph of the press release: "These arrangements have been decided upon with the aim of facilitating an orderly Presidential decision making process while assuring the President of multiple sources of information. Of course, the White House organization will continue to evolve."[22]

The Ford White House is an excellent example of structuration at work. In the early weeks of the administration, staff attempted to organize the work of the White House by establishing regular meeting times to develop the president's work and travel schedules, discuss weekly activities and issues needing analysis by the senior staff, and coordinate senior staff conferences at which Ford's briefing books for news interviews and press conferences were reviewed. When Rumsfeld began working at the end of September, structurational processes continued. For instance, lists were developed that included the names of individuals whose calls could be routed to the president without Rumsfeld's approval. Mindful of organizational problems that had existed in Nixon's White House, where a number of individuals were not assigned to a functional unit, Rumsfeld determined to avoid "floaters" in the Ford White House. According to Ron Nessen, Ford's press secretary, "Rumsfeld insisted that everyone work for someone."[23] Additionally, the appointment of deputies at the behest of the staff coordinator was an attempt to impose additional structure on the policy development and implementation process in the White House. Rumsfeld stated in a press conference on December 18, 1974, when the news release on the structure of the White House was distributed to the press:

> We felt that it would be desirable if the principal people on the staff did in fact have a deputy in every sense. That is to say, an individual who was personally used to working with the President, and with whom the President was used to working. An individual who, when a meeting was called, in the event the principal in that office was not available to be there could fill in so the work of the Government could go on.[24]

Rumsfeld also developed a mechanism for tracking items discussed at meetings with the president. He requested the lead staff member (the person who had functional responsibility for the topic under discussion) at each meeting to report what actions had been directed by the president, who was responsible for follow-up on those actions, and when the follow-up was due. In a memo dated June 13, 1975, Rumsfeld wrote: "You should submit your reports to me and to Jim Connor . . . within twenty-four hours of the meeting."[25] The lead staff member was responsible for submitting the briefing paper for each meeting. If the lead staff member was not present, those staff members attending the meeting would determine who should prepare the meeting report before the session began. Through these attempts at structuring the White House, the staff wielded considerable power—not only in their areas of responsibility but in the operation of the White House in toto.

The individuals most important to the creation and maintenance of structure, either formal or emergent, during Ford's years in the White House were his chief of staff and the staff secretary. As will be seen in Chapter 5, the system of information flow, the "staffing system," created by Donald Rumsfeld and operated by the staff secretary to ensure an orderly flow of information into the Oval Office from multiple sources, was of significant assistance to Gerald Ford as the manager and organizational leader of his White House.

Donald Rumsfeld wielded considerable power as the anchor of the formal structure in the Ford White House and as the person in charge of the development of the emergent structures needed to organize and accomplish the tasks of his staff. A former congressman and director of the Office of Economic Opportunity under Richard Nixon, Rumsfeld came to the White House at Ford's request, leaving his position as ambassador to the North Atlantic Treaty Organization. He was one of four people asked by the president to chair a "transition team" that made suggestions to the new president on the type of formal structure he should initiate in his White House organization. That structure called for the establishment of a spokes-of-the-wheel arrangement with a staff coordinator in charge of organizing the flow of people and paper into the Oval Office. Gerald Ford, concerned that making major organizational changes in structure and personnel during the first few weeks of his presidency would further disrupt an already chaotic environment, decided to retain Alexander Haig as the overseer of White House operations. According to Ford:

> Someone . . . had to be responsible for scheduling appointments, coordinating the paper flow, following up on decisions I had made and giving me status reports on projects and policy development. I didn't like the idea of calling this person chief of staff, but that in fact was the role he would fill. And Haig was the obvious choice.[26]

During the ensuing weeks, however, major conflicts developed between Haig, the former president's chief of staff, and the senior aides appointed by President Ford. In part this conflict was due to a sincere interest, on the part of former vice presidential aides like Robert Hartmann, to protect the new president from perceived attempts at undermining his control of the White House. Whatever the reasons for the conflict, which were also attributable in part to Haig's commanding presence in the White House organizational structure, Ford decided to ask Donald Rumsfeld to join his staff as assistant to the president for White House operations. According to Rumsfeld, the president said:

> He was going to move Haig, that there was staff conflict, and asked me to be chief of staff. I declined and told him I had no desire, that I had been in the White House and didn't care to come back. He pushed and pushed and I believe it was then that he told me that Betty had cancer and I really had to do it for a period. So I agreed to do it.[27]

However, Rumsfeld agreed to accept the position only if the president would consent to delegating some form of coordinative control over access to the president. According to Rumsfeld, the president needed someone "who serves to bring . . . disparate threads in and put them through a needle head in a reasonably coherent manner."[28]

Rumsfeld's role in Gerald Ford's White House was the one most significant to the initiation and continuance of both formal and informal structures in the organization. He initiated many, if not most, of the structurational processes discussed previously, in large part because that is the nature of the staff coordinator or chief of staff role. At times Rumsfeld was quite directive in his attempts to establish control over both structure and functions in the White House. On August 5, 1975, for instance, he sent a terse memo to Ronald Nessen that read: "From now on, we will have a policy whereby the press office will release nothing until it has been signed off on by Rumsfeld, Cheney, Jerry Jones, or Connor."[29]

Nevertheless, in response to presidential concern about the appointment of anyone as chief of staff, and his own perceptions of what the position's responsibilities should entail, he viewed his role as one of managing, not necessarily restricting, staff access to Ford. According to Rumsfeld, his principal responsibility was to ensure that "people who had statutory or appointed responsibility for given subject matters and areas of interest did in fact have a chance to participate in the decision-making process as well as the implementation of whatever was decided."[30] Consequently, he insisted on the development of a tightly structured system of information flow into the Oval Office. This "staff system," as it came to be called, was responsible for eliciting White House staff and Cabinet member input on virtually any proposal requiring a presidential decision. It was a system closely monitored by the staff secretary as well as the chief of staff.

The staff secretary was perhaps the second most important organizational role related to the initiation and maintenance of structure in Ford's White House, with the possible exception of the deputy chief of staff. The position was intended as part of a formal structure that imitated the staff secretariat created in the Eisenhower White House. James Connor, who had White House experience and was working for the Atomic Energy Commission during the last months of the Nixon administration, was selected by Rumsfeld to be Cabinet secretary at the beginning of the Ford administration. He retained that position and also became staff secretary in late spring of 1975. In an interview with the author he defined his responsibilities as follows:

> If anyone wished to communicate in writing with the president it would come through me. If that communication entailed a presidential decision, it would come back through me from the president at which point I would be the one who would convey to the person requesting the decision what the outcome of the decision was.[31]

As will be discussed in more detail in Chapter 5, Connor therefore played a significant role in the flow of information to and from the president during the Ford administration.

One other person who sought, but did not attain, more control over the organizational structure in Ford's White House was Nelson Rockefeller. At the time the president selected the former New York governor for the vice presidency, he decided to put him in charge of domestic policy. Not only did this assignment cause conflict between Rockefeller and White House staff already working on domestic issues, it apparently created in the vice president's mind a need for his increased involvement in the operation of the entire White House organization. As he became more involved in domestic policy discussions, and entrenched in, as well as critical of, the structure and operations of the White House, he began to see an expanded role for himself in the Ford administration. According to Robert Donovan, the vice president would return from a meeting in the Oval Office and tell Ann Whitman, his secretary (and former personal secretary to President Eisenhower), that "he was going to 'run' the White House."[32] At other times he would excitedly talk about becoming Ford's chief of staff, and allegedly told Ford "that the only way he would serve in a second Ford administration was as White House chief of staff and not as vice-president."[33] In an interview with Trevor Arbrister, who assisted Ford in the preparation of his memoirs, the president recalled Rockefeller's interest in being chief of staff.

> He would be very blunt in his criticism of certain individuals and the West Wing organization. . . . One time he said that the West Wing is so badly run, why don't you let me come in here and clean house and organize it. I said, Nelson, I don't agree with you that it's as badly run as you emanate [sic], and for obvious reasons it couldn't be done that way.[34]

Rockefeller, in an interview with Robert Hartmann on December 2, 1977, recalled the same conversation.

> I said, "Mr. President, the morale of your organization is going down, the efficiency of the operation in the White House is going down," and I said, "this is very serious for you going into a campaign. . . . It is to my disinterest, it is against my interest, but I would like to volunteer to accept the responsibility of Chief of Staff of the White House. I can do a job for you both internally in the White House on organization and in improving

the morale of your Cabinet and the handling of issues.'' He thanked me and said that he didn't think he would change the structure.[35]

According to Rumsfeld, Ford's decision to put Rockefeller in charge of domestic policy created a problem within the president's staff. The arrangement ''just didn't work,'' essentially because the vice president of the United States, considering his other official functions, is unable to assume day-to-day responsibility for the analysis of domestic issues.[36] James Connor observes that Rockefeller ''was not constitutionally, physically, mentally, psychologically a staff person.''[37] As former governor of New York, he was used to being a decision maker, not a source of information for other decision makers. He had not been, and would not have been, comfortable in a subordinate staff relationship with Gerald Ford, who, as a long-time congressman and a short-term vice president, had not shared Rockefeller's presence in the national political limelight.

Formal structure within an organization may precipitate conflict within that organization as individuals who are assigned roles and functional areas of responsibility strive to maintain control over their assigned ''territory'' or turf. Such was the case in the Ford administration when Rockefeller was assigned primary responsibility for domestic affairs and when units such as speechwriting and the press office had to transmit their draft work to other White House aides for review, at the behest of Rumsfeld. Another type of conflict developed when the president chose not to continue his vice presidential chief of staff, Robert Hartmann, in a similar role in the White House. Hartmann felt that Alexander Haig, as Nixon's former chief of staff, could not serve Ford's best interests, and indeed was out to prevent Ford's success as president. Hartmann had been a loyal adviser and speechwriter for the new president for many years, and did not trust several of the new staff members who now saw the president as much as or more than he did.[38] Rumsfeld explains, Ford ''had put in place people who had come in on the basis that they would be interacting directly with him on everything. . . . He had . . . structured it [the White House] with people and organization and then changed his mind, but didn't change the people. It was hard because suddenly their circumstances were changed.''[39] Hartmann was one of the nine spokes of the wheel who reported to Ford, but he no longer enjoyed unrestricted access to the president, whom he had served longer than anyone in the White House.

Organizational role conflict also developed between the vice president and Rumsfeld, which in great part was the president's fault. Ford asked Rumsfeld to coordinate all White House operations, as chief of staff or staff coordinator, and promised that Rockefeller could oversee domestic policy-making within the White House. Ultimately, a conflict developed between the chief of staff and Rockefeller because the president had agreed to let the vice president oversee the Domestic Council. ''Even though he wasn't going to be put in by name, the commitment was that he could be in charge of the development of policy and the execution of policy. I think that conflict probably is what highlighted the subsequent differences between Nelson and Don.''[40] These differences decreased, but did not disappear, when Rumsfeld was appointed secretary of defense and Richard Cheney was promoted to the position of staff coordinator.

The White House organization of Gerald Ford was beset by conflicts due to the integration of two presidential staffs under one roof, disagreements between the president's chief of staff and his vice president concerning the appropriate reporting relationship for domestic policy-making, the ineffectiveness of coordinative efforts in the White House, and ongoing battles over turf. As is the case in other types of organizations, Ford, as organizational leader, was disturbed, even angered, by some of these conflicts but found it difficult to stop, or control, some of those which were ongoing and eventually made public. In James Connor's opinion, such conflict ''conveyed a notion . . . that Ford was not in control'' of his White House.[41] As will be discussed in Chapter 6, Gerald Ford was a creature of the Congress, and, particularly as minority leader, had developed skills in the art of consensus building among colleagues, not managing and leading subordinates. His selection of Rumsfeld was, in part, due to his realization of this fact. When he eventually understood the need for a staff coordinator in the White House, he selected someone with managerial and administrative skills to compensate for his lack of them.

During the last eighteen months of his administration, Ford finally felt comfortable with the organizational structure that had evolved within his White House.[42] He had fashioned a balance of openness and control within his organization by modifying the spokes-of-the-wheel concept to permit the coordination of the flow of both information and people into the Oval Office. In his words: ''Anybody who had a particular problem could come in and see me but had to be channeled through at least one person who had some control over the schedule.''[43] Ford worked within the structure he and others had devised. He saw Donald Rumsfeld, and later Richard Cheney, most frequently during the day, compared with other members of his senior staff, but their role in the organization required such access. Nevertheless, to prevent the isolation that surrounded his predecessor, Ford sought information and opinions from individuals outside the formal White House structure, including several who had served other presidents in other times. The staff coordinator consciously worked to make these individuals available to the president.[44]

Ford's initial organizational response to the Watergate scandal was short-lived. Within two months of Richard Nixon's resignation Ford essentially had adopted the organizational structure used by his predecessor. As will be seen in Chapter 5, what made his office more accessible to staff was his willingness to accept information from multiple sources and his interest in talking with his senior staff as part of the evolutionary process that resulted in decisions. Additionally, the president selected a staff coordinator, or chief of staff, who valued the use of structure as a means to facilitate, not inhibit, communication between the president and his key aides.

At the end of 1976, the Ford administration compiled briefing books to assist the Carter administration in its transition efforts. The internal structure within the Ford White House was described as follows:

> The Ford White House does not have a Chief-of-Staff in the sense that one individual controls the flow of all information to the President. Mr. Cheney does, however, have responsibility for insuring the smooth operation of the White House Office. He carries out this responsibility by coordinating the appointments function with the flow of paper to and from the President, by meeting with the President each morning and evening, by managing the administrative operation of the office and by conducting senior staff meetings each morning. While all senior staff members have direct access to President Ford, there is a strict centralized paper flow system for controlling and disseminating all materials flowing to and from the President[45]

When he left the White House on January 20, 1977, Richard Cheney left behind a gag gift his fellow staff members had given him—a beat-up bicycle wheel with its spokes bent and broken. "I set it up on the bare desk so Ham Jordan could find it, and I put a little handwritten note right beside it. It said, 'Dear Ham: Beware of the Spokes of the Wheel.' "[46] However, within a few days after the inauguration the Carter administration announced that the new president had decided to adopt an organizational structure in his White House known as "the spokes of the wheel."

THE PROCESS OF STRUCTURATION IN JIMMY CARTER'S WHITE HOUSE

According to Jody Powell, Jimmy Carter's press secretary, the Watergate scandal had a "significant impact" on the type of organizational structure Carter chose to implement in his White House.[47]

> There was, and justifiably so, a sense of concern about having an excessively powerful White House staff in general and a chief of staff in particular, a feeling that the danger was that it could tend to choke off the flow of information to the president. It would place too much power in the hands of personal staff and not elected officials.[48]

As a result, Carter adopted the spokes-of-the-wheel organizational arrangement, with nine senior aides representing functional areas reporting to him directly, with no chief of staff or staff coordinator. Initially Carter's White House operated under a less formal structure than had Ford's or Nixon's; it was reminiscent of those under other Democrat presidents. Like Roosevelt, Kennedy, and Johnson, Carter had as his primary goals policy origination and execution, and he was, or seemed to be, more interested in the generation of policy ideas than in the structures needed to develop and implement decisions. Ironically, as will be illustrated later in this chapter, Carter's attempts at policy-making were thwarted by a structure too inadequate to plan, develop, and implement the policies he envisioned. Indeed, the Carter staff spent much time and effort in the process of structuration, in part to compensate for the lack of a designated organizational role in the formal structure with the duties of a chief of staff.

Comparing Herbert Hoover and Carter, who both had engineering backgrounds, Michael Medved wrote:

> Both men came to office with overdeveloped reputations as administrative experts and proceeded, with much fanfare, to institute new staff arrangements in which several coequal aides with clearly defined responsibilities replaced a strong staff leader. In both cases the results were the same: a crushing burden on the President himself as even the smallest issues went to him for final decision.[49]

According to Bruce Mazlish and Edwin Diamond, "Carter straddled the worst of both worlds, administratively; he tried to do more than even activist Democrat Presidents did, with less of the orderly hierarchical organization that Republican Presidents have depended on."[50]

Jimmy Carter began his administration in a spirit of openness and accessibility, walking, not riding behind bulletproof windows, in his own inaugural parade. He also intended the Oval Office to be accessible to those he chose to bring with him to Washington—loyal and trusted companions and advisers. He writes in his memoirs, "I had made a private promise to myself to call on some of the talented Georgians who had served me as governor and as a candidate for President. My decisions about how to use them were not made casually."[51] Although Carter was well aware that his predecessors had been assailed in the press for surrounding themselves with trusted "cronies," he chose to follow their lead, despite the fact that most of his aides had no experience in Congress, the Executive Branch, or other Washington political circles. "But when I considered the alternatives, I decided without any doubt that my predecessors had chosen wisely. The selection of loyal and well-known associates is the result of a need for maximum mutual confidence and a minimum of jealousy and backbiting within a President's inner circle."[52]

Just as Gerald Ford's long-time aides had been wary of Nixon holdovers and new appointees in Ford's White House, so Carter's closest aides were protective of their president. Although Carter began his administration stressing the need for Cabinet government, it did not take long for the Democrat's administration to follow the example of his predecessors. Those aides closest to him, and most protective of him, "took personal affront at any examples of what they perceived to be a Cabinet official undercutting a presidential initiative. This led to several confrontations and internal disputes that ill-served Carter, and conveyed the image of an administration in disarray."[53] As a result, over a period of time control over policy development and execution moved quietly but steadily into the White House. By the summer of 1979, Cabinet members were unhappy with their decreased roles in the Carter administration, and several of them were publicly voicing their displeasure.

As previously mentioned, the initial formal structure of the Carter White House was the spokes-of-the-wheel arrangement with nine senior aides reporting directly to the president. Hamilton Jordan was recognized among his colleagues as the "first among equals," and his title was assistant to the president. He was a general adviser to the president. Each of the following individuals was responsible for a functional area of activity within the White House:

Jody Powell—press secretary

Zbigniew Brzezinski—assistant for national security affairs

Stuart Eizenstat—assistant for domestic affairs and policy

Frank Moore—assistant for congressional liaison

Jack Watson—assistant for Cabinet and intergovernmental affairs

Midge Costanza, and later Anne Wexler—assistant for public liaison

Robert Lipshutz, and later Lloyd Cutler—counsel to the president

Tim Kraft—special assistant for appointments.

According to Jack Watson, "Carter really was conceptually true to his 'spokes of the wheel.' He really did honestly, not just nominally and not just on paper . . . look to the different ones of us for advice in different areas."[54]

It should be emphasized that the formal structure of the organization underwent several changes during the four years Carter was in office, and individuals in addition to those listed had direct access to the president. One of those individuals was the vice president, who was a major force in the development of emergent structures within the White House to assist in planning presidential initiatives. Walter Mondale was the first vice president to have an office in the west wing of the White House; his working quarters were down the hall from the president, between the offices of Brzezinski and Jordan.

Despite the selection of aides who were competent and trustworthy and who appeared to have a good working relationship with each other, the president's attempts to push his preferred policies through Congress suffered continuous setbacks, in large part because of the lack of adequate structure and supervision needed to coordinate the efforts of all the "spokes" in his wheel. Stuart Eizenstat recalls, "It's that critical early period when we overloaded the congressional circuits with a lot of major priorities and didn't make those strategic judgments we needed to make when opinions of him were formed."[55] The president's former assistant for domestic affairs emphasizes that "things improved after a year, when Mondale was put in charge of setting priorities," and Carter's White House adapted organizationally, to some degree, to its tasks.[56] Unfortunately, Eizenstat suggests, "first impressions are damn difficult to reverse. The first 100 days were a disaster, but after that it got a lot better," yet "there is a caricature of the Carter years which is largely a caricature of the first six months."[57]

The efforts to rectify organizational problems in the Carter White House, through the process of structuration, is of particular interest to this study. To compensate for an inadequate formal structure, most notably the absence of someone in an organizational role, other than the president, to coordinate the internal operations of the White House, some presidential aides were involved almost continually in attempts to organize and complete a variety of tasks, as the following archival materials reveal.

In a memorandum to Carter and Mondale, dated December 27, 1976, Hamilton Jordan proposed a process for managing and scheduling projects and programs of the Carter administration. His proposal included tabular listings of projects, the designation of a person responsible for each one, and a time line by month and year for follow-up of progress. Jordan prefaced this proposal by writing:

We should develop a system for identifying goals and objectives of this Administration. We should translate those goals and objectives into specific tasks and assign each task to a responsible person with a work plan and a timetable. Finally, we should develop a system for monitoring progress and problems. We should also develop a system for scheduling the major activities of the President and Vice-President that reconciles their limited time with the priority activities of the Administration.[58]

The Carter White House began its operations with a Management Committee comprised of nineteen people, including Hamilton Jordan, Jody Powell, Stuart Eizenstat, Jack Watson, Frank Moore, Zbigniew Brzezinski, Richard Harden, and Rick Hutcheson (staff secretary). On January 3, 1977, Harden, who was in charge of information management in the White House, wrote a memo to Robert Lipshutz and members of the White House Management Committee summarizing items agreed to at a meeting of the committee the previous day. One decision described in the memo was the following:

There are to be fifteen responsibility centers within the White House Office. These centers will be headed by the Counsel to the President, Press Secretary, eight assistants to the President, Assistant to the First Lady and four special assistants to the President. This latter group will be handling functions that relate to the White House Management Committee on a continuing basis.[59]

Although this memo was in draft form when seen by the author in one set of files in the Carter archives, it is assumed it was sent, for Harden was engaged in a variety of similar structurational attempts during the Carter presidency. In late January 1977, for instance, he outlined special projects requiring oversight by Management Committee members in an internal memorandum. Two such projects, identified as important work to be undertaken during the first weeks of the Carter administration, were the development of a system to manage paper flow to the president and the initiation of a system to coordinate review of policy papers going to the president. Rick Hutcheson, staff secretary, was put in charge of the first project and Jack Watson, Cabinet secretary and assistant for intergovernmental affairs, who had a talent for administration, was responsible for the second.[60]

In the meantime, senior staff responsible for functional areas in the White

House were in the process of suggesting ways their areas of responsibility could be organized efficiently. On January 3, 1977, two and a half weeks before Carter took office, Stuart Eizenstat wrote the president a seven-page memorandum that outlined a suggested organizational structure for the domestic policy staff and proposed its size and functions. He prefaced his organizational plan as follows: "As you are aware . . . I would like to be Assistant to the President for Domestic Affairs and Policy."[61] He also emphasized the importance of White House control over domestic policy-making, continuing a trend that had begun in the Kennedy administration. "Regardless of whether or not the Domestic Council is kept, the domestic *staff* function must continue to be performed for the President by a staff within the Executive Office or White House whose loyalty is to the President, and *not* to the department and their constituencies."[62]

At the same time Eizenstat was assuming major responsibilities for domestic policy-making, Jack Watson was selected to serve in a linking role within the White House as assistant to the president for intergovernmental affairs. According to Watson, when Carter chose him for this position, the president emphasized: "You are a manager and I want you to help me manage the execution of domestic policy by being a problem solver and a reconciler between and among the agencies and departments of government. I want you to be a convener. I want you to be a coordinator."[63] Watson also was appointed Cabinet secretary, a role in which he served as a link between the federal departments and the White House.

But all the individual and group attempts to plan, organize, and accomplish the multiple tasks within the White House did not seem to be working one month after the inauguration. In a memo to senior staff (Costanza, Eizenstat, Jordan, Lipshutz, Moore, Powell, and Watson), dated February 25, 1977, Richard Harden discussed the importance of "setting priorities and getting things done," which was the title of his memo. Harden's correspondence stemmed from an observation that "we are potentially getting ourselves in the posture of trying to do too many things so that we end up not doing anything well."[64] According to Harden, there were several causes for the problems the White House was then facing:

> We have not developed and implemented a simple system for setting up and monitoring projects that have been initiated by the President and staff members.
>
> We have been busy getting our own shops in order and haven't had the time to sit down and decide how we are going to work together to achieve a limited number of accomplishments.[65]

Additionally, Harden suggested, "we really haven't spelled out in detail what we hope to accomplish during the next 12 months."[66]

Harden suggested several ways to organize the staff's work; all are attempts at structuration. One of his proposals was the identification of major projects.

> There is a need to identify the 10–15 major projects the President wishes to emphasize during the next several months and to develop a work plan for each. The work plan

would indicate the persons to be involved, the major activities, the person responsible for each major activity, an estimate of the time involved, and the start and completion dates.[67]

He also suggested a project management system, through which a notebook would be compiled for the desk of the president listing current projects, and the preparation of monthly status reports from each senior aide:

I think it would be good for each of you to begin preparing a simple yet comprehensive monthly status report. It should be a maximum of two pages single spaced and should include what you did the previous month, what you anticipate doing during the coming month and a brief discussion of any problems you are encountering.[68]

Additionally, Harden announced the initiation of a study of paper flow in the Executive Office of the President ''to determine ways to eliminate bottlenecks and permit all involved parties to have adequate review time.''[69] Finally, Harden emphasized the need for improved communication within the White House. ''As things heat up, the need for good internal communications is going to increase. To ensure that the existing good communication doesn't break down, we should develop a full understanding of the communications equipment we have available and develop some guidelines governing its use.''[70] Of course well-functioning equipment does not ensure communication within any organization, but Harden was expressing his interest in, and appreciation of, that process among a president's staff.

The components of Harden's memo illustrate the time and effort Carter's senior aides were expending to find successful ways to structure and complete their tasks. Indeed, it appears that continual attempts at structuration may have impeded the completion of the work they were appointed to do. James Fallows, a Carter speechwriter, wrote in a notorious description of the president's White House during his reelection campaign: ''Run like a bureaucracy, the White House took on the spirit of a bureaucracy, drained of zeal, obsessed with form, full of people attracted by the side-dressings of the work rather than the work itself.''[71] Although the White House, like any formal, centralized organization, is bureaucratic to some extent, Fallows emphasized that the Carter White House was spending too much time focusing on the procedures and processes used to organize work, and not enough on the work itself. As a result, the president's dreams of creating myriad public policies to cure the ills he had identified during his 1976 campaign were turning into nightmares.

By the middle of 1977 the Executive Committee, chaired by the vice president, had been assembled in the White House. Recommended in a study reviewing the possible reorganization of the Executive Office of the President, it was comprised of ''senior advisers with responsibility for building and continually updating the President's decision-making agenda, setting priorities among issues and dealing with interrelationships among them.''[72] Additionally, on July 15,

1977, the White House issued a press release describing a new process for the formation of domestic and economic policy, the Policy Management System. According to the release, policy agendas would be recommended by the new Executive Committee, to be chaired by the vice president. Although the process was allegedly designed to strengthen the role of the Cabinet in policy development by involving departments in the early stages of policy formulation, the news release also stated that the "Domestic Policy Staff and National Security Staff will coordinate the process and assure that the resources of the government are brought to bear on the issue," and that "the views of Congress and the public are taken into account."[73]

These continuous attempts at developing structures and processes to organize the work of the White House reflect an organization in disarray. Moreover, it appears the reason for its lack of procedural cohesion was the absence of an individual who could oversee and coordinate the very processes and structures discussed in the plethora of memoranda circulating throughout the White House during the Carter presidency's first two and a half years.

When he assumed the presidency, Jimmy Carter sincerely believed that he could act as his own chief of staff. As Jody Powell has said, the image of a powerful gatekeeping staff surrounding the president, with a chief of staff reminiscent of H. R. Haldeman, was not one this president wanted to convey. He also was exceedingly confident in his own ability to manage the White House—he paid attention to detail, was a voracious reader, and was interested in the intricacies of policy development. Moreover, other Democrat presidents of the modern era, who shared his passion for policy origination, had been their own chiefs of staff, running the White House and the country with a handful of trusted aides. The major difference between Carter and those chief executives, however, was his lack of congressional and/or administrative experience in Washington, a weakness shared by most of those he designated as his chief aides. Considering the work he wished to do, the complexity of the White House organization he inherited, and the overwhelming demands other presidential tasks placed on his time, Carter should have appointed a chief of staff, or staff coordinator, as part of his initial organizational structure. According to Medved: "The absence of a staff coordinator . . . contributed to a lack of discipline and consistency among Carter's various aides."[74]

Additionally, the lack of one person to oversee and manage the distinct, yet overlapping, functional areas within the White House sometimes fostered intrastaff competition as well as duplication of work. According to Anne Wexler, assistant to the president for public liaison, Carter "would sometimes ask two or three people to do the same thing while he was delegating. Whoever got the job done first, that was fine with him. He would often ask me to do something and I'd find out in the process of getting it done that he also had two other people doing the same thing."[75] Unlike the conflict generated by this approach in FDR's White House, Carter's aides just seemed concerned that their combined work sometimes ended in duplicated effort and wasted time—problems a chief of staff might have prevented.

Ironically, a review of memoranda in various Carter White House files reveals that several aides in the White House pursued the possibility of establishing the role of chief of staff throughout the president's first years in office—without initial success. For instance, Hamilton Jordan requested an opinion on the advisability of a chief of staff in the Carter White House in the fall of 1977. In response to Jordan's inquiry about the matter, A. D. Frazier, a staff member of the president's Executive Reorganization Project, wrote on October 19, 1977, that "designating someone as chief of staff or better, as staff coordinator, would be most helpful to the President."[76] During the months that the Executive Reorganization Project was under way, Carter apparently had made it abundantly clear that there was no need for such a position in his White House. According to Frazier,

> We were aware of Mr. Carter's feelings about a "chief of staff" function when we did the EOP study. We concluded, and I still believe, that the President can operate without a person being so designated. But, he will continue to find it difficult to operate without some management system that ensures . . . his office is functioning smoothly.[77]

Hence the Project's recommendations to establish an executive committee chaired by the vice president, and supported by a policy management system.

In discussing the possibility of establishing a coordinative role within the White House, Frazier suggests eight general responsibilities for the individual, assuring Jordan that because of the close relationship between the president and his senior aides, "I am quite sure the staff coordinator's role would not be allowed to become overbearing."[78] The eight responsibilities were coordinating activities of the White House staff; preparing the president's plan for dealing with issues, such as the selection, timing, and allocation of resources; ensuring implementation of presidential decisions; ensuring "broad political input into the decision-making process"; screening personnel for presidential appointments; ensuring broad-based substantive information for each presidential decision; "resolving differences of opinion among White House staff units"; and "auditing the performance of White House staff units."[79] In his memo Frazier emphasizes that the person appointed for these purposes would coordinate activities and information, not isolate the president. In short, he or she would be a facilitator, not a dictator, inside the White House.

Approximately two months after this interchange between Jordan and Frazier, and *eleven* months after Carter's inauguration, Stuart Eizenstat wrote to the president, expressing his concerns about the lack of coordination inside the White House: "I continue to believe that our most serious structural problem is the lack of internal White House coordination."[80] Continuing, Eizenstat emphasizes that

There is no mechanism by which, on a regular basis, we can find what the other is doing that may have impact on an area in which we are working . . . no one has been given the directive to sort out the various priorities of our work, to coordinate our work and make sure it is all going in the same direction, before it all pours in to you.[81]

This function, Eizenstat recommends, "can be done by a key 'coordinator' to whom we would all look as a point of coordination between us. This would be particularly useful also in making sure that there was domestic input into foreign policy decisions and likewise that there was foreign policy input into domestic decisions."[82]

Jordan's and Eizenstat's interest in pursuing the possibility of a staff coordinator in the White House may have affected a detailed plan for the reorganization of the White House completed in early 1978 by Harrison Welford and A. D. Frazier. According to Medved, "Their investigation, never fully revealed to the public, 'led inescapably' to the conclusion that Carter needed a Chief of Staff. Despite the President's stubborn resistance to that idea, he did authorize Jordan to expand substantially his area of responsibility."[83] This "area" included foreign policy as well as the coordination of White House staff activities.

Growing increasingly concerned about the president's inability to work effectively with Congress, and the role of his staff in that endeavor, Jordan apparently arranged a meeting to discuss the state of the Carter presidency with friends and advisers, both in and outside the White House, in the summer of 1978. After the meeting, Lloyd Hackler, president of the American Retail Federation and the individual who would later replace Robert Lipshutz as White House counsel, sent Jordan correspondence discussing the organizational problems he perceived in the Carter White House. He began his assessment by stating there was "insufficient structure in the White House staff to execute the President's decisions, to give them proper political consideration and to explain them publicly."[84] He emphasized the need for someone whom the president trusted to coordinate the administrative processes within the White House. "I do *not* advocate a Haldeman-type operation of central White House control, but there should be someone close to the President to advise, execute, follow through, coordinate, politically evaluate and convey the President's wishes to the bureaucracy."[85] According to Hackler, "The coordinator needs to be someone of the status of Jordan or Powell or Strauss. A new face, preferably a non-Georgian and non-Southerner, would be even better."[86]

Still there was no appointment of a staff coordinator or chief of staff. However, on December 18, 1978, Jordan sent a confidential memo to the senior staff outlining a proposal for improved staff coordination, stating that the reasons for the communication to them were a "crucial gap in our current structure," and a lack of "time, space and materials necessary to work on the design and implementation of general strategies."[87] Part of Jordan's new coordination process included regular staff meetings.

Beginning Monday, December 18, the senior staff will meet for a period of approximately two hours every other week. . . . In these meetings, we will focus the discussion, making the agenda as narrow as possible. We will distribute background material in advance. I will chair each meeting. Participation in the meeting will be limited to principals only; no substitutions.[88]

Jordan also announced the establishment of task forces that would include staff from his office and those functional areas headed by other members of the senior staff. These task forces would focus on specific issues or proposals, according to Jordan, and would develop a work plan outlining a general strategy, staff resources needed by the task force, use of the media, use of presidential and vice presidential time, major themes for the issue, a plan for involvement of congressional members and staff, and records needed by the task force. Each task force leader was to provide a weekly report, and all leaders were to meet together every two weeks.

In some ways, it appears these task forces were reincarnations of Richard Harden's organizational ideas in early 1977; since that time senior staff had focused on process and not on the substantive issues with which they were supposed to be dealing. Jordan concluded his memo by saying:

This new program of coordination is an attempt to build upon the experience of the past two years. While there is nothing revolutionary in it, it does reflect a slightly different approach to staff coordination and issue management. In order to make sure that it works properly, the new program will require cooperation from everyone, as well as criticism and suggested changes. I hope you will be able to help on all counts.[89]

In short, Jimmy Carter's White House, because of his opposition to a chief of staff, spent two years attempting to structure its work through policies, procedures, regularly scheduled meetings, task forces, and projects. Senior aides apparently were doing everything possible to create a substitute for a chief of staff, when what they really needed was the real thing.

The result was that by the summer of 1979 the White House staff had increased "their respective jurisdictions" over policy development but White House operations were in disarray; "there was no central administrator controlling staff activities."[90] Moreover, the president and several senior aides were increasingly disenchanted with specific members of the Cabinet, some of whom had publicly criticized the inefficiency and ineptitude of the White House staff and/or the president. In mid-July 1979, President Carter, in a major restructuring attempt, asked for the resignations of his Cabinet and White House staff. He accepted resignations only from those Cabinet members such as Joseph Califano and Michael Blumenthal who had been critical of his policies or staff. Additionally, he announced the appointment of Hamilton Jordan as chief of staff. Figure 1 is a copy of the memo Jordan sent to the president before Carter was to meet with his staff and Cabinet after the restructuring had been announced.

This memo, which Carter initialed in the top right-hand corner, assumes a

Figure 1

July 79

C

TO: PRESIDENT CARTER

FROM: HAMILTON JORDAN HJ

This should serve an a briefing memorandum for both the Cabinet and staff meetings with a couple of exceptions which I will mention.

1. It is important that both the staff and the Cabinet understand the Camp David process and the basic change in attitude and approach that you have agreed to.

2. They should see and share your basic sense of confidence about our collective ability to deal with the country's problems, but they should also know that just as you have changed your attitude and approach, they must also.

3. With the staff, you should tell them that we have had a good two years together, but that to accomodate this new attitude and approach, changes here will have to be made. You should say that you have asked me to assume the duties of chief-of-staff, and to have responsibility and authority over White House personnel, over policy and political coordination and over operations. Also, that I will no longer be their peer, but that I will be their boss. You should not stay too long at the senior staff meeting. It should be a crisp appearance and departure.

Figure 1 (continued)

4. With the Cabinet, you should meet with them alone and with me present. You should not tell them or the senior staff that they are all doing a great job. If we had all done a great job, we would not be in the shape that we are in today. You should make points #1 and #2 of this memo, plus these additional thoughts:

-That you do not intend to get bogged down any more in interdepartmental fights - that you will look to me and Stu to resolve more of these things; on bigs things you expect to be involved;

-That I will serve as Chief-of-Staff for the purpose of coordination, personnel and accountability, and that a request from me should be treated as a request from you. If they find it to be unreasonable, they can appeal it directly to you

-You should say that neither the Cabinet nor the staff has served you well as a group; changes in process and attitude are necessary in both the White House and the government;

Source: Reproduced courtesy of The Jimmy Carter Library.

tone of authority not seen in earlier memos from Jordan to his colleagues. In it he indeed appears to be taking charge of the White House staff.

As Figure 2 illustrates, Jordan took his organizational role seriously. By late July he had taken actions to make the internal operations of the White House more efficient, and most were agreed to by the president, as is indicated in Carter's handwriting.

By the end of October 1979, Jordan had redone the White House organizational chart to ''clarify certain areas of responsibility,'' and to reflect his role as the coordinator and controller of the flow of people and paper in the Oval Office. As can be seen in Figure 3, however, Carter wanted to ensure that direct access to him by key aides would be maintained in the new organization chart.

As a result, on November 26, 1979, the White House senior staff received the organizational chart that is Figure 4. The president's personal secretary, Susan Clough, was shown as having direct access to the president and an inset was included in the final version to emphasize that all senior staff had direct access to the president on matters relating to their areas of responsibility.

Jordan served as chief of staff for less than a year; he was replaced by Jack Watson when he left the White House to work in Carter's reelection campaign. The Carter White House had gotten its chief of staff, two and a half years after the president was inaugurated. But it was too late. The president was already

Figure 2

THE WHITE HOUSE

WASHINGTON

Ham
J.

July 26, 1979

MEMORANDUM TO: PRESIDENT CARTER

FROM: HAMILTON JORDAN HJ.

After assuming my new responsibilities, I began to focus on the personnel changes that need to be made here, along with adjustments of process that are obvious to us both. But along the way, I have stumbled on a number of other problems which have compelled me to conclude that we need to take a fresh look at a number of things here in the White House, and that our problems here can only partially be solved by changes in personnel.

In trying to take a look at the larger scheme of White House functions, we have discovered a series of major problems which we will move on immediately, pending your approval and/or guidance. Some of the problems we have discovered are:

1. There is little relevance or equity in our system of titles or salary levels. *I agree*

2. It is clear that office space has not been allocated on the basis of any rational system. People who need to be near your office because you need to have frequent contact with them are housed in the White House complex in a haphazard way. People who don't need to be near your office are housed near you. We are developing a rational system, based on the need for proximity to your office and will develop a plan for space allotment. *I agree*

3. We are grouping the staff in logical units because what we have found is that (theoretically) there are upwards of 40 people who have direct reporting relationships to you. We are moving quickly to streamline the staff organization by putting people into groups or clusters to report through unit managers to you and/or me. Along with this we intend to use these clusters to have people do planning based on the use of management teams or groups rather than the *good*

Figure 2 (continued)

- 2 -

system we have been using which has bean a proliferation of individual memoranda gathered together by one person, put into a single memorandum and then forwarded to you. We hope these groups will be able to come up with plans based on their own interaction and eliminate this profusion of memoranda.

4. We have done a survey of meetings within the White House and what we have discovered is that there are over 200 regular meetings scheduled and held every month. I might add that these meetings which we have uncovered are only meetings which are attended by your top staff (Assistants and Deputies). The 200 number does not include meetings held by any Special Assistants and only a few of the regular unit staff meetings. We are investigating methods for integrating these meeting times and trying to control what seemed to be a maelstrom of meetings.

5. Following the individual personnel reviews we are doing, we will be doing a unit by unit review of the functioning and structure of every unit in the White House complex. Additionally, we are reviewing the ways in which units work or don't work together and will come up with an orderly operational plan for how these units might best operate.

6. We are doing a systematic review of the skills, competence and loyalties of Sub-Cabinet personnel, so that we can be sure that both the Secretaries and the White House have a team which they can operate.

7. We are also looking at the decision-making process within the White House with a view toward developing a system which will work more effectively for both you and the rest of your staff. The reason we are doing that is that at this stage in the game the decision-making process deserves serious scrutiny and adjustment.

Figure 2 (continued)

- 3 -

8. Finally, a review of current staffing levels by Jim McIntyre and Hugh Carter. There is no way for us to bring in new people, enhance our quality of work, and create a new planning unit without additional staff persons.

The team is composed of members of the staffs of Jim McIntyre, the Vice President and Frank Moore. Jim, the Vice President and Frank have given us the services of their people, and in addition Frank made available Leonard Hirsch and Jan Esbeck who have been working with him on his organization. Further, Frank has given me as much of Les Francis' time as I need, and I have Les overseeing and coordinating this effort. We have a planning group composed of myself, Les Francis, Landon Butler and Len Hirsch, and we meet daily to assess our progress and to create a comprehensive organizational development plan for the White House. Our deadline is to be able to make the important changes which need to be made by August 15; thereafter, to monitor continuously -- and improve constantly -- the effectiveness of the White House as an organization.

Let me hasten to add that we are not going to go through an exhaustive and extended management study and produce a report that is not implemented. Our intention is to take a quick but complete and fresh look at the way we function and conduct business and make the changes immediately. I wanted you to be aware of this process and have your general approval to proceed.

Source: Reproduced courtesy of The Jimmy Carter Library.

stereotyped as an inefficient administrator who could not mobilize a team to push his programs through a Congress whose recalcitrance he helped create by perpetuating his ignorance of congressional and Washington politics. As most of his senior aides knew, or learned, a chief of staff was needed in anyone's White House by 1977, because the information needs and coordination demands on the president and his staff were part of an increasingly complex organization. However, the specter of Watergate, at least in Carter's perception of the public's memory, was still too frightening to justify the appointment of another chief of staff—particularly by a president who in his election campaign stressed his worth as a Washington "outsider."

In retrospect several of Jimmy Carter's former senior staff have commented on the problems that the lack of a chief of staff caused the president's White House organization. In an interview with the author, Jody Powell remarked, "I think we should have had one. There can always be too much of a good thing and I think there were probably too many people involved. I think that a chief of staff could have saved time for everybody, including the president.''[91] According to Stuart Eizenstat, ''Without question, I think one of the most serious errors that was made, I would say near fatal error, was not having a chief of staff.''[92] Because that role was not filled, ''the White House was not as cohesive a unit as it should have been in the Executive Branch.''[93] Carter's administrative strength was his desire to be his own chief of staff, Eizenstat emphasizes, because ''he wanted to be on top of everything, to manage everything, to know everything, and therefore he really did know what was going on.''[94] On the other hand, attempting to be his own staff coordinator also was one of the president's weaknesses, because he initially failed to realize that presidents assuming this organizational role have too broad a span of control to attend adequately to all issues and activities within the White House. ''They have to prioritize. They need other people to whom they delegate other things. President Carter realized that . . . after the first year and a half.''[95]

Jack Watson admits that Carter ''should have designated a chief of staff almost immediately.''[96] But Watson provides some insight into the reasons Carter may not have initially included this role in his formal structure.

> One reason was he was reluctant to put one [staff member] above the other. Second, he did not want to impede or impair the ability of any one of us to communicate directly to him. He felt very strongly that he didn't want to set up any barriers or obstacles between the free and full expression of opinion to him directly from Stu, Jack, Hamilton, Jody, Frank. And, he didn't want it to be filtered. Third . . . he felt that he didn't need that intermediary.[97]

Despite the organizational problems caused by a lack of coordination in Carter's White House, the environment within his organization was relatively free of intrastaff conflict. According to Anne Wexler, there was a ''minimum of turf battling'' because ''there was a clear understanding among the senior staff'' as to who Carter's closest associates were.[98] Similarly, Eizenstat observes, ''There was not a lot of backbiting or effort to be first among equals. People knew what their roles were. They were comfortable with their relationships.''[99] In short, there was no *need* to fight for territory in the Carter White House; several of the senior aides had known each other for a number of years before coming to the White House and were forged into a team loyal to Carter. Others quickly learned who Carter's close aides were and saw the political futility in attempting to wrest power and authority away from one of these individuals. Moreover, the staff seemed satisfied with the roles they had been assigned by the president, and to his credit, he returned their loyalty with support—sometimes to the detriment of certain Cabinet officers who publicly criticized the intrusion of White House staff into Cabinet areas of responsibility.

Feigenbaum writes that Carter's efforts to reinvigorate the concept of Cabinet

Figure 3

THE WHITE HOUSE
WASHINGTON

October 29, 1979

Ok c me, but
a) Does Lloyd agree?
" Zbig " ?
b)
They should have direct access to me except for "administration" matters
J
cc Same c Susan

MEMORANDUM FOR THE PRESIDENT

FROM : HAMILTON JORDAN
AL MCDONALD

SUBJECT: White House Organization

As you know, we have re-examined the White House organization to clarify certain areas of responsibility. Attached is an organization chart that depicts how the organization looks as of November 1, 1979.

We would welcome any guidance or suggestions on this line up. Otherwise, we will use it as our operating base and publish it as appropriate.

THE WHITE HOUSE OFFICE

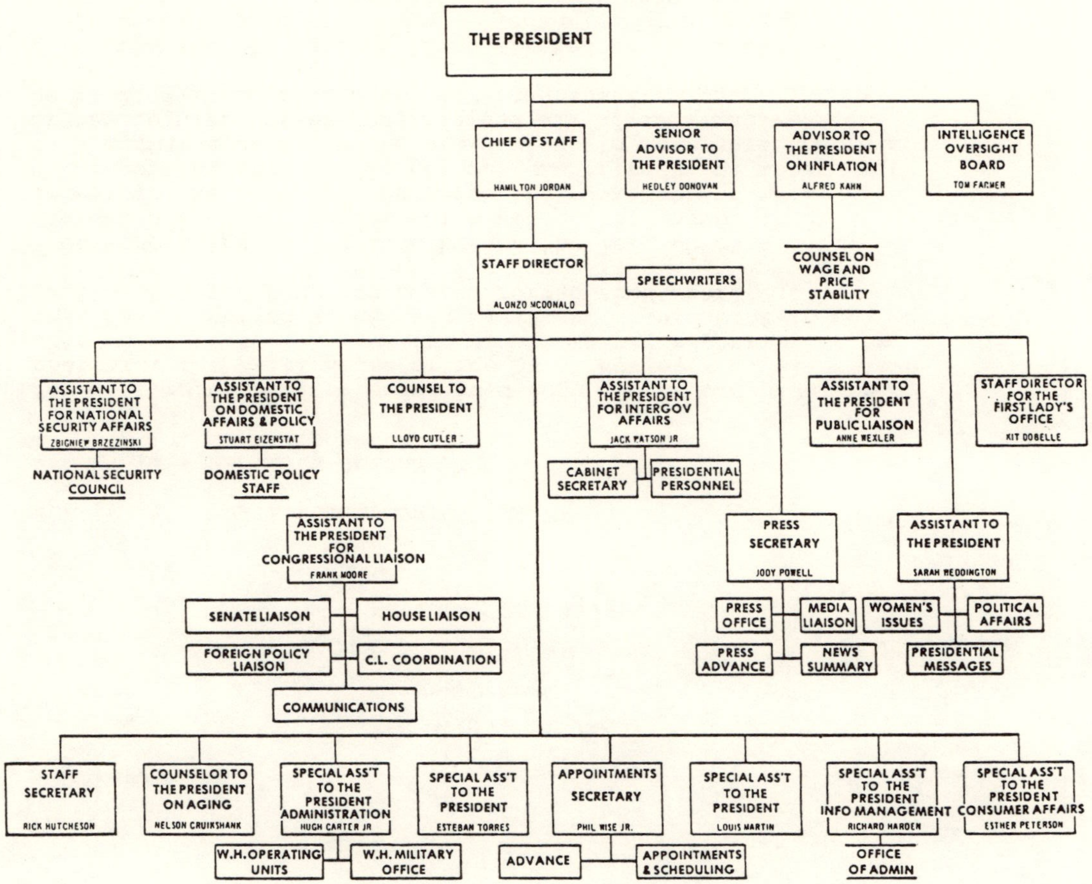

Source: Reproduced courtesy of The Jimmy Carter Library.

Figure 4

MEMORANDUM

THE WHITE HOUSE

WASHINGTON

Barbara

November 26, 1979

FOR : WHITE HOUSE SENIOR STAFF

FROM : HAMILTON JORDAN H.J.

For your reference, attached is a copy of the organization chart for the White House office as of November 1. I believe this reflects the changes and transfers of responsibilities that have occurred since Camp David and should contain no shifts that you have not been informed about earlier.

Please note the dotted line box on the left which clearly indicates that all Senior White House Staff have direct access to the President on major policy issues in their area of responsibility. It is not our aim to restrict in any way this normal access, but we are anxious to make sure that all of the regular issues possible and all administrative items be handled in line with the revised organization.

This organization chart will be altered periodically as needs and assignments change. Please let me have any suggestions you have that should be considered in our next revision.

THE WHITE HOUSE OFFICE

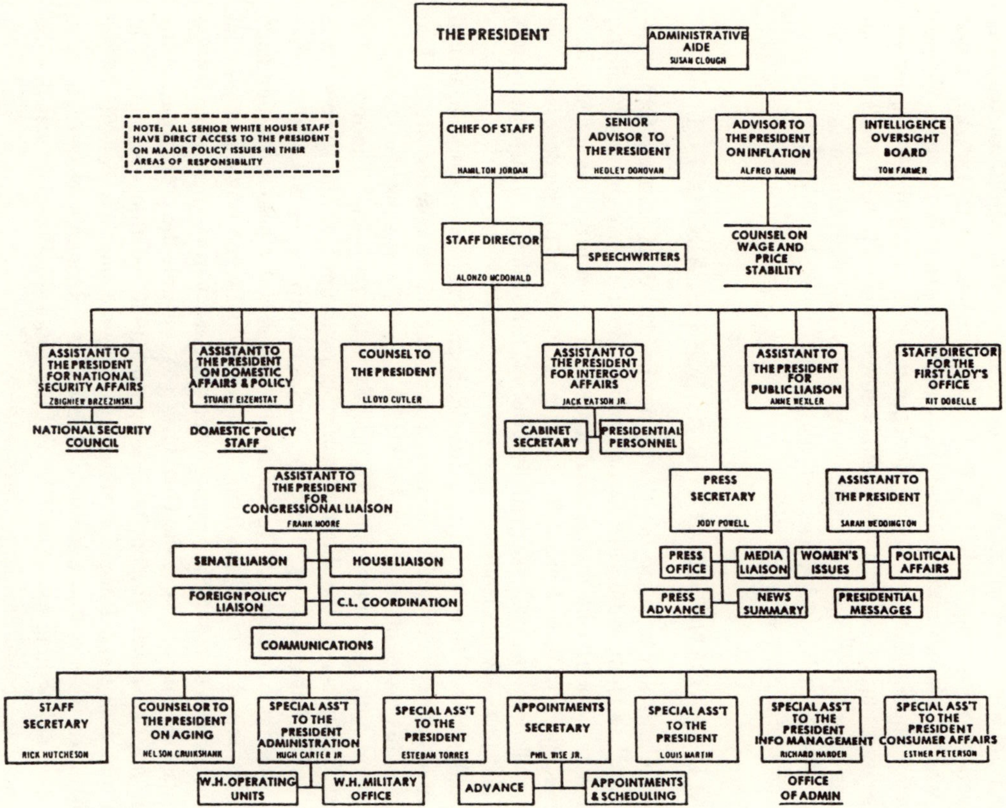

Source: Reproduced courtesy of The Jimmy Carter Library.

government "were hampered by a White House staff overly sensitive to Cabinet members not precisely toeing the Carter line, and certain agency employees who did not have the President's best interests in mind at all times."[100] Hedley Donovan, who served the president for a short time as a senior adviser, observed that there were many competent individuals in Carter's Cabinet and on his White House staff, but they were not brought together as an administration. "It was something of a puzzle why so many capable individuals didn't coalesce more effectively as a working body."[101] Perhaps one answer to that puzzle is that Carter was an administrator in theory, but not a manager in practice. He was *not* a team builder—he was unable to adopt the role of organizational leader, moving his group of senior aides together toward mutually held goals. Social architects must understand that establishing a structure does not ensure its success. It must be massaged, corrected, and guided through the president's continual communication with his staff.

RONALD REAGAN: THE ACTOR AS SOCIAL ARCHITECT

Jimmy Carter's reaction to the Watergate scandal, or at least the formal organizational structure within the Nixon administration that, rightly or wrongly, became synonymous with that scandal, created its own problems for him as a chief executive. In turn, Ronald Reagan's perceptions of his predecessor's organizational problems at least partially affected the structure that initially was established in his White House.

Unlike his post-Watergate predecessors, Reagan established an organizational structure at the beginning of his administration that stayed successfully in place throughout his first term in office. Ironically, it also was a spokes-of-the-wheel arrangement with four aides reporting directly to the president. The rest of the senior staff members in the White House reported to three of four spokes in the wheel: James Baker, Edwin Meese, or Michael Deaver. The national security adviser was the fourth spoke. This arrangement was both a help and a hindrance to the president during his first term. Four individuals reporting directly to the president seemed to represent a manageable span of control—there were not too many aides seeking access to the Oval Office to consume the greater part of his working day. However, the potential for presidential isolation was inherent in such a structure since Reagan preferred to delegate most, if not all, of the administrative tasks within the White House. "As Reagan saw it—and those around him did nothing to dissuade him of the notion—a President was like the chairman of the board of a large corporation."[102]

In analyzing Reagan as a social architect it is appropriate to study his two terms separately, since the structure of the White House changed significantly in the second term. In his first term, the structure Reagan imposed to organize his White House was based on that used in the California statehouse when he was governor, and on "knowledge . . . from people who had been experienced in the Nixon and Ford White Houses."[103] According to Edwin Meese, "our ideas for a structure were an amalgamation of problems they had or experience that had taught them things.''[104] Meese recalls that Watergate was not a significant event affecting Reagan's choice of formal structures ''because our feeling was that that was not particularly a result of structure as it was a result of the politics of the time and maybe some of the personalities.''[105] Failing to remember some of the mistakes created by people in that structure, Reagan, especially in the second term, was doomed to repeat them.

As had his Republican predecessors, Reagan expressed a commitment to Cabinet government when he assumed the presidency. Indeed, Bob Schieffer and Gary Gates report that he and his advisers ''had envisioned a staff structure in which all members of the Cabinet would operate from offices within the White House.''[106] However, the idea was soon abandoned as being impractical, ''and the concept of Cabinet government—as it had been for a long line of Presidents who had tried it—was pretty much discarded once the new administration settled in.''[107] To his credit, however, and that of Edwin Meese, who was responsible for the endeavor, Reagan established a Cabinet Council system through which Cabinet members were organized into committees that met regularly to discuss issues and suggest policies. Fashioned after a similar system used during Reagan's years as California's chief executive, this attempt at structuration within the Cabinet was planned and administered by Meese, and therefore was under White House control. Indeed, the formal organizational structure initiated in Reagan's first term—the troika or triumvirate comprised of Baker, Meese, and Deaver—was instituted specifically to maximize control over the Cabinet, the rest of the White House, and, it sometimes appeared, over the president himself. This structure suited the president's managerial style—he preferred to delegate than personally to coordinate the work of the White House. In an interview published in *Fortune* magazine in September 1986, Reagan stated: ''I believe that you surround yourself with the best people you can find, delegate authority, and don't interfere as long as the overall policy that you've decided upon is carried out.''[108]

John Sears, the president's former campaign manager, once suggested that Reagan's approach to the use of structure in the White House, and his concomitant belief in delegation, were the result of his experience in the organizational environment within which he made movies.

> A lot of people in political and corporate life feel that delegating is an admission that there's something they can't do. But actors are surrounded by people with real authority—directors, producers, scriptwriters, camera-men, lighting engineers, and so on. Yet their authority doesn't detract from the actor's role. The star is the star. And if the show's a hit, he gets the credit.[109]

Soon after the 1980 election, Reagan asked James Baker to be his chief of staff, to the alleged surprise and chagrin of Edwin Meese, perhaps because the president realized the value of placing someone in that position with experience in Washington's political circles. The decision was based, at least in part, on the lesson Reagan learned by watching problems created by a lack of that experience in Carter's White House. Baker moved quickly to assert himself as the major coordinating and controlling influence within the White House. On November 13, 1980, just a few days after the election, he presented the president with a piece of paper proposing his duties and those of Meese, with Meese in attendance. The three agreed to the outline of duties, and appointments were announced the next day.

As chief of staff, Baker's tasks included coordinating and supervising White House staff functions; hiring and firing members of the staff; sharing the coordination and supervision of several White House administrative units (e.g., the Office of Management and Budget and the Council of Economic Advisers); participating as a principal in all policy group meetings; coordinating and controlling the paper flow to and from the president and the president's schedule and appointments; and presiding over meetings of the White House staff.[110]

Meese's duties as counselor to the president for policy included participating as a principal in all meetings of the Cabinet (he held Cabinet rank); coordinating and supervising the secretary to the Cabinet; coordinating and supervising the work of the domestic policy staff and the National Security Council; and participating as a principal in all policy group meetings. Both Baker and Meese were made members of a Super Cabinet Executive Committee.[111]

Meese summarizes the organizational roles of the Reagan troika as follows: he was responsible "for policy development and for the liaison with the departments and agencies of the Executive Branch"; Baker, "for the internal administration of the White House and congressional relations and press relations"; and Deaver, for "travel and schedule and security and the executive residence."[112] In Baker's case, however, some of his responsibilities overlapped with other areas of White House activity—he rather quickly became first among equals because of the nature of the responsibilities he had carved for himself from the menu of possibilities in the White House structure.

According to Helene von Damm, Reagan's first personal secretary and later head of his personnel office, the "Big Three" worked well together initially, meeting at 7:30 in the White House each morning to discuss the day's activities and other issues. "That the Troika worked as well as it did was the result of a certain balance of power and competition. Ed Meese made sure the policies and issues reflected Ronald Reagan's philosophy. Mike Deaver protected the body and image. Jim Baker made sure the apparatus worked and moved."[113] While Franklin Roosevelt purposively had created competition and conflict in his organizational structure to reap the benefits of divergent opinions, Reagan (assisted by the efforts of Baker) created the troika as a group of three cooperating generalists who could manage the large tasks of policy development, congressional and press relations, and the minutiae involved in the day-to-day administration of White House work. Nevertheless, the three-man structure was naturally susceptible to the development of competition and conflict. As von Damm writes, "frictions had to develop and periodically tempers would fray."[114]

A structure comprised of three strong individuals, two of whom had been close to the president for many years, and all representing diverse political and personal orientations to their organizational roles, was bound to foster some degree of intrastaff competition, if not conflict. Von Damm has described the professional effects of each individual's personal characteristics as follows. Jim Baker "was a superb administrator, dynamic and decisive. . . . His keen attention to detail never let anything slip through the cracks."[115] Meese, a "slow and deliberate" worker, would frequently let the papers on his desk "pile so high that no wood was visible, and when there was no more room on the desk, the papers would settle happily on the floor."[116] As a result, von Damm asserts, Baker took advantage of Meese's work habits "by burying Meese with paper when he wanted to thwart him on something. By the time Meese had gotten to the paperwork, the decision would already have been made."[117] Additionally, she suggests, Baker and Deaver formed an alliance when presenting suggestions to the president, often at the expense of Meese. While she characterizes Meese as a team player who would wait to present a policy recommendation to Reagan in Cabinet meetings with the rest of the troika present, Baker and Deaver often spoke with the president ahead of time, presenting their idea or position first, to ensure a positive presidential response.[118]

Nevertheless, the troika did sometimes speak to the president as one voice and act as one adviser. Jane Mayer and Doyle McManus suggest: "At times the troika worked as a protective shield around the president, preventing interlopers from getting too close to him."[119] Such "interlopers," according to Mayer and McManus, included William Casey, whose foreign policy approach was less moderate that that of the president's inner circle. Larry Speakes, former press secretary to Reagan, has recalled that the protective shield also served to prevent unrestricted access to Reagan by some members of his own staff. "During the Baker–Meese–Deaver days no one was allowed in the Oval Office unless one of them was present. I don't know what they were afraid of, but it was just not done."[120]

To supplement the formal organizational framework within which the White House operated, an informal, emergent structure evolved, through the efforts of James Baker. Internally it was referred to as the LSG, the Legislative Strategy Group, and David Stockman describes it as having "managed the enactment of what the press labelled as the most sweeping revolution in national economic policy since the New Deal."[121] Larry Speakes presents the following description of this structurational device in the Reagan White House.

> The membership was limited to . . . as many as could sit around Baker's conference table, six or seven, the elite of the White House decision makers. That meeting became the engine that ran the White House. Meese had the policy apparatus, but it was slow and

creaky. Baker's legislative strategy group had to react immediately to legislative developments. His group quickly became a policy group as well as a legislative group; the fast-breaking give-and-take of the legislative process required that policy decisions be made on the fly. What happened around Baker's conference table was the key as Baker seized control of the White House from Meese.[122]

Stockman, Reagan's first director of the Office of Management and Budget, recalls that LSG meetings were often held in the late afternoon, when White House principals probably had the time to convene with a minimum of interruptions. "There was always a hand calculator next to my place at the table and a TV remote control switch next to his [Baker's]."[123] At 6:30 P.M., when the early edition of the network news programs began, "the remote control switch always won. The meeting shifted from the policy problem in the numbers to the political problem on the screen."[124] In other words, at that point another major role of the troika was assumed; the three key Reagan advisers became viewers of their internal efforts to shape the public persona of Ronald Reagan.

The major strength of the troika as an organizational structure in Reagan's first term was due to its composition: James Baker possessed a brilliant political mind, an ability to communicate with multiple constituencies, particularly those in Congress, and a facility for administration. Meese was Reagan's political conscience and knew the president's strengths and weaknesses as well as, or better than, anyone else. Deaver was an intimate friend of the president and the first lady, and seemed to know how to translate every presidential action or appearance into an effective public relations event and/or strategy. However, the structure was also successful because of the diversity in style and viewpoint represented by each of the three. Differences of opinion sometimes had to be settled in front of, if not by, the president. As a result, such sessions brought problems and possible policies to the president's attention. Such was not always the case in the second term. On the other hand, the legislative effectiveness generated by Reagan's triumvirate apparently served to lull the president into passivity about staffing matters. When he was approached about the possibility of structural changes in the White House for the second term, he agreed without question. That passivity would cost him dearly during the second four years of his presidency.

As Ronald Reagan began his second term, he discovered that his chief of staff and secretary of the Treasury had discussed their mutual interest in trading roles within the Reagan administration. Apparently with little, if any, questioning of the principals involved, Reagan agreed to appoint Baker as Secretary of the Treasury, and Donald T. Regan became chief of staff atop a pyramidal structure like that used in the Nixon administration. According to Mayer and McManus:

While the troika had functioned somewhat in the manner of Franklin Roosevelt's loosely defined and often overlapping staff, allowing the president to benefit from the clashes of viewpoint, Regan fashioned himself in a different mold, more like Eisenhower's aggressive chief, Sherman Adams, or Nixon's strongman, H. R. Haldeman. His primary concern was efficiency, and he set out to create a system streamlined for action, one that allowed the president to be only as involved as he wanted to be.[125]

According to Regan, he and the president never discussed what the organizational structure of the White House should be in the second term.[126] Writing in his memoirs that he wanted the chief of staff position "to bring a semblance of managerial order to the affairs of the Presidency," he found "an environment in which there seemed to be no center, no structure, no agreed policy"—in other words, no organizational leadership in the Oval Office.[127]

This discussion of Ronald Reagan as a social architect began with a reference to the president's acting experience and its relationship to his view of structure. In the Reagan White House, Regan observed; "The Chief of Staff was a sort of producer, making certain that the star had what he needed to do his best; the staff was like the crew, invisible behind the lights, watching the performance their behind-the-scenes efforts had made possible."[128] In Reagan's second term, the senior staff met "every week or two," in contrast with the weekly, if not daily, meetings of staff during the Ford administration—a reflection of the lack of importance ascribed to such forums for internal communication by the president and/or his chief of staff.[129] Moreover, under Regan the number of assistants to the president was reduced from seventeen to eleven. The Cabinet councils Meese had created were condensed into one discussion group on economic policy and one on domestic policy. Where once a trio of senior aides had coordinated the functions of the White House organization, now Regan managed all key areas of responsibility. "He placed himself in charge of long-range planning . . . thus becoming the supervisor of an entire group of legislative, communications, and advance men."[130]

Regan also restricted access to the president. Whereas six people had unrestricted, unannounced access to the president in the first term, only four had the privilege under Regan's rule, including the National Security Council adviser and the president's personal secretary.[131] In both terms the vice president had direct access to Reagan. Evaluating the White House's second-term structure, Edwin Meese mentioned the restriction of access to White House staff in an interview with the author:

> I think that it [the second term's organizational structure] could have worked particularly if the chief of staff at the time had had more people at the higher levels of the White House staff having almost continuous access to the president. I think the fact that access was fairly limited to one or two people probably tended to restrict too tightly the ability of people to meet regularly with the president.[132]

At least two of Reagan's former aides have compared Regan's enactment of his organizational role with that of James Baker. According to Michael Deaver, "Regan's style was the opposite of Baker's. Regan was his own man, and expected people to be courteous and even deferential. Baker was a great delegator. His staff would tell him he was nuts or blow up at him in meetings, and he would tolerate it. He had no problems with their form of communication.''[133] Similarly, Robert McFarlane, one of Reagan's National Security Council advisers, observed:

In the second term, had he kept his first organization, things would definitely have gone better, but they would have gone as well if he would have had Jim Baker instead of Don Regan as a single voice. Meese, Baker, Deaver brought him diverse perspectives that were all useful. And those were lost in the second term. Yet most of what those three brought would have been carried forward if Jim had still been there.[134]

Comparing Deaver's efficiency in the role of developing the president's schedule with that of Regan, Speakes writes:

Mike Deaver not only had a feel for which events would be best for the President and the pace that should be set for Reagan, he held scheduling meetings once a week. Regan would go for weeks without holding a meeting scheduling the President, and things would just end up haphazardly on the President's schedule. Without as much input from other staffers, the planning of the President's schedule under Regan lacked the spark for using it as a tool for communication, legislative efforts, foreign policy, and the whole range of issues.[135]

On the other hand, Speakes observes, Regan's staff meetings were more productive than Baker's because he ''encouraged open give and take'' and ''unlike Baker, always relayed our deliberations to the President.''[136]

The problem, of course, in citing reactions of former senior staff members to the actions of their colleagues is that each individual's perspective is colored by his own relationship with that peer. Nevertheless, both the primary and the secondary sources used in this study paint a picture of Donald Regan as not only authoritarian but also rather inefficient, and in terms of being the chief assistant to Reagan, generally ineffective. Schieffer and Gates write that Regan planned to end the factional infighting that existed when the troika ran the White House ''by tightening the reins on the staff and gathering as much power as possible for himself.''[137]

This did result in a more peaceful atmosphere for Reagan, but the White House became a two-level world where conflict went on at a layer the President never saw. But as Baker's people had come to understand, an executive of Reagan's work habits *needed* to see ideas being thrashed out because he was too passive to explore issues on his own.[138]

Consequently, they conclude that the organizational structure in the second term exacerbated Reagan's managerial weaknesses.

A President who had never shown any interest in detail now had been left all the more isolated from the problems of his presidency. The decision making had been more free-form during the first term, and as Richard Darman . . . later said, "Seeing the interplay between us, a lot of things happened. First of all, Ronald Reagan learned much more about reality."[139]

Donald Regan's problems as chief of staff did not stem solely from his authoritarian behavior or from the reporting relationships he established in the White House. When Ronald Reagan, the person responsible for the social architecture within his own White House, agreed without question to the abandonment of the three-person organizational structure, he became responsible for the dissolution of the decision-making infrastructure in the White House. The aides to Baker, Meese, and Deaver, like their superiors, had either federal government experience or a personal understanding of, and loyalty to, Ronald Reagan. Donald Regan, and those who came with him to the White House, did not possess those attributes. Most important, however, the president's lack of interest in being an organizational leader, in exerting some degree of control over the management of his White House, placed an enormous burden on his chief of staff and gave him the potential for the accumulation of personal power. Mayer and McManus write, "The chief of staff's job derives all of its power from presidential delegation; in the Reagan White House, the job was enormous."[140]

Despite a growing reputation within the staff and among the press corps as a tough, autocratic chief of staff, Regan began to feel comfortable with his structure and his staff as the Reagan administration worked through its second term. According to Mayer and McManus:

> Management by objective was becoming second nature in the West Wing. The staff was now firmly in the habit of identifying issues, developing them, and bringing them to the President for decision. The two new councils, on Economic and Domestic Policy, worked more swiftly and efficiently under the chairmanship of Jim Baker and Ed Meese than the former system of seven Cabinet councils.[141]

However, in the area of foreign affairs, other aides with other agendas were pursuing their personal goals as steadfastly as Regan was working toward his. The Iran-Contra debacle, a controversy over whether the U.S. government had sold arms to recover hostages, diverted some of the profits to Contra rebels in Nicaragua, and defied federal law with the president's blessing, tore some of the protective coating off the "Teflon president." In so doing it called into question the culpability of the president and his senior aides.

Three individuals were appointed by the president to study the possible role of the Executive Branch in the operation. Reagan selected Edmund Muskie, Brent Scowcroft, and John Tower, chairman of the group, to conduct an investigation and make its findings public. It did so in February 1987, and reported in part, that the Iran initiative was organized outside the formal structure of the White House with a corresponding lack of opportunity for the president to benefit from a full hearing on the components of the plan or its implications. The commission faulted the president's management style for placing a "heavy responsibility on his key advisers" and, of particular concern to Donald Regan, it found that he shared in the responsibility for the fiasco, since "he asserted personal control over the White House staff" more than "almost any chief of staff of recent memory" and "as much as anyone, should have insisted that an orderly process be observed."[142]

On Friday, February 27, 1987, Donald Regan resigned as Ronald Reagan's chief of staff, amid controversy over the degree of their individual and collective involvements in the Iran-Contra scandal, alleged continuing attempts of the first lady to have Regan fired, and growing concerns about his autocratic style of management in the White House. Had it not been for the concern over his apparent lack of ability to detach the president form the Iran-Contra controversy, his autocracy ultimately might not have mattered. Months later, a joint congressional investigating committee cleared Regan of any wrongdoing in the Iran initiative. In his memoirs, Regan gives his reasons for the movement that resulted in his abrupt departure from the White House.

> President Reagan and I were too well suited to each other. The psychic and administrative support that I attempted to provide to him as a means of helping him to achieve his own fundamental objectives, rather than supporting the choices that others wished to make for him, created the impression that he was depending too much upon me. The fear arose that I was dominating him, and the press campaign that portrayed me as a martinet who had made himself into an ex officio prime minister fortified the impression.[143]

Regan's perception of the president he served was essentially the same when he left the White House as when he entered it. The president's shortcomings, he has written, included a "baffling reluctance to give orders, or even guidance, to his close subordinates" and "the tendency to permit some of his advisers to manage the Presidency for effect rather than for results."[144]

Howard Baker, a former senator from Tennessee, a former member of the Senate committee that had investigated the Watergate scandal, and a well-respected Republican politician, was selected by Reagan to replace Regan. Baker's demeanor and managerial style resembled those of James Baker, and he moved quickly to restore some semblance of order to a rather chaotic organization. He brought back into the White House some of the competent staff who had left with members of the troika. Additionally, he was sufficiently respected outside the White House that he was able to direct the actions and activities of those within it, and make strong recommendations to a president open to advice in the wake of private anxieties and public criticism stemming from doubts about the extent of his involvement in a foreign policy fiasco. Baker brought calm to the White House as it reached its final organizational stage. The president left office with very high popularity ratings, due in no small measure to the steady control of the White House that Howard Baker maintained during the organization's final months.

Gerald Ford, Jimmy Carter, and Ronald Reagan came to the presidency from different personal and political backgrounds. Ford and Carter reacted similarly to perceived effects of the Watergate scandal on public perceptions about the influence of a close cadre of advisers surrounding a president. Reagan, in the first term, eschewed the appointment of a chief of staff in a pyramidal structure, mainly through the influence of the individuals who became the basis for his formal organizational structure: the troika whose power in the White House was as significant as, if not more than, that of Sherman Adams or H. R. Haldeman. But the very nature of the three-man structure sometimes required presidential review of, and participation in, discussions and debates held by them. Consequently, in the first term, Reagan, the great delegator, seemed more in touch with the events and activities transpiring in his White House than he would in his second term. The appointment of Donald Regan altered that opportunity for the president, and the Iran-Contra scandal was only one example of situations from which the president had been protected . . . or isolated. After Regan's embarrassing departure from the White House, the appointment of Howard Baker showed presidential, or staff, sensitivity to the problems created by placing the wrong person in a seemingly appropriate structure. Nevertheless, the president who apparently could communicate his vision of America and its goals for the future to a public audience could not efficiently oversee the management of his own organization.

Regardless of their political and policy successes and failures, the post-Watergate presidents, and their senior staffs, worked to establish formal and emergent structures through which to exercise their legislatively and publicly defined duties. As we shall see in Chapters 5 and 6, formal structures and the process of structuration assist in the elimination or diminution of equivocality, of ambiguity, within the White House. Together they also provide a framework of reference that shapes and significantly affects the communicative relationship between a president and his senior staff.

As social architect, the president and/or those he designates as senior aides develop formal and informal structures to organize and coordinate the work of the White House. As is illustrated in the next chapter, such structures allow for the development of social systems to facilitate and guide the flow of information to the president for his use in decision making.

NOTES

1. Stephen Hess, *Organizing the Presidency*, 2d ed. (Washington, DC: The Brookings Institution, 1988), p. 174.

2. Gerald R. Ford, *A Time to Heal* (New York: Harper & Row and The Reader's Digest Association, 1979), p. 147.

3. See Robert D. McPhee, "Formal Structure and Organizational Communication," in Robert D. McPhee and Phillip Tompkins, eds. *Organizational Communication: Traditional Themes and New Directions*, (Beverly Hills, CA: Sage, 1985), pp. 149–77.

4. Marshall Scott Poole, David R. Seibold, and Robert D. McPhee, "Group Decision-making as a Structurational Process," *Quarterly Journal of Speech*, 71, 1985, p. 76.

5. Patricia Riley, "A Structurationist Account of Political Culture," *Administrative Science Quarterly*, 28, 1983, p. 415.

6. Jerald Hage, Michael Aiken, and Cora B. Marrett, "Organization Structure and Communication," *American Sociological Review*, 38, 1971, p. 863.

7. See Jay Galbraith, *Designing Complex Organizations* (Reading, MA: Addison-Wesley, 1973).

8. Staff of the White Burkett Miller Center of Public Affairs, University of Virginia, *The Ford White House* (Lanham, MD: University Press of America, 1986), p. 12.

9. Ibid.

10. *A Discussion with Gerald R. Ford* (Washington, DC: American Enterprise Institute for Public Policy Research, 1977), p. 4.

11. Terrence O'Donnell, interview with the author, November 4, 1987.

12. Richard Cheney, interview with the author, November 4, 1987.

13. Gerald R. Ford, interview with the author, April 21, 1987.

14. Ford, *A Time to Heal*, p. 147.

15. Ibid., p. 186.

16. Ibid.

17. Typed notes of Jack W. Hushen, October 1974, folder: "Rumsfeld," box 44, staff files of Ron Nessen, Gerald R. Ford Library.

18. Cheney, interview with the author.

19. Ronald Nessen, interview with the author, November 5, 1987.

20. White House press release, December 18, 1974, folder: "White House Organization: Press Release," pp. 1–2, box 21, staff files of James Connor, Gerald R. Ford Library.

21. Ibid., p. 2.

22. Ibid.

23. Nessen, interview with the author.

24. Transcript of Press Conference of Donald H. Rumsfeld, Assistant to the President, December 18, 1974, p. 4, Box 21, Staff Files of James Connor, Gerald Ford Library.

25. Memorandum from Donald Rumsfeld, June 13, 1975, folder: "Presidential Meetings; Follow-up on Directives," box 15, staff files of James Connor, Gerald R. Ford Library.

26. Ford, *A Time to Heal*, p. 147.

27. Donald Rumsfeld, interview with the author, August 10, 1987.

28. Ibid.

29. Memorandum from Donald Rumsfeld to Ron Nessen, August 5, 1975, folder: "Rumsfeld, 7/75–11/75 (2)," box 132, papers of Ron Nessen, Gerald R. Ford Library.

30. Donald Rumsfeld, interview with the author, August 10, 1987.

31. James Connor, interview with the author, July 15, 1987.

32. Robert J. Donovan, *Confidential Secretary: Ann Whitman's Twenty Years with Eisenhower and Rockefeller* (New York: E. P. Dutton, 1988), p. 187.

33. Ibid., p. 189.

34. Interview of Gerald R. Ford by Trevor Arbrister, p. 22 of transcript, folder: "Interview with GRF by Arbrister," box 34, papers of James Cannon, Gerald R. Ford Library.

35. Interview of Nelson Rockefeller by Robert Hartmann, p. 44 of transcript, folder: "NAR Interview with Bob Hartmann, 12/2/77," box 35, papers of James Cannon, Gerald R. Ford Library.

36. Rumsfeld, interview with the author.

37. Connor, interview with the author.

38. For Hartmann's discussion of his view of the Ford White House, see Robert Hartmann, *Palace Politics* (New York: McGraw-Hill, 1980).

39. Rumsfeld, interview with the author.

40. Interview of Gerald R. Ford by Hugh Morrow, p. 25 of transcript, folder: "Interview with GRF by Hugh Morrow (1979)," box 34, papers of James Cannon, Gerald R. Ford Library.

41. Connor, interview with the author.

42. Ford, interview with the author.

43. *A Discussion with Gerald R. Ford*, p. 4.

44. Connor, interview with the author.

45. "Analysis of Present White House Office, Staff Management," folder: "Transition—Analysis of White House Organization," box 12, Richard Cheney files, Gerald R. Ford Library.

46. Quoted in Michael Medved, *The Shadow Presidents* (New York: Times Books, 1979), p. 347.

47. Jody Powell, interview with the author, June 16, 1989.

48. Ibid.

49. Medved, *The Shadow Presidents*, p. 362.

50. Bruce Mazlish and Edwin Diamond, *Jimmy Carter: A Character Portrait* (New York: Simon and Schuster, 1979), p. 243.

51. Jimmy Carter, *Keeping Faith* (New York: Bantam Books, 1982), p. 40.

52. Ibid., pp. 40–41.

53. Edward D. Feigenbaum, "Staffing, Organization, and Decision-making in the Ford and Carter White Houses," *Presidential Studies Quarterly*, Summer 1980, p. 371.

54. Jack Watson, interview with the author, August 19, 1988.

55. Stuart Eizenstat, interview with the author, June 16, 1989.

56. Ibid.

57. Ibid.

58. Memorandum from Hamilton Jordan to Jimmy Carter and Walter Mondale, December 27, 1976, folder: "Management and Scheduling of Projects and Programs," box 234, files of domestic policy staff–Eizenstat, Jimmy Carter Library.

59. Draft memorandum from Richard Harden to Robert Lipshutz and members of the White House Management Committee, January 3, 1977, folder: "Organization," box 62, White House Administration Office files, Jimmy Carter Library.

60. Memorandum from Richard Harden to Members of the Management Committee, January 24, 1977, folder: "Organization," box 62, White House Administration Office Files, Jimmy Carter Library.

61. Memorandum from Stuart Eizenstat to the president, January 3, 1977, p. 1, folder: "DPS (General), 1/3/77–3/29/77," box 118, domestic policy staff—Eizenstat, Jimmy Carter Library.

62. Ibid., p. 2.

63. Watson, interview with the author.

64. Memorandum from Richard Harden to Midge Constanza, Stu Eizenstat, Hamilton

Jordan, Bob Lipshutz, Frank Moore, Jody Powell, and Jack Watson, February 25, 1977, p 1, folder: "Memoranda: Harden, Richard, 1/31/77–4/7/77," box 43, Press Office—Powell, Jimmy Carter Library.

65. Ibid.

66. Ibid.

67. Ibid., p. 2.

68. Ibid., p. 4.

69. Ibid.

70. Ibid., pp. 4–5.

71. James Fallows, "The Passionless Presidency II," *The Atlantic*, June 1980, p. 79.

72. Attachment to a memorandum from the vice president to Executive Committee members, undated but initialed, p. 7, folder: "White House Executive Committee," box 51, Office of Counsel—Lipshutz files, Jimmy Carter Library.

73. White House press release, p. 5, folder: "Executive Office of the President—Reorganization Decisions [1]," box 26, White House Administration Office files, Jimmy Carter Library.

74. Medved, *The Shadow Presidents*, p. 362.

75. Anne Wexler, interview with the author, June 15, 1989.

76. Memorandum from A. D. Frazier to Hamilton Jordan, October 19, 1977, folder: "Reorganization—WH/EOP, 1977 (2)," box 37, chief of staff—Jordan files, Jimmy Carter Library.

77. Ibid., p. 1.

78. Ibid., p. 4.

79. Ibid., p. 5.

80. Memorandum from Stuart Eizenstat to the president, "Year-End Summary," December 27, 1977, Eizenstat personal collection, quoted in Bradley H. Patterson, Jr., *The Ring of Power* (New York: Basic Books, 1988), p. 302.

81. Ibid.

82. Ibid.

83. Medved, *The Shadow Presidents*, p. 362.

84. Memorandum from Lloyd Hackler to Hamilton Jordan, July 7, 1978, p. 1, folder: "Informal Advisers Group," box 47, chief of staff—Jordan files, Jimmy Carter Library.

85. Ibid., p. 2.

86. Ibid., p. 3.

87. Memorandum from Hamilton Jordan to the senior staff, December 18, 1978, p. 1, folder: "Senior Staff Coordination Notebook," box 55, chief of staff—Jordan files, Jimmy Carter Library.

88. Ibid., p. 2.

89. Ibid., p. 5.

90. Feigenbaum, "Staffing, Organization, and Decision-making . . . ," p. 372.

91. Powell, interview with the author.

92. Eizenstat, interview with the author.

93. Ibid.

94. Ibid.

95. Ibid.

96. Watson, interview with the author.

97. Ibid.

98. Wexler, interview with the author.

99. Eizenstat, interview with the author.

100. Feigenbaum, "Staffing, Organization, and Decision-making . . . ," p. 377.

101. Hedley Donovan, *From Roosevelt to Reagan: A Reporter's Encounters with Nine Presidents* (New York: Harper & Row, 1985), p. 215.

102. Bob Schieffer and Gary Paul Gates, *The Acting President* (New York: E. P. Dutton, 1989), p. 23.

103. Edwin Meese, interview with the author, June 15, 1989.

104. Ibid.

105. Ibid.

106. Schieffer and Gates, *The Acting President*, p. 24.

107. Ibid.

108. Interview with Marshall Loeb, Lee Smith, and Ann Reilly Dowd, "Reagan on Decision-making, Planning, Gorbachev, and More," *Fortune*, September 15, 1986, p. 36.

109. As quoted in Ann Reilly Dowd, "What Managers Can Learn from Manager Reagan," *Fortune*, September 15, 1986, p. 35.

110. Schieffer and Gates, *The Acting President*, p. 83.

111. Ibid.

112. Meese, interview with the author.

113. Helene von Damm, *At Reagan's Side* (New York: Doubleday, 1988), p. 255.

114. Ibid., p. 254.

115. Ibid., p. 166.

116. Ibid., p. 167.

117. Ibid.

118. Ibid., pp. 168–69.

119. Jane Mayer and Doyle McManus, *Landslide: The Unmaking of the President, 1984–1988* (Boston: Houghton Mifflin, 1988), p. 31.

120. Larry Speakes, *Speaking Out* (New York: Charles Scribner's Sons, 1988), p. 31.

121. David Stockman, *The Triumph of Politics* (New York: Harper & Row, 1986), p. 4.

122. Speakes, *Speaking Out*, p. 70.

123. Ibid., p. 12.

124. Ibid.

125. Mayer and McManus, *Landslide*, p. 40.

126. Donald T. Regan, *For the Record* (New York: St. Martin's Press, 1988), p. 262.

127. Ibid., pp. 256 and 161.

128. Ibid., pp. 252–53.

129. Ibid., p. 323.

130. Mayer and McManus, *Landslide*, p. 40.

131. Regan, *For the Record*, p. 261.

132. Meese, interview with the author.

133. Michael Deaver, *Behind the Scenes* (New York: William Morrow, 1987), pp. 134–35.

134. Robert McFarlane, interview with the author, June 16, 1989.

135. Speakes, *Speaking Out*, p. 76.

136. Ibid., p. 75.

137. Schieffer and Gates, *The Acting President*, p. 199.

138. Ibid.

139. Ibid., p. 200.

140. Mayer and McManus, *Landslide*, p. 240.

141. Ibid., p. 372.

142. John Tower, Edmund Muskie, and Brent Scowcroft, *The Tower Commission Report* (New York: Bantam Books and Times Books, 1987), p. xviii.

143. Regan, *For the Record*, p. 422.

144. Ibid., p. 425.

Chapter 5

The President as Decision Maker: Systems of Information Flow and Use, 1974–1988

All White Houses, as dynamic organizations, are continually engaged in the creation of social architecture. As we have seen, the Ford and Carter White Houses particularly used the process of structuration to define and organize tasks conducted by senior aides. In the Reagan adminstration, the formal structure of the organization was changed significantly in the second term to accommodate changes in personnel, specifically the dissipation of the White House troika.

Structure not only defines reporting relationships and organizes the process through which tasks are identified, coordinated and conducted; it provides the framework through which a president and his staff organize the systems of information flow he will use when making decisions. As the president's information needs change during the various stages of his presidency, structural changes are made to accommodate these needs. Such changes help the White House match its information-processing capabilities with its information-processing requirements.

The post-Watergate presidents sought and processed information and made decisions in different ways, due to differences in their backgrounds, personalities, and managerial philosophies, and in the ways they chose to communicate with senior staff. Before analyzing these chief executives individually, and comparing them collectively, it is beneficial to consider observations about information flow and decision making within organizations in general, and inside the White House in particular.

INFORMATION FLOW AND DECISION MAKING: THEORETICAL OBSERVATIONS

Information is power because it is the substance of which decisions are made.

Analyzing the interrelationship between information flow and decision making therefore is an important consideration in understanding communication between presidents and their senior staffs. Emphasizing the interrelationships between information acquisition and use, Charles O'Reilly, Jennifer Chatman, and John Anderson note that "in order to understand how individuals in organizations typically make decisions we must understand both how they acquire information and how, once acquired, they process or use this information.[1] Similarly, K. J. Arrow described decisions as being a "function of information received. . . . In turn, the acquisition of information must be analyzed, since it is itself the result of decisions.[2]

In their analysis of message flow and decision making in organizations, O'Reilly et al. discuss the effects that structure has on these processes.[3] As was seen in Chapter 4, the organizational roles of staff secretary and chief of staff affected the flow of information into the Oval Office, as did the formal hierarchical structure of reporting relationships adopted by each president. Additionally, it was observed that the key aides serving Presidents Ford and Carter, and the troika under Reagan, developed communication networks that greatly influenced the flow of information to these presidents and ensured "the presence of certain types of information," as well as the availability of sufficient and reliable information for the presidents' needs.[4]

Hierarchy, one component of structure, may constrain information available to decision makers, as O'Reilly et al. observe and as was illustrated in the previous chapter. In the White House, as in other organizations, the superior–subordinate relationship may affect both the quality and the quantity of information a president receives and perhaps, ultimately, the quality of the decisions he makes.

> Since many important decisions in organizations are made at higher levels, these decision makers need accurate, reliable, and relevant information to define problems, generate alternatives, and ultimately make choices. This information is often acquired through messages exchanged from subordinates to superiors. Therefore, the variables that influence this relationship also influence the decision outcome by affecting the content and quality of information transmitted.[5]

The change from a troika-led White House, comprised of two personal friends and a competent administrator, to a chief of staff who represented a single channel of information flow to the president, affected the quality and quantity of information Ronald Reagan received in his second term. In the Iran initiative, for instance, the Tower Commission found that the pyramidal structure operating in the Reagan White House at the time contributed to the president's lack of information about the arms-for-hostages deal. O'Reilly et al. observe that "structure, while serving to channel information flows, may also act under some circumstances to deny decision makers relevant data."[6] The use of Donald Rumsfeld as staff coordinator allowed Gerald Ford more time to seek information from a variety of sources during his years in the White House. Jimmy Carter's stubborn resistance to the appointment of a chief of staff until late in his presidency seems to have denied him an orderly flow of information from divergent viewpoints until key aides created processes and procedures to enhance the flow of information to the president.

Access to the president, of course, does not ensure that one has communicated with him, or even that one has imparted all relevant information to him on a given issue. As is the case in other organizations, those sending information to superiors may eagerly transmit some information and avoid the presentation of other data, either to reap rewards or to prevent punishment. At the same time, the superior bears responsibility for those times when he sends "a clear signal. . . . that only certain types of information are desired."[7] He may, for instance, prefer oral, as opposed to written, information. He may deem only information provided by certain individuals as trustworthy. As we shall see later in this chapter, Gerald Ford preferred the oral give-and-take of interpersonal communication settings; Jimmy Carter was more comfortable studying, and reacting to, briefing papers. Gerald Ford sought information from a variety of individuals representing multiple viewpoints. Carter relied on his staff and key Cabinet members; and Ronald Reagan, under most circumstances, was content to listen to opinions of his closest aides.

Regardless of an individual's preferred sources of information, and the process used to transmit that information to him, "both the information transmitted to the decision maker and the decision maker's framing of it can act to affect the decision outcomes."[8] Moreover, as O'Reilly et al. suggest, "The quantity and quality of information may have direct effects on the types of decisions to be made and on how decision-makers behave."[9]

INFORMATION FLOW AND DECISION MAKING IN THE WHITE HOUSE

Theodore Sorensen has written that, theoretically, presidents should use a decision-making process based on the following: agreement on the facts and the overall policy objective; a precise definition of the problem; a canvassing of all possible solutions; a list of all possible consequences that might flow from each solution; a recommendation and final choice of one alternative; and then the communication of the decision and provision for its execution.[10] However, as all organizational leaders are aware, decisions are not made under theoretical conditions. In the circumstances in which a president is continually involved, any of these elements may be in doubt or under dispute. Moreover, the White House, like other organizations, is a set of coalitions of individuals where differences are settled by bargaining and domination.[11] Decision making, as a result, is a linear process only in theory, certainly not in reality. A particular president's White House is undergoing constant change—moving through a series of organizational stages—and the process of decision making changes as these stages evolve from one to another.

Paul Light, who has applied contributions of organizational theory to the study of the presidency, observes that decision making in the White House

will always involve a mixture of. . . . three models of organization choice. At times the office will resemble a garbage can, with streams of problems, solutions, and participants; decisions will be more accidental than planned. At other times it will resemble the ordered efficiency of the rational model, with attempts at comprehensive choice. Usually, however the Presidency resembles the *behavioral* system: choices are the result of either bargaining or domination.[12]

Interpersonal communication between a president and his staff, consequently, increases as these processes develop.

While Light is particularly concerned with group decision making in the Executive Branch, this study focuses on decision making solely from the perspective of the president—the person unilaterally responsible for decisions made in his White House. An individual who has studied presidential decision making from this perspective is Alexander George, who focuses on the chief executive's use of information and advice from his key aides. In looking at the process of decision making among executives in general, George writes:

Executives who find personal contact with too many advisers inefficient or wearing, or who find exposure to the rough-and-tumble of vigorous debate within the advisory group incompatible with their habitual or preferred mode of decisionmaking, will seek to limit their direct involvement with others in the search and evaluation phases of policymaking that precede the final choice of action. The type of communication network that an executive develops around him will reflect not only his cognitive style but also his conception of the role he should play in the management structure and in the decision-making process. Some executives prefer to restrict their role to making the final choice of action; others prefer to involve themselves more actively in the search and evaluation activities that precede the final phase of decisionmaking. But all executives rely to some extent on a relatively small number of advisers and staff to ferret out information, make suggestions, develop and appraise policy options, and to monitor the implementation of decisions taken.[13]

Henry Kissinger discusses decision-making criteria for U.S. presidents in his account of White House service during several administrations. According to Kissinger, the set of criteria used by chief executives should meet the following requirements.

It must be compatible with his personality and style. It must lead to action; desultory talk without operational content produces paralysis. Above all, it must be sensitive to the psychological relationship between the President and his close advisers: it must enable the President's associates to strengthen his self-confidence and yet give him real choices, to supply perspective and yet not turn every issue into a test of wills. It must give scope for genuine Presidential discretion without promoting the megalomania that often develops in positions where one encounters few equals. At the same time, if every single decision is funneled into the President's office, he will lose the benefit of the technical competence and accumulated experience of the permanent officials.[14]

When analyzing the process of information flow and decision making used by presidents, one must consider their personalities as well as the influences of the inner circle around each of them. In so doing, one must ascertain the "decision rules" that guide a chief executive's policy-making deliberations. Kissinger suggests that "The decision rule that a leader chooses to follow may importantly affect the quality of the information processing and appraisal that takes place and, hence, the policy outcome."[15] Some leaders value unanimity among participants in the decision-making process, at times forcing a consensus among participants in a discussion. Others value the give-and-take of debate and discussion, and reach their decisions after encouraging advisers and aides to share multiple, sometimes conflicting, points of view. Most presidents follow another decision rule:

authoritative choice by the executive, after consultation. While in this case the executive is not bound to seek either unanimous or majority support for the action he decides to take, nonetheless, the nature of his consultation becomes a critical factor in determining the quality of the search and evaluation provided him by the advisory system.[16]

The decision-making process in the White House is fraught with pitfalls, as the president attempts to make decisions based on what he hopes is, or accepts as, adequate information. Moreover, a number of malfunctions in the decision-making process may occur during deliberations between a president and his advisers. Such malfunctions, according to George, include the following:[17]

- When advisers discuss their own disagreements without the president's knowledge and present him with a unanimous recommendation, as was sometimes the case when Reagan's troika agreed upon a course of action in their meetings and then presented it to the president for approval.
- When the president is dependent on a single channel of information, as was often the case in the second Reagan term, when Donald Regan served as chief of staff.
- When there is no advocate for an unpopular decision option, which may often be the case in the White House, as in other organizations, when a staff member is hesitant to adopt a position that may alter his status as the right or left hand to power in the White House, that is, as one of the president's favored aides.

Whatever the role of senior staff in decision making within the White House, the president must understand and assume his decision-making responsibilities. Light has written: "Unless the President is willing to enter the decision process, the movement toward domination [of one coalition over another] will ultimately appear."[18] As was illustrated in Chapter 4, Ronald Reagan's detachment from the decision-making process on a day-to-day basis created more power for his troika and allowed them to dominate other coalitions or individuals in the Reagan White House.

Sorensen wrote in 1963, while serving as one of President Kennedy's closest aides, that a chief executive's decisions are limited by permissibility, available resources, available time, previous commitments, and available information.[19] It is on this last resource that this chapter focuses, for as Sorensen emphasizes, "the essence of decision is choice; and, to choose, it is first necessary to know."[20] Developing formal systems of information flow within the White House, and cultivating other sources of information outside the White House, call for presidential and staff awareness of the organization's information-processing requirements and the relative richness of various media. The working environment around the president must create and maintain an information-processing capacity to meet the president's needs, to avoid his making a decision based on too little information, or to ensure he is not the victim of information overload. Leonard Hawes's observations about information overload in organizations are pertinent to the White House:

> Only certain types of information permeate the boundaries of a closed, highly structured, bureaucratic system; the rest is systematically filtered out. The result is minimum overload but also minimum flexibility. In an open, loosely structured, learned environment a wide variety of information permeates the system's boundaries. The result is a potential for maximum overload but also maximum flexibility. The dilemma confronting today's organization is which information can be filtered to reduce unnecessary overload without, at the same time, crippling the organization's ability to process new types of information.[21]

As is discussed in this chapter, staff members in each post-Watergate presidency endeavored to fashion systems of information flow that attempted to avoid the pitfalls of sending either too much or too little information into the Oval Office for use in decision making. Additionally, each president selected sources of information that provided varying degrees of richness, such as face-to-face meetings with one or two individuals, small group meetings, or written memoranda. While Carter preferred reacting to written communications, Ford and Reagan valued the use of information-rich media such as individual consultations with aides or small group meetings. Sorensen states, "The interaction of many minds is usually more illuminating than the intuition of one. In a meeting representing different departments and diverse points of view, there is a greater likelihood of hearing alternatives, of exposing errors, and of challenging assumptions."[22] The greater the number of individuals attending such meetings, however, the more disadvantages they hold for decision makers. The larger the group surrounding the president, the less rich the information being shared—some verbal and nonverbal cues are lost in communication interactions among a large number of individuals.

Presidents read daily newspapers, see some of the letters sent by citizens to the White House, call on friends and former officials for advice, and seek information from a variety of other sources. This chapter, while discussing informal sources of information used by each president, focuses on the formal system(s) of information flow developed by the president and his senior staff within the White House, including the system used to channel written information to the president for his use in policy deliberations and decision making. Additionally, individual styles of decision making used by the post-Watergate presidents are analyzed, remembering Harry Truman's observation that "no one can know all the processes and stages of [a President's] thinking in making important decisions. Even those closest to him. . . . never know all the reasons why he does certain things and why he comes to certain conclusions."[23]

The communicative relationship between a president and his senior staff is crucial to the effectiveness and efficiency of the processes of message flow and decision making used in the White House. Those closest to the chief executive, personally and professionally, are responsible for sharing their ideas and the information they collect in the conduct of everyday responsibilities; they also transmit data and opinions accumulated by other members of the administration, and they are generally responsible for arranging the president's contact with sources of information outside the White House. Before comparing the post-Watergate chief executives as users of information, it is first important to look at how each of them sought ideas and opinions, remembering that presidents, like other organizational leaders, may react to, if not learn from, the perceived mistakes of their predecessors.

INFORMATION FLOW IN THE FORD WHITE HOUSE

To foster a smooth transition between administrations in late 1976, the Ford White House prepared an "Analysis of the Present White House Office."Describing the formal system of information flow used by President Ford and his senior staff, the document first listed several of the objectives the Ford administration followed when managing paper flow in the Oval Office. The objectives were listed as follows:

—Screen material that the President does not need to see.

—Insure that the President receives background material on a timely basis.

—Insure that each document is well-prepared—as short as possible, comprehensive and accurate.

—Insure that the views of all principal advisors are reflected in memos requesting a Presidential decision.

—Insure that the appointments and paper flow functions are properly coordinated.

—Insure that differences in opinion are properly narrowed and sharpened prior to being brought to the President.[24]

The system of paper flow used by the Ford White House was described in the following manner:

These objectives are accomplished by requiring that all papers going to the President flow through the Staff Secretary's Office where they are logged, distributed for staffing, if appropriate, and sent to the President at the appropriate time. Likewise, papers flowing from the Presidential Office go through the Staff Secretary's office for control and proper dissemination. The staff also asks that Presidential memos be kept to a maximum of two pages and follow a standard format. Any required supplemental information is included as an attachment. The President and senior staff members also receive a daily news summary in order to minimize the time required to keep abreast of the events of the day.[25]

Obviously the objectives for the control of paper flow into the Oval Office were not always achieved, but the formal system through which Gerald Ford received briefing papers and formal memos was one of the more orderly and more open systems of those used by modern presidents, in part because of the Eisenhower legacy that several key staff respected, and in part because of the president's determination to include input from multiple sources. This determination was fueled by Ford's years of consensus building in the Congress, and by his perception of weaknesses in Richard Nixon's approach to decision making that were magnified in the Watergate cover-up.

In Ford's White House the "staff system," as it came to be called, was responsible for eliciting White House staff and Cabinet member input on virtually any proposal requiring a presidential decision. It was closely monitored by the staff secretary and the staff coordinator. James Connor, staff secretary from late spring 1975 until the end of Ford's term, describes the system as follows:

I would receive a memo from anyone basically in the position to ask the president . . . to make a decision. Those were sometimes from Cabinet officers, requests from the director of OMB [Office of Management and Budget], from the president's counsel, from any one of a number of people who were charged with orchestrating the policy process. . . . My purpose was . . . to review the paper to the president requesting the decision; it was to ascertain that, at least in my own judgment . . . that the issue being presented had in fact been adequately staffed, that potential problems were identified, risks identified, alternatives clearly explained, and to show that paper to anyone . . . I thought ought usefully to comment on it before the president saw it. To elicit . . . any inputs that I thought the president ought to have before he made his decision. Most of the inputs that I would be eliciting would be internal, White House and Executive Office inputs. In other words, to create a . . . fully staffed paper that would not . . . determine the way the president made his decision, but basically create an environment in which he wouldn't be surprised after he made his decision that the . . . end fell off because somebody should have told him that it was going to fall off if you loosened the screw.[26]

The staffing system used by Ford was similar to that used in the Nixon White House. However, H. R. Haldeman insisted on seeing every document before and after it went to the president. Under Ford, the staff secretary assumed greater responsibility and autonomy while under the supervision of Donald Rumsfeld and, later, Richard Cheney.

Each memo or document received by Connor was sent for comment to appropriate senior aides and Cabinet members, giving the date and time a response was due in the staff secretary's office. Written responses and the original paper were compiled, and Connor would develop a short cover memo summarizing the issue and identifying who supported which alternatives.

The purpose of the cover was especially to indicate to the president . . . there was one essential unanimity on the part of his advisors, in which case I would identify that in the cover memo, and in which case hopefully he wouldn't spend his time plowing through the fact that it was complex, or to flag to him that in this particular case, "boss, we got the guys all over the lot on this one."[27]

Sections of the document judged to be particularly important for presidential review were "red-tagged." The original proposal, written responses to it, and the cover memo were sent to the president as a packaged "decision memorandum." According to Connor, most of these documents were three to five pages in length, since some staff members' responses would be one-word comments agreeing with the original proposal. Other memoranda would be "thick with tabs."[28]

In one memo disseminated by Donald Rumsfeld, Cabinet officers and agency heads were given five days to prepare their responses to memos for inclusion in a decision memorandum.[29] Some documents, Connor recalls, were shown to Rumsfeld before being taken to Ford. According to Cheney, however, during his tenure as chief of staff *all* documents went through his office before and after a presidential decision was made. Connor would take stacks of these papers directly to the president or to Terrence O'Donnell, the appointments secretary, whose office was outside the Oval Office. Records were kept to show when a document entered the Oval Office and when it was taken from Ford's "out box." These logs kept track of each paper's progress in the system of information flow.

According to both Rumsfeld and Connor, Ford carefully read the packaged sets of papers prepared for him. Rumsfeld, for instance, recalls that

Ford was a real workhorse. He really plowed through stuff. You sent in a stack and out it would come with writing on it, check marks, "approve" or "disapprove," or "What about this?" or "Let's do this," or . . . "I think I want to do this." There would be a number of little note pad papers with that left-hand scrawl of his where he would say, "I've been thinking about this and it's something I want to do."[30]

Connor emphasizes that Ford

was the only human being I've ever known in the world who's read Tab G of the decision papers. . . . I'd get this stuff back and go back through it, and I'd look at it carefully and I found the . . . man had been annotating, making notes far back into the paper. I mean, if you ever want to bury something in the policy process, put it in Tab G.[31]

Connor would convey a presidential decision to the originator of the request, and to other affected parties, in writing. If the need for a presidential response was urgent, he telephoned Ford's answer and then sent the written reply. In this way an organizational "paper trail" of requests and decisions was maintained. According to Connor, this staffing system did not determine the way Ford made a decision, but it did create an environment that allowed a variety of staff input and fully assessed the implications of decision alternatives. Due to the nature of his duties, the staff secretary in Ford's White House obviously was a conduit of information to and from the president and among key staff members. In his words: "My job was basically to keep all of the white knights in the same shoe box and . . . when they chewed their way out to shepherd them back in and patch up the hole and still have them in the shoe box."[32]

Rumsfeld and Connor may have been responsible for establishing this formal system of information flow, and continuing the organizational legacy of the Eisenhower White House, but President Ford soon became aware of its advantages. Connor emphasizes that "If people tried to raise issues . . . that had not been fully staffed, Ford, Rumsfeld, and myself and the other players would generally say . . . 'put that in the staff system; create a paper for it. We won't meet until the papers are ready.' "[33] Richard Cheney recalls that over time Ford began to appreciate and expect thorough analyses of proposals, that is, those which appeared to consider the effects of various alternatives and resulting implications for affected departments and agencies throughout the Executive Branch. "Lots of times a decision memo would come in that he wasn't satisfied with and he'd ask me in, give it back, and say, 'Look, these guys aren't ready for the meeting yet. Scrub it. Don't let them in until they get their act together.' "[34]

Moreover, Ford usually would not accept papers brought to him by Cabinet members and White House staff who attempted to circumvent the "staff system." When documents were left with the president during a meeting, they were returned with other memoranda to Connor. In these instances, the staff secretary purposely did not convey the president's decision, feigned ignorance about the proposal, and sent the document through the "system." Instead of gaining time, individuals might wait two or three weeks for a decision, and then receive an angry telephone call from the chief of staff about the importance of following White House procedures. (Exceptions to the routinized system of information flow were documents relating to national security issues that General Brent Scowcroft, national security adviser, might take directly to the president to maintain confidentiality. Even Scowcroft, however, tried to use the staff secretary's system for most other items of business.)

Despite the presidential and staff allegiance to this system of information flow, certain individuals, such as Cabinet members and the vice president, were guaranteed that papers submitted by them would reach the president quickly. According to Cheney, "We would try to put it through the system, but within so many hours it had to land on his desk even if it hadn't been staffed out yet, just so he would know it was there. Cabinet members knew they could get through."[35]

The "staffing system" in Ford's White House served at least two main purposes: to provide the president with input from more than one staff member on an issue and to lengthen the decision-making process sufficiently so that potential problems or disadvantages resulting from a decision could be uncovered or discovered as information was evaluated. As will be discussed later in this section, the strength of the staff system was giving a decision time to "cook" among the president and his staff; however, in crisis situations the system was not used to the extent that the president was prevented from making a decision quickly if a situation warranted immediate action.

Members of Gerald Ford's senior staff interviewed for this study generally were very supportive of the organization's staffing system. One criticism, however, was articulated by Robert Hartmann, who served Ford as chief of staff during his vice presidential years and became counselor to the president, in charge of speechwriting, when Ford assumed the presidency. Hartmann, who was skeptical of the loyalty of former Nixon staff members to President Ford, often was in conflict with Alexander Haig during the first weeks of the administration and, at times, with other members of the senior staff. Although he was included on the distribution list for decision memoranda covering a wide range of issues, he explains one potential problem with the staffing system:

> When they're preparing those decision papers, they send them around to a great circle of people for comments before they take them to the president. But by whom you include in that circle and by whom you leave off the list for distribution for this piece of paper, you could pretty well decide whether there's going to be a great majority of opinion on your staff . . . that we should do this or not.[36]

Despite these concerns, which are germane to the use of a reliable formal system of information flow in a White House, the senior aides interviewed for this study believe that the routing system used for decision memoranda in the Ford White House did not exclude input from those who could contribute ideas and opinions to the discussion of an issue requiring a presidential decision. Nevertheless, Ford sought information from other sources to ensure exposure to a variety of viewpoints.

The president read the *New York Times* and the *Washington Post* each morning in the residence and, like his predecessors, received daily intelligence briefings upon arriving at the Oval Office. He also received a Weekly Domestic Activities Report from the domestic policy staff that included updates on congressional legislation in specific domestic areas. Results of conferences and meetings affecting domestic legislation were mentioned in this document, as were any plans to present the president with decision memoranda on a specific piece of legislation he might wish to send to Congress. Additionally, according to Hartmann: "He got all this mail: professional publications, trade publications, and in his limousine he'd keep a great stack of papers. . . . He'd go through them to see if he could find something interesting in them. He had that quality which I know Nixon didn't have."[37]

Ford, like FDR, was particularly interested in getting information orally, from senior staff as well as individuals outside the White House. In his autobiography he mentions Jack Marsh, counselor to the president, as an important informal source of information.

> Jack seemed to know everything about the internal workings of the White House. He would tell me who was feuding with whom and what the problems were, and he would give me his recommendations for smoothing everything out. More than anyone else, he was the man who bridged the gap between the Nixon and Ford staffs. He had a knack for getting along well with everyone, his suggestions were almost always good and I could give him the worst conceivable problem to solve.[38]

The president also was concerned that Cabinet officers have sufficient access to him, not only through their written comments in the decision memoranda packages but also in face-to-face meetings. According to Connor, who served Ford as Cabinet secretary as well as staff secretary, regularly scheduled meetings were held between the president and individual Cabinet officers ''on a one-on-one basis—just the two of them and me and that was it. There was no chief of staff there, no other White House staff there.''[39] Additionally, Ford sought to increase internal communication between White House staff and the Cabinet departments. In a memo sent to members of the White House staff on May 1, 1975, Connor wrote: ''The President has indicated that he would like to have a greater involvement of Sub-Cabinet members with the Senior White House Staff. Such involvement should include regular briefings and discussions with the Sub-Cabinet members as well as social contact using some of the facilities available to the White House.''[40]

As a creature of Congress, the president also valued input from his former colleagues. In an interview with the author he emphasized:

> That . . . is an advantage for a person who comes from the Congress rather than a person who comes from the outside, like Mr. Carter and Mr. Reagan. They don't have the luxury of going to leaders in the Congress on a personal basis, whether you agree philosophically or not . . . I would reach out and not always at the initiation of my staff.[41]

In fact, Ford writes in his autobiography, ''From the moment I became President, I set aside several hours a week for any member of Congress who wanted to come and see me privately.''[42] The president often telephoned certain congressmen or senators regarding specific legislation, and senior staff would provide him a written overview of the issue and suggested points he might make during the conversation. Ford also used a ''kitchen cabinet,'' comprised of friends and former congressional colleagues, to supplement the viewpoints provided by his senior staff. It included a former governor, representatives of business and industry, and officials from previous administrations. According to Ford:

> At least once every six weeks they would troop into the Cabinet Room, roll up their shirtsleeves and tell me what they thought of the job I was doing as President. They were

free to praise or criticize. When things were getting tough, they gave me encouragement and said the Administration was pursuing the right course. When things were picking up, they kept me from getting carried away with myself. . . . And they gave me blunt advice when I needed it most.[43]

FORD AS DECISION MAKER

Aware of the problems Richard Nixon created for himself by limiting the number of people involved in decision making, and responding to his personal preference for discussion and debate fostered during his years in Congress, Gerald Ford encouraged the use of small group meetings in the White House to enhance his review of information after reading the packaged sets of papers and other written materials sent to him. Indeed, "the mechanism that was developed was consciously an attempt to pattern itself on much of what had been the Nixon structure with an overlay of personal meetings."[44] According to Terrence O'Donnell, Ford preferred "to have contact with people who were recommending the decisions and to talk it over at the table and . . . have a lively debate."[45] Obviously the amount of discussion a decision warranted varied, depending on the nature of the decision and its potential consequences—and whether it was a decision prompted by a foreign or a domestic crisis. According to Rumsfeld, "Sometimes a major issue would get discussed fifty times," and there might be ongoing discussions for several months on a legislative proposal.[46] However, in crisis situations the president might make a decision in a meeting with four or five advisers in attendance. Ford recalls his preferred decision-making process as follows:

I preferred on major decisions where I knew there might be a difference of opinion between Cabinet officers, that we . . . have the Cabinet meeting and the pros and cons would be discussed and then I would usually not make the decision right there. I would say within twelve hours or at the most twenty-four hours I would give the decision to the chief of staff to then relay it to the various departments.[47]

During the first weeks of Ford's presidency, when the White House was in a state of disarray, Alexander Haig as chief of staff would bring lists of options to the new president at least once a day, and often more frequently. Over time, however, Ford abandoned this dependence on Haig, to decrease his influence over decision making and generally to improve the decision-making process by allowing for increased debate and deliberation before decisions were made. Nevertheless, Ford made some decisions by choosing between alternatives provided by his staff in written memoranda. Alan Greenspan, head of economic policy formulation in the Ford White House, occasionally sent several pages of economic policy options on long-term issues to the president, who would check off responses such as "yes," "no," "talk to me."[48]

As a former congressman, Ford appreciated the importance of discussion before making a decision. As president, he soon realized the necessity of presidential–staff communication because of the nature of the decisions facing him:

Almost by definition, the decisions that must be made in the Oval Office are difficult. If they're easy, they're made elsewhere in the federal bureaucracy. Invariably, those that wind up on the President's desk have an equal number of supporters and opponents, an equal number of pluses and minuses, and an equal number of people who will scream bloody murder when the decisions are announced.[49]

Accordingly, Ford approached decision making as a deliberative process, as did Franklin Roosevelt, allowing his advisers time to discover the potential ramifications of the options he considered. Staff members recall his approach to decision making, in the presence of key aides and advisers, as follows. According to Ron Nessen, "He would sit back and . . . puff on his pipe and not really say very much and listen around the table as people discussed and argued and stated their positions, and he'd just sit there and puff on his pipe. And then after he'd heard enough, he would lean forward and then you knew he was going to make his decision."[50] Philip Buchen, White House counsel, recalls: "He certainly wasn't abrupt. . . . I think he liked to see the paper first but then liked to get into give-and-take. He wasn't shy about that."[51] Richard Cheney, who as Ford's second chief of staff sat in many meetings with the president, describes Ford as follows:

A man who loved the give-and-take of political debate and dialogue. The kind of guy you could go into and argue with over policy. He would never deny you access because you disagreed with him. You could come back two hours later and do it all over again. He was very good at sitting down around the table and listening to the debate and the dialogue and having issues argued out in front of him. He was good at receiving bad news, things that a lot of people wouldn't want to hear. . . . He wouldn't kick you out because you came in and gave him some tough, hard-nosed advice. . . . He was a good decision maker in the sense of being able to make a decision and not look back. He'd weigh the options and alternatives . . . make his decision and . . . move on to the next one.[52]

In an interview with Trevor Arbrister on October 21, 1977, Nelson Rockefeller assessed Gerald Ford as a decision maker, describing his patience during decision-making sessions with staff. Rockefeller was somewhat critical of the effort Ford made to listen to the viewpoints of his staff.

He would listen with a patience . . . equal to that of Job to different points of view way beyond the point of [sic] which I would have listened. And then when somebody would finish and sometimes in my opinion it was very repetitive . . . going way beyond the simple statement of a position, when he got through he would make no indication whatsoever of his reaction so that you had no way of telling in a meeting what he was thinking. He might at the end of a meeting say what he thought, what decision he had made, or he might not. At some time later he would then state his position or he would say he wanted more information. And he was a prodigious reader of papers, getting up at 5 o'clock in the morning and reading all this mass of material. Personally I thought people abused his patience by talking too much and writing reams of material which were what I would call rationalizations of a point whereas you can put down precisely and concisely the facts without all the rationalizations and save a lot of time. But he had this tremendous patience.[53]

Rockefeller's views illustrate his concern about the administration of the decision-making process specifically and the operation of the White House in general. It is therefore not surprising that he entertained thoughts of becoming Ford's chief of staff while simultaneously serving as vice president; neither is it surprising that his idea was not popular with the president or Ford's closest aides (see Chapter 4). Rockefeller's observations were, however, echoed by Juan Cameron. According to Cameron, the decision-making process in the Ford White House sometimes suffered from delays while options and alternatives received considerable discussion.

Staff meetings have sometimes deteriorated into "brainstorming sessions" in which, according to one participant, "too many people were popping off with ideas that obviously came right off the top of their heads." The result, according to the same critic, was that decisions were left hanging—and were made by the President later in consultation with his political advisers.[54]

Nevertheless, Ford's insistence on receiving information provided orally during group meetings afforded the president an opportunity to hear opinions that might have been omitted from written material. Philip Buchen acknowledges that in many instances Ford's staff purposely avoided putting candid remarks on paper because of changes in information disclosure laws prompted by the Watergate scandal. A review of numerous White House memoranda and discussions with archivists in the Gerald Ford Library confirm that many documents lack the richness of personal opinion and candor that apparently characterized internal memoranda in other administrations. Ford's use of discussions to supplement written information therefore gave him the opportunity to assess the depth and breadth of support or disagreement individual staff members had about a given issue—contextual information not always apparent in a memorandum.

Within two months of Richard Nixon's resignation, Ford essentially had adopted the system of written information flow into the Oval Office used by his predecessor. What made his office more accessible to staff and Cabinet members was his willingness to accept information from multiple sources, using more than one channel of communication, such as group discussions and individual consultations.

Terrence O'Donnell, who worked for both Nixon and Ford, summarizes their differences as users of information:

President Nixon saw fewer people and had many, many less appointments than did President Ford. He preferred to make decisions based on well-crafted staff papers with all the views of the various players stated therein. Ford . . . preferred . . . to have contact with the people who were making recommendations. Ford would have long meetings with these people and would hear everybody out oftentimes before making a decision. Nixon . . . wanted to have this done by the staff. He wanted a concise statement of their positions . . . a good, concise briefing paper and he'd act on that. Only reluctantly, if he felt that he really needed to see people, would he schedule a meeting to help him make a decision. At the president's request, Bob Haldeman really had control of this process—every appointment with Nixon and every single piece of paper, total control.[55]

James T. Lynn, director of the Office of Management and Budget in the Ford administration and secretary of housing and urban development from 1973 to 1975, has compared the decision-making processes of Nixon and Ford, praising Ford's use of orally presented information. "Because . . . in a world where not everyone can get the exact nuance in a writing of what their position really is, a head-to-head discussion gives the President an opportunity to verify various positions of the players, to sniff out nuances and the tradeoffs. Now this was a fundamental difference between those White Houses."[56] In Brent Scowcroft's opinion, however, the principal difference between Nixon's and Ford's decision-making processes was due to their different personalities.

Both President Nixon and Bob Haldeman were more formidable people personally. They were not open and warm in the sense of accessibility. And one thought very seriously before you asked to go in and get a decision reversed. Because the cabinet officers and the staff members knew that if you went in there frivolously there were going to be problems and penalties down the road. That was not true with President Ford. The result was that the process tended to not only open up but be treated a little more cavalierly because the people knew they would always have another word.[57]

The system of information flow to the president in both the Nixon and the Ford administrations was essentially the same. However, the chief of staff in the Ford White House sometimes was bypassed because Rumsfeld and Cheney had confidence in Connor's abilities, intuition, and tenacity. Connor apparently could distinguish those items which needed to be seen by the chief of staff before taking them to the president, and he was entrusted with the task of making that distinction. Additionally, Rumsfeld particularly was known for instilling in his staff an appreciation of the importance of adequate information flow to the president. During his years in the Ford White House he disseminated "Rumsfeld's Rules," which he had begun compiling while serving in the Nixon administration. These "rules" were his guidelines for being an effective White House staff member, and include recommendations related to staff involvement in information flow and decision making:

A President needs multiple sources of information—work to insure adequate success. Avoid overly restricting the flow of paper, people or ideas to the President, even as you strive to avoid wasting his time.

Don't be a bottleneck in the flow of paper or decisions.

Don't allow people to be cut out of a meeting or an opportunity to communicate because their views may differ from the President's views, the views of the person setting up the meeting, or your views. Include them. The staff system must have discipline to serve the President well.

The staffing system on Presidential decisions must have integrity, and be known to have integrity. When the President is making a decision, either be sure he has the recommendations of appropriate people, or conversely, that he knows he does not have their views and is willing to accept the disadvantages that will inevitably result, such as key people being out of phase, unhappy, or less effective as a result of being seen as having been "cut out."[58]

This last rule is particularly important because the staffing system used in the Ford administration depends on the integrity of those charged with eliciting input from all appropriate sources on matters requiring presidential decisions. Such a system is successful only if it provides the president with information from a variety of sources with divergent viewpoints. A president is not well served by a chief of staff, staff secretary, or information distribution system that orchestrates the input of opinion from a few staff members in agreement on an issue, and fails to solicit responses from those who may hold differing opinions or have access to data that conflict with the majority's recommendation.

According to several of the individuals interviewed for this study, Gerald Ford apparently did make the decision to pardon Nixon without soliciting a variety of staff input on the options open to him, although he convened most members of his senior staff to inform them of the decision before it was made public. Perhaps no other decision in his presidency prompted as much public criticism of Ford, and there are those among his former advisers who claim it cost him a second term in office. Yet Ford did not believe the decision to pardon Richard Nixon was an appropriate one for staff comment because of the unique circumstances surrounding the issue. According to Ron Nessen, Ford's decision in November 1975 to initiate major personnel changes in his Cabinet, dubbed "the Sunday night massacre," and the pardon decision were made "in a similar, secretive manner. He seemed to be following a pattern of acting alone and instinctively on important matters about which he had strong personal feelings."[59]

Over a decade after leaving the White House, Gerald Ford still praised the systems of information flow used during his administration. "I don't know of any major decision I made where I didn't have adequate information. I made some bad judgments, but it wasn't for lack of information at my disposal. The process was not faulty."[60]

INFORMATION FLOW IN JIMMY CARTER'S WHITE HOUSE

The relative success of the formal system of information flow instituted in the Ford White House was directly related to the decision to *modify* his "spokes-of-the-wheel" organizational structure, and put the "staff coordinator" and staff secretary in charge of information flow into the Oval Office. Until he appointed Hamilton Jordan as chief of staff in the summer of 1979, Jimmy Carter utilized the spokes-of-the-wheel structure, and the formal system of information flow was affected accordingly. Documents, memoranda, and notes came into the office from more than one channel, even though the staff secretary, Richard Hutcheson, attempted to organize and transmit information to the president via a system similar to that used in the Ford White House. However, several avenues were open to senior staff through which they could communicate to the president in writing. Sometimes memos were sent directly to the president, bypassing the staff secretary; other times memoranda and correspondence reached Carter through his personal secretary, Susan Clough.

According to a senior archivist at the Jimmy Carter Library, some documents in the Carter archives indicate that important messages, or those from the president's close friends and/or advisers, would be taken to the president by Clough "without going through the staff secretary mechanism."[61] According to Zbigniew Brzezinski:

> I could take a memo directly to him outside the system. In other words, it didn't go through whomever was there routing memos. My memos went to Susan Clough, if I chose to give them to Susan Clough, or I could walk into his office when he wasn't there and just leave it in his in-box.[62]

The staff secretary's frustration with aides' attempts to circumvent the formal system of paper flow to the president is evidenced in a memorandum written by Hutcheson to Robert Lipshutz on December 19, 1977, almost a year after Carter's inauguration.

> As recently as last Monday, the President asked again that all members of his staff cooperate with the established system, and submit papers to him through my office rather than directly. . . . Either Bill Simon or I are in the office every day of the year. If we are not in at the time you have finished with a memo, it can be left on my desk, or, if it is classified, left in the Situation Room with a note to me that it can be picked up there. Please cooperate with the system in the future.[63]

Part of the frustration evidenced in this memo was based on concerted attempts, since the first days of the Carter term, to decrease the amount of written material reaching the president. Carter writes in his autobiography:

> At first, sixty or seventy documents arrived on my desk each day, some of them consisting of many pages of detailed analysis. There would be proposals from Cabinet officers that

I had to approve; correspondence to sign; presidential appointments . . . to be considered; reports from meetings in the Situation Room on foreign, intelligence, or defense subjects; facts about legislation before Congress; or proposals we were developing to send to Capitol Hill. Throughout the day, I would also receive copies of news bulletins and diplomatic reports that Jody or Zbig thought I should see.[64]

Carter acknowledges that after several weeks he realized the amount of written material flowing into the Oval Office had to be reduced. Consequently he met with staff to review the documents he regularly received and arranged to have some delegated to staff for analysis; others were abbreviated. Concurrently, some senior staff actively attempted to curtail the amount of written information they were routinely sending to the president.

Zbigniew Brzezinski describes how he worked to prevent information overload on the president after Carter's first few weeks in office:

At first I would send him a great deal with a cover memo saying, ''Please look at the introduction, look at the conclusion, look at the clipped pages. Here is my analysis. Here are the other points of view. You have some options.'' And the whole thing would come back to me annotated from beginning to end. He would read the whole damn thing. And so after awhile I realized if I sent him something, he was going to read it, and I better not send as much as I used to. Initially I used to send him most of the stuff that was meant for him from the principal secretaries—Defense, State, CIA. . . . He would read it all, and then be spending hours each day, hours, hours. That was in multiple scores of pages. At one point I did a little . . . study of how much paper was destined for him [just from Brzezinski's office]. It averaged almost 300 pages a day. So then I pared it down very drastically to about 30 to 40 pages a day and the rest of the stuff I either summarized or did not send to him. I would simply send the memo back to the department secretary, saying ''It has been received and unless subsequent action is needed, it's being digested.''[65]

Protecting the president from reams of written material apparently was a concern to Carter aides other than Brzezinski. For instance, a memo dated December 14, 1977, prepared by an anonymous author and found in the archival files of Robert Lipshutz, stresses several ways that senior staff could reduce paper flow to the president. The writer suggests that staff members encourage the president to be more critical of long and unnecessary memos from his senior staff, submit fewer memos to the president, send weekly summaries of their ideas and accomplishments rather than daily ''reports,'' and be more critical of documents circulated to them for comment, and urges staff and Cabinet officers to write joint memos whenever possible.[66] According to the memo:

The greatest paperwork burdens generally are associated with major decisions or major policy proposals. . . . A major reduction in the President's paperwork will result only from: (a) a conscious decision by the President to study fewer of the details of his major decisions; or (b) limiting the easy access—on paper, in person and by telephone—presently accorded to the Senior Staff and Cabinet.[67]

Consequently, it appears the spokes-of-the-wheel concept had major deleterious effects on the amount of information flowing into the Oval Office, at least during Carter's first year in office.

Part of the paper flow problem that apparently faced the president was of his own making. He preferred to receive information in writing to conserve time. "Instead of holding a five- or ten-minute conversation (at least), I could read a brief memorandum and make a decision in a matter of moments and I could do this at odd times throughout the day."[68] Additionally, Carter preferred to send written feedback to his aides, rather than communicating with them face-to-face. He sent responses to written questions by making comments in margins and then returning memos to their authors. Often he sent handwritten comments and instructions to senior staff on notepad paper. The president thought this form of written communication saved him time and personalized his messages.

It is not clear that Jimmy Carter's preference for responding to memos and documents from his aides in writing did indeed save him time. The perceptions of members of his senior staff are that it was a relatively time-consuming form of feedback. However, they were impressed by his attention to each subject they presented in writing, and by his recognition of their work. According to Anne Wexler, "He never, ever didn't read or send back a piece of paper. I have books full of memos with Carter's writing all over them in the margins."[69] Nevertheless, Wexler emphasizes that Carter's interest in thoroughly informing himself about a subject, and his writing questions and reflections about it in memos to aides, were wrongfully criticized as too much attention to detail.

> I don't think he was immersed in too much paper. I think he was a man who was interested in . . . not only the things that he got from his staff and from his Cabinet, but he read a lot of newspapers and a lot of magazines. . . . If you're really going to make decisions and when the buck really does stop at your desk, you better damn well know what the intricacies of that decision really are. And he did.[70]

According to Stuart Eizenstat, the standard method of communication in the Carter White House was the written memorandum.

> I was responsible for preparing decision memoranda on domestic positions. Frequently, though not always, I would suggest that if there was a particular important . . . or divisive issue . . . those memoranda [should] be followed up by meetings with the principals, in which I would participate. But more often than not, the president liked to make decisions from paper and I would get back . . . his handwritten comments.[71]

In Eizenstat's opinion, Carter might have been too immersed in paper and overly attentive to policy details in his first year in office, but not thereafter.

> He felt like he had a steep learning curve and he wanted to have a body of knowledge under his belt. . . . He did a lot of reading. He did enjoy getting the details of issues from the beginning to the end of his presidency, but he did a much better job after a year or

year and a half of insisting on shorter memos. Indeed, the first Camp had, at which the whole relationship between the White House and th changed, came as a result of the fact that he was getting too much paper, . . . He wasn't satisfied making a decision unless he felt he really kn it. In that respect, I think he demanded more material than other p would really not say it was excessive after the first year to year and a half.[72]

Zbigniew Brzezinski reiterates that attention to detail was not necessarily a presidential fault in the Carter White House even during the first months of his administration.

He was so fast, so intelligent and so scrupulous that when you gave him a document, he felt that he shouldn't just look at the annotated parts . . . but look at the whole thing, because he may not agree with my annotations. . . . He was compensating for the fact that he knew less [than his principal foreign policy advisers] and he wanted to learn.[73]

According to Carter's national security adviser, the president's attention to detail was exaggerated as an information-processing problem during his administration, in part because the president possessed the ''ability to grasp complicated memos very quickly, the capacity to digest an enormous amount of information and to respond to it intelligently and promptly.''[74]

Nevertheless, Jack Watson confirms that some Carter staff advised the president to limit the number of personal notes he wrote to them. ''Communication of information via writing is . . . really sort of one-dimensional and communication in person is multidimensional. . . . I think that he would have benefited from a somewhat more informal, more give-and-take, more personally interactive style.''[75] Although Watson emphasizes that Carter's review of written material was ''superimposed on top of all the meetings,'' and that his dedication to reading documents and memoranda was possible largely because he was a speed reader and put in a long day's work, he advised the president to spend more time in face-to-face communication.[76]

It has always been my opinion, and I said to him . . . both in person and in written communication . . . that personal interactions would be very valuable, that while he had a truly remarkable capacity for gathering, assimilating, sorting, applying information via the written word, and that would serve him well, that he needed to be very careful not to rely on that too much.[77]

Watson's major form of communication with the president was through short memos and notes.

Carter's interest in understanding informational details prior to making decisions perhaps was due in part to his training as an engineer and in part to personal preferences in the assimilation and evaluation of information that developed during his years as Georgia's governor. Hans Mark, secretary of the air force under Carter, suggests that the president's hunger for information was related to "his mental frame, maybe even his fundamentalism, his sense of duty, and last but not least, his nuclear training, where you are taught to be very attentive to detail which in a nuclear submarine you have to be."[78] On the other hand, Hamilton Jordan traced the president's use of written information to his years as governor of Georgia. In a published interview in February 1977, one month after Carter's inauguration, Jordan explained that he began writing memos to the governor to avoid being outdebated by him. "I learned in the Governor's office that if I went in prepared to argue five points with him, I would never get past the first point before he started arguing back. So now I put it down on paper first and then go in and discuss it with him."[79]

Whatever the reasons for his attention to detail, for which he was much criticized by the press and some political pundits, Carter states the philosophy that guided his interest in absorption of facts, figures, and concepts in his autobiography.

> From the beginning, I realized that my ability to govern well would depend upon my mastery of the extremely important issues I faced. I wanted to learn as much as possible and devoted full time to it, just as I had done as a young submarine officer, a businessman, a governor, and a political candidate running against enormous odds to be elected President.[80]

The criticism of Carter's attention to detail was underscored during his presidency in press accounts of his supposed administration of the White House tennis court schedule. According to several senior aides interviewed for this study, Carter's secretary, not the president, kept a listing of when the tennis court was available for staff use. Jody Powell emphasizes that the president attempted to share that recreational facility with staff members when he had no plans to use it, and instead was criticized for monitoring its use. Powell and other aides to Carter believe the president's interest in informational details was exaggerated during his presidency—that there were substantive reasons, such as those mentioned in this chapter, for his interest in the facts and figures that flowed into the Oval Office each day in the form of memos and briefing papers. Another possible reason for the president's concern about the letter, as well as the spirit, of proposed policies and legislation is that he sought personally to compensate for a senior staff comprised mostly of individuals with little or no federal legislative experience, who were outsiders in both the political and the social circles within Washington. In other words, to ensure that his organization would be adequately informed on issues and potential policies, he felt compelled to read and understand the details presented in position papers and decision memoranda.

Additionally, Carter's personal investment of time in the study of written material may have been related to a concern that he not repeat Richard Nixon's mistakes and become isolated from the policy-making process. Even though he and Nixon both preferred the perusal of documents to frequent participation in discussion and debate with several staff present, Carter had no interest in divorcing himself from the day-to-day work of the White House. It appears, however, that there might have been a middle ground between isolation and saturation that he did not find. Whatever the reasons for his interest in details, he paid a political and public relations price for what appeared to be unnecessary presidential involvement in the review and assessment of the written information that reached the Oval Office. And yet, despite perceptions of Carter as a devotee of only the written word, he did receive information from his staff, as well as from sources outside the White House, in a variety of communication formats.

Among Jimmy Carter's staff, those from whom he received most of his information were Jody Powell, Hamilton Jordan, and Zbigniew Brzezinski, because of the organizational roles they assumed in his organization. According to Edward Feigenbaum:

> Where Powell served to relay information to Carter from the outside world, Jordan was firmly ensconced in the White House machinery, feeding internal information to the President in his ever-increasing daily walk-in visits. . . . He sought to establish discipline and accountability among the presidential staff, while screening both people and paperwork and making routine decisions for the President.[81]

The president's first scheduled meeting every day, however, was with Brzezinski, who would bring to Carter the Presidential Daily Briefing. This document, distributed to only five individuals, summarized defense and foreign affairs developments on a day-to-day basis. In addition to these regularly scheduled meetings, Carter would see his national security adviser "several times during the day at different hours."[82] According to Brzezinski, "I . . . could walk into his office unannounced . . . anytime—whether he had an appointment or was due at an appointment . . . I could phone him anytime I wanted—night or day."[83] He emphasizes that Carter did not rely solely on written information in the process of decision making—he also brainstormed with aides. "On foreign policy issues he did a lot of talking, particularly with Vance [Secretary of State Cyrus Vance], Brown [Secretary of Defense Harold Brown], myself, and, to some extent, Mondale."[84]

Although he did not meet as frequently with his senior staff as some of them might have preferred, the president did meet with a small group of senior aides at 10 A.M. each day, at least during the latter months of his presidency.[85] His support for these meetings generally hinged on his assessment of whether each was worth his time. Prior to the meeting with the president, the senior staff convened at 8 A.M. for thirty to forty-five minutes to discuss, in Wexler's words, "the problems of the day, what we had to do with the president, the president's schedule, speeches for the future, ideas, whatever it was we needed to talk about."[86] In mid–1979, after appointing Hamilton Jordan chief of staff, Carter gave the responsibility of convening staff meetings to him. Additionally, he allowed the chief of staff to participate in those meetings involving the president's principal foreign policy advisers.

In addition to meeting with his senior staff, Carter visited with several "senior advisers" he appointed toward the end of his term to provide ideas and insights from external perspectives. According to Hedley Donovan, who came to the White House from *Time* magazine, the president's appointment of these "outsiders" was an admission that he needed an "older, broader, more diversified staff," and that he had an "isolation problem," or at least a perception of one.[87] Consequently, Donovan recalls:

> I had a number of private meetings with the President. Usually every other week we would have a formally scheduled thirty to forty-five minute meeting. It was understood I could get at him any time between those meetings if I had something I felt should be brought up right away. When I did want to see him, I would get to see him the same day. Those were brief five, ten, fifteen minute meetings, almost entirely on my initiative, seldom his.
>
> He urged me to write him memos when I was so moved and I was so moved quite often. . . . He would read my memos very promptly. I would almost always get his comment back by the end of the same day, or the following morning.[88]

Donovan's comment does not depict a president overwhelmingly interested in advice and counsel from those he selected to advise him. Nor did Carter apparently spend much time during his workday in discussions with staff to supplement information obtained in written communications. According to Professor Robert J. Thompson, who has conducted a comparative analysis of the Daily Diaries from the Ford and Carter White Houses, Carter's staff

> had private contact with him over 150 more times [than did Ford's staff], but . . . they spent less than 50% of the amount of time with him that Ford's staff spent with him in comparable interactions. Carter apparently preferred more frequent contact with more people, but preferred it in relatively small amounts of time. Even Hamilton Jordan and Jody Powell did not spend much time with him on an individual basis. The only person in the sample who stands out is Bert Lance. . . . He appears to have been the only close Carter aide with whom the president was willing to interact with [sic] on a private basis for any extended period of time.[89]

Interestingly, Thompson's study reveals that Carter spoke to Charles Kirbo, an Atlanta lawyer and the president's closest friend, at least every other day by telephone.[90]

The evidence substantiates comments from interviews with several of Carter's senior aides that the president relied more readily on written, rather than orally presented, information. However, the information he sought from sources outside the White House generally came to him through group discussions, particularly at the beginning of his term.

Carter writes with great pride in his autobiography about his efforts to seek ideas and advice from congressional leaders, including a meeting he held in Georgia with key senators and congressman shortly after his election.[91] Additionally, in early January 1977, he met with Congress's Democratic leadership as well as the members of both parties who served on committees related to foreign policy. In Carter's words:

> No President-elect had ever held such a conference. We covered the gamut of issues in international relations we would face together. These extensive discussions allowed me to learn more about the congressional committee structure, to size up the individual members, and to let my diplomatic and defense teams learn from and be known by the leaders of Congress.[92]

After his inauguration, at least for a time, Carter held working breakfasts with the Democratic leaders in Congress and participated in meetings with legislative committees: "I spent many good evenings having supper and then a lively discussion of domestic and foreign affairs with groups of as many as a hundred members of Congress."[93] The quality of information shared in meetings with this many individuals is certainly questionable—one wonders how much information of use in decision making was shared in this setting. Also in question is the degree to which Carter used the information he supposedly sought in various meetings with congressional leaders. As is the case with all organizational leaders, presidents must listen as well as speak during interactions with those invited to offer opinions. In Carter's case, considering his lack of success in working with the congressional leaders of his own party, convening meetings did not ensure that communication took place among the parties involved—or that information sought was ultimately information used.

At one point in the middle of Carter's term, Hamilton Jordan apparently recognized the president's propensity to insulate himself from opinions of those who did not support his programs and policies. In a confidential memo to the president, Jordan suggested the president develop a mechanism for hearing ideas and opinions from individuals other than the White House staff.

> I have been concerned that you and all of us talk too much to one another and don't have the benefit of different points of view that challenge some of the basic premises on which our decisions are made. I think the real challenge is to assemble a small group of people that you trust and are comfortable with and have the collective experience to provide you with advice on foreign policy, domestic issues, your image and the politics of the Presidency. . . . .
>
> There are several criteria that are important:
>
> —The people in the group should be able to keep their mouths shut.
>
> —They should not be people actively involved in the political process . . .
>
> —They should not be a part of your Administration.[94]

Jordan suggested a meeting of individuals such as Clark Clifford, Harry McPherson, Lawrence O'Brien, Jack Valenti, Willard Wirtz, and Arthur Goldberg—voices from past Democratic presidencies. He also recommended that Rosalynn

Carter and Vice President Mondale be invited to all meetings, along with Charles Kirbo. Carter returned this memo to Jordan, indicating in handwriting on its first page that he'd been "waiting for weeks" for such a suggestion but emphasized, "no commitment or prediction of any additional meetings until after we assess this one."[95]

By July 1979, when Carter restructured his White House, appointed Jordan chief of staff, and dismissed certain Cabinet members, little advice from outside the White House had been enthusiastically sought by the president. An excerpt from his diary, written after several days of intensely analyzing his presidency with several groups of external advisers, reveals that the reassessment of his presidency had forced him to spend 90 percent of his time listening. "I worked hard all week, some of the more strenuous work of my life. Also, it's not easy for me to accept criticism and to reassess my ways of doing things. And this was a week of intense reassessment."[96] It was a reassessment, however, that came too late with too little impact on the remainder of his presidency, in part because for some time Carter had limited, on a daily, ongoing basis, the sources from which he sought information to make decisions important to the development of the administration's goals, policies, and legislative agenda.

CARTER AS DECISION MAKER

Like Gerald Ford, Carter made decisions after he had read briefing documents and then discussed options with small groups of White House staff and appropriate Cabinet members. In his words:

> I found through experience that a collegial approach—with a group discussing the issue as equals—is good, provided the gathering includes primarily those who will be directly involved in carrying out the decision or explaining it to the public. Most often, the smaller number of people, the more productive the discussion. A President's time is too precious to waste on many bull sessions among those who have little to contribute; but I cannot deny that . . . I sometimes permitted people to come into a discussion just so they would not be embarrassed or upset about being excluded.[97]

According to Carter, he informed his close advisers about significant decisions he intended to make, giving them an opportunity to appeal. "But once I made a final judgment, I expected them to honor it even if they had strongly advised a different course of action."[98]

In describing the president's approach to decision making, most of the individuals interviewed for this study discuss his use of small group meetings to substantiate and enrich the information received in written briefing materials. According to Wexler: "He would read the paper, look at the options, and have a meeting . . . in which the various . . . people who were agreeing or disagreeing about the policy would make their cases. He would listen and then he would decide."[99] Jody Powell also recalls the president's preference for reading and then listening to discussions of issues. "Not in every case, but on things it seemed to me that . . . he liked to have a chance, if not to p in, to listen to the arguments and debates of people making the case fo courses of action. . . . Sometimes . . . he would make a decision rig ere. Sometimes he'd sleep on it."[100] According to Powell, Carter might share "some particular directions or inclinations" with staff as the decision-making process began "so you would know where he was coming from."[101] His tendency to discuss policy options with aides before making a decision may have caused him to err "on the side of openness," in Powell's opinion. "His deep concern about making the best decision that he possibly could and for giving people a chance to state their case when they felt strongly meant that some people always took advantage of that and there were probably times when he allowed people to come back one more time to argue their side."[102] Echoing Powell's comments, Cyrus Vance, Carter's secretary of state, writes in his account of his role in the Carter administration:

> He listened carefully and wanted the fullest discussion before making decisions. He was, if anything, willing to permit debate to go on too long and to try to absorb every detail and nuance before making his decision. The president encouraged frankness and accepted disagreement on policy from his advisers. He did not want to be shielded from unpleasant facts, hard options, or difficult decisions.[103]

Brzezinski remembers that Carter tended to "go along" if there was unanimity of opinion among his advisers on a given foreign policy, but convened a meeting of his principal foreign policy aides if there was a division of opinion among them.[104]

Except in times of crisis, a president's thorough review of facts and his interest in discussing decision alternatives with key advisers, time-consuming practices though they may be, are not weaknesses. They allow for time to assess the ramifications of potential solutions so as to select the one that appears to be the most appropriate at a given point in time. However, a president's concern about making the right choices may cause him, like other organizational leaders, to avoid delegating decision-making responsibility—even for decisions that might appropriately be made at lower organizational levels. According to Brzezinski: "He [Carter] did not like to delegate what I would call non-presidential level issues to his immediate subordinates. . . . He was reluctant to do that. . . . I would report to him . . . actions that I would take on his behalf and while he never really violently objected, I could tell he was extremely uneasy about it."[105]

Brzezinski speculates that the reason for Carter's unwillingness to delegate such decisions stemmed from

> a reaction to . . . a kind of feeling that Ford delegated too much and, secondly, and much more specifically, a desire not to have anyone be perceived outside the White House as playing the role in foreign policy that Kissinger played in relationship to Ford. He was very much afraid that he would be viewed as a president that was excessively influenced by . . . me.[106]

Brzezinski was not afraid to stand by the decisions he made or the policy options he recommended to the president, even if they were at odds with the secretary of state. As a result, part of Carter's uneasiness when hearing reports of Brzezinski's decisions may have related to a concern that he would be caught in the middle of policy differences between his secretary of state and his national security adviser, and that he would be placed in the role of mediator in intra-administration conflicts.

Carter has written that he delegated as much decision-making responsibility as possible, and Wexler confirms that the president "was a much better delegator than anybody in the outside had any reason to believe . . . because there is all this mythology about attention to detail."[107] The president's response to comments about his tendency to avoid delegation of decision-making responsibilities is that:

> the more difficult an issue is to resolve, the more likely his [a president's] advisers are to be equally divided about it and the less eager they are to go on record with an answer that might later be criticized. I tried never to duck the more controversial issues nor to put an onerous responsibility on others when it was rightfully mine. After the laborious staff work and study were completed, I usually made decisions without delay. Option papers describing the choices I had to make rarely stayed on my desk overnight, unless it was necessary for me to consult a few more people.[108]

However, Carter's inclination to control decision making in the White House, aside from his belief that it was a presidential prerogative, may relate to his reasons for generally basing decisions on written information. An organizational leader has an element of control over written information that he loses when people with varying viewpoints convene in his office to discuss and debate. A president can choose what and how much to read in a decision memorandum—the cover sheet, the entire document, or selected sections. In the presence of more than one other person in a meeting, what he listens to and accepts or rejects is a matter of record—"private" though it may be. And more than one president has fallen victim to news leaks that sprang from meetings with senior staff inside the White House. Carter was plagued by such leaks, as was Ford, but Carter's presidency, and the president himself, seemed more vulnerable to the publication of those leaks, especially in the area of domestic policy-making, where his legislative program sometimes floundered in a hostile Congress.

In reviewing Carter's approach to decision making, Stuart Eizenstat aptly describes the greatest problems Carter faced as a decision maker. A president has

> got to be able to put . . . decisions into a broader context or under a broader umbrella. . . . The decisions have to have a common thread. They have to hold together so people have a sense of what it is you're trying to do. I think that the common thread was not always as clear as it should have been.[109]

In short, decision making in the White House, as in any organization, is a set, sometimes a continuum, of related decisions, not an ad hoc practice in the formulation of policy. Hedley Donovan observed that

> Carter's joy in digging into the factual detail of a complex subject may have absorbed too much of his intellectual energy that he didn't always have the time or disposition to sit back and reflect on the implications of these facts, how they related to other facts he knew, which sets of facts might be more important or, so to speak, more true.[110]

As a result, the coherency of policy-making in the Carter White House sometimes seemed suspect, perhaps in part because of the president's inclination to focus on the papers sent to him rather than to seek actively multiple sources of diverse viewpoints until late in his presidency. Nevertheless, Jimmy Carter was steeped in the information he did receive, knowledgeable about the major issues with which he had to deal, a devotee of the learning process—even if he sometimes failed to use that process successfully. Such was not the case with his successor.

INFORMATION FLOW IN THE REAGAN WHITE HOUSE

Analyzing Ronald Reagan as a decision maker one year after the end of his presidency creates some disadvantages for a scholar interested in the inner workings of his White House. Archival material is not yet categorized and available from a presidential library; memoirs of some key aides, as well as the president, have not yet been written; and some of Reagan's former senior staff have continued in government service and therefore are either unavailable as interviewees or are understandably unwilling to discuss communication inside the Reagan White House as candidly as they might otherwise. As a result, the information used to describe Reagan as a decision maker and a communicator within the White House in this book come from available primary and secondary sources.

The passage of time is often the friend of the scholar—it allows for the ongoing assessment of a presidency and its components from a variety of perspectives. We know more about, and perhaps judge differently than we did in 1960, the White House of Dwight Eisenhower. The same is becoming true of the Johnson and Ford presidencies. What follows is a description and analysis of Ronald Reagan as a decision maker, based on secondary sources, memoirs of several of his key staff members, and interviews with two members of his senior staff and other individuals who worked in his administration.

Before looking at the processes used by Reagan to seek and use information, it is important to underscore that these processes differed to some degree in his two terms. During his first four years in office, information flowed to the Oval Office through the troika established to oversee the administration of Reagan's presidency. In the second term much of his information was channeled through Donald Regan, with the exception of foreign policy documents, memos, and oral reports that came directly from the national security adviser. In short, the organizational structure imposed on the White House in each term directly affected information flow into the Oval Office as well as the extent to which other sources of information were used in the decision-making process.

According to Robert McFarlane, "analytical material as well as background information to enable him to make policy decisions" were sent to Reagan through a pyramidal staff structure "with a National Security Adviser and domestic policy advisers sending their material through the chief of staff."[111] Major sources of information for presidential decision making also included documents prepared by the Cabinet councils discussed in Chapter 4. These councils utilized teams of assistant secretaries who met to address specific issues and develop recommendations for each council's consideration. Reports from these groups were circulated before council meetings, which were attended by Cabinet members, White House staff, and *occasionally* the president. As Edwin Meese explains:

> Normally these councils would meet in a planning session where they would refine the issues relating to a particular topic and often assess the different points of view that might be presented and then these would be presented at a Cabinet meeting . . . usually in the form of a series of issues on which the president had to make a decision. He would then decide either at the Cabinet meeting or sometimes afterward.[112]

The advantage of these councils is that the process of policy development moved quickly compared with the slow pace of task accomplishment for which the Cabinet, as a large, unwieldy committee, is famous. White House staff and Cabinet communication was facilitated by the working councils. In the past, competition and conflict had characterized their relationship, especially under presidents who sought to initiate, develop, *and* execute policy through the work of key aides and not the federal departments. A disadvantage of the council system, however, was the distance at which this process put the president from the review of information and the generation of options. Reagan was at the end of the process, not a participant in it, and the quality of a decision, and/or his understanding of the ramifications of that decision, potentially were always suspect.

Other sources of written information sent to Reagan were decision memoranda developed in preparation for meetings and briefing books prepared for visits with foreign leaders in Washington or the president's trips abroad. During Reagan's years in office a perception developed that he was not a wellspring of information and certainly did not immerse himself in written material, as had Carter and Ford. Meese recalls, however, that Reagan "read everything that was given to him. He took homework home with him every night and was very disciplined in reading everything that was presented to him. This is why we had to exercise some discipline ourselves in how much we gave him so he wouldn't be totally overloaded."[113] Reagan's White House reading habits were not out of character, according to Meese, one of his close aides and confidants for many years, including those spent as California's governor. "I've known him reading constantly—books, magazine articles on current affairs subjects . . . I can't ever remember him not being occupied on plane trips . . . with reading something that was background material for speeches or . . . for issues he was dealing with."[114]

Helene von Damm, Reagan's personal secretary during the early part of his administration, confirms Reagan's interest in seeking information from written sources. "Whenever he had time to spare, in cars, on airplane trips, or between meetings, the President would open his briefcase and dig in. He was also a tireless reader of newspapers and magazines."[115] Moreover, von Damm emphasizes, Reagan was "forever circling and checking items he found in newspapers and magazines like *National Review* and *Human Events*."[116] However, Larry Speakes, Reagan's press secretary during most of his presidency, wrote that Reagan did not read newspapers thoroughly. "He glances at the *Washington Post*, *The New York Times*, the *Washington Times*, the *Los Angeles Times*, and *USA Today*. They all come into his office each morning, but he doesn't have much time to read newspapers."[117]

Like his predecessors, Reagan received a news summary, prepared overnight by the Press Office, to give the president what Speakes characterizes as a "total diet of national and international news each day."[118] Such summaries are, of course, the creation of White House staff, selectively compiled and presented. The president also valued the comments from correspondence he received from private citizens. According to Jane Mayer and Doyle McManus, "one senior aide estimated that he opened more than half of his fifteen-minute national security briefings by reading selections from them."[119] These journalists present a different perspective on Reagan's interest in seeking and using information that factually does not conflict with Meese and von Damm but portrays a president who was a nondiscriminating reader.

> Reagan obligingly read whatever he was given—all of it—at least in the early years. One aide early on was surprised to find that the president was staying up until the early hours of the morning trying to read all the materials his staff had sent him. "He read indiscriminately. . . . If you gave him eight hundred pages, he read every word. He used no judgment." Nancy Reagan finally stepped in and explained that her husband's workload needed to be reduced.[120]

This statement confirms Edwin Meese's comments to the author that shortly after the beginning of his term, the White House staff worked to control the amount of written information sent to the president.

Robert McFarlane acknowledges that Reagan read briefing materials "and would absorb and understand written analysis."[121] As a result, McFarlane sent memos and other briefing materials to Reagan on a regular basis. Indeed, when the national security adviser realized that Reagan had some interest in pursuing a "thaw" in the Cold War relationship with the Soviet Union, he determined to educate the president about that nation.

I began to give him about a paper a week, twenty-five pages, on the key dimensions of Soviet and, separately, Russian culture—the state, how it is organized, where the centers of influence are in the party, the KGB, the military, how historically these have worked together. A separate paper on Soviet negotiating doctrine. . . . The current Soviet leadership and their personal histories and how they arrived where they are. Religion in the Soviet Union. The nationalities problems they have. In short, a kind of short course in Russian–Soviet history. Twenty-five papers of about twenty pages each in the course of about six months, by the end of which he had absorbed a pretty good grasp of the foundation factors which influence Soviet behavior and of how to deal with them. . . . It led in 1985 to the summit at which a lot of this new direction in the relationship was charted.[122]

Ann Reilly Dowd discusses the president's review of written information in a *Fortune* magazine article published in 1986:

Insiders confirm that he is not a detail person, but they insist he receives enough information to make the right decisions on the most important issues. On each one, he gets a two- or three-page memo prepared by Cabinet Secretary Alfred Kingon's office outlining options and their pluses and minuses, and detailing which Cabinet members and top White House aides are pushing what. The agencies involved also prepare longer papers, which, aides say, the President reads and remembers.[123]

Despite personal testaments to Reagan's commitment to the review of written information, the evidence that he personally absorbed and actively used this information is not overwhelming. According to Donald Regan, the president's first action each morning was to give his "homework" to his personal secretary or to Regan for filing or dissemination to appropriate individuals. "Reagan's discipline and study habits were unique—but once he had completed an assignment he seemed to lose interest in it. Only occasionally did he talk about what he had read the night before.'[124] However, George Church wrote in *Time* magazine in 1987 that Regan hindered, rather than helped, the president's exposure to information when he presented the president with "sanitized position papers" that did not present major differences of opinion on decision alternatives.[125] Additionally, Church observes,

Regan sits through two-hour meetings, then gives the President a two-minute synopsis. . . . During his first term, Reagan was occasionally pushed into greater involvement with his policies. Aides such as Edwin Meese, James Baker, Michael Deaver and William Clark would argue issues in his presence. The disputes forced Reagan to focus on and drew him toward decisions.[126]

In other words, the president's participation in these information-rich communication settings fostered a better understanding of what he was reading. Listening to a short report that did not call for his active involvement, however, adversely affected his participation in the analysis and evaluation of information as well as the decision-making process in which this information was supposedly used.

In addition to written information, Reagan's staff provided him facts, ideas, and opinions from a variety of sources in other communication formats. According to McFarlane, "I arranged a number of sessions with academics . . . scholars on Russia and on the Soviet Union. The scholars would have lunch or spend time in the morning or afternoon in the Cabinet Room talking about some aspect of Russian life. The president liked those."[127] The national security adviser also used his daily briefings to "educate" the president on foreign policy since it was not a subject well known by him. During these sessions, McFarlane would relate one of the day's headlines to an issue facing Reagan in the foreign policy arena.

There would be a headline that said something about the Russians "walk out of arms talks" and I would talk about why that happened in the context of their efforts to split us from our European allies and Soviet political doctrine. There were a lot of these half-hour sessions on a daily basis that contributed [to Reagan's understanding of foreign affairs], but all . . . avenues were needed because he was not a man who was very deep in foreign matters.[128]

McFarlane's one-on-one session with Reagan, which was scheduled at 9:30 each morning and was the first meeting on his daily agenda, was supplemented by two thirty-minute private meetings each week with Secretary of State George Schultz. Shultz insisted on more than one meeting per week with the president to discuss foreign affairs. According to Speakes, "those sessions were good for Shultz and good for Reagan," as were the communications Reagan initiated with Richard Nixon.[129]

Reagan would reach out to him for advice on arms control, Soviet relations, and other foreign matters. In addition, Nixon often wrote memos to Jim Baker while Baker was chief of staff, and White House emissaries would travel up to Saddle River, New Jersey, where Nixon lived, to seek his advice in person. We usually tried to keep these communications secret, but the fact is, Nixon was very helpful to Reagan.[130]

In the early part of the Reagan administration, another form of foreign policy information was provided by the president's first national security council adviser, William Clark. According to Jane Mayer and Doyle McManus, short movies were produced showing the president the places he would go and the people he would meet during overseas trips.[131] In these "training films" the narrator would describe the president's itinerary as the geographical stops on his schedule appeared on the screen, along with still photos of dignitaries he would meet. The narrator would also supply information about that individual germane to discussions planned between the two leaders.

One unifying thread that runs through the comments of Reagan's former aides is the characterization of the president as a reactor to, rather than a seeker of, information. He employed a "delegating style" of information scanning in the White House, assigning the search for information to others rather than seeking information "actively and constantly."[132] Mayer and McManus write: "Unlike other presidents, Reagan seldom requested information beyond the briefings and talking points his aides gave him. He enjoyed occasional luncheons with outside experts when they were brought in, but he rarely initiated invitations."[133] Unlike Eisenhower, Johnson, and Ford, "the president rarely initiated calls unless his staff asked him to. Nor did he keep in touch in other ways with those who were reputedly his oldest friends and advisers, on or off the White House staff."[134] As a result, as Vicky Martin and Donald Martin discovered in their study of senior managers in a banking organization, relying on the delegating style of information scanning led to "a dependency on subordinates."[135]

According to Donald Regan, the president did not give him specific instructions on how to discharge his responsibilities as chief of staff. The one request Reagan made was that Regan ensure that he heard both sides of every issue. " 'And if there are more than two sides, I want to hear all of them. I don't mind making decisions as long as I know what everybody thinks.' "[136] Regan eventually would learn, however, that the president entrusted this responsibility to him totally—he did not intend to *seek* diverse viewpoints from a variety of sources, as had been the case with the modern presidents who preceded him (although their seeking behavior varied in degree). Nevertheless, no strong evidence exists to suggest that Regan encouraged Reagan's solicitation of diverse viewpoints from individuals outside the White House or in discussion with members of his own staff. For instance, in contrast with the amount of time Robert McFarlane spent with Reagan, the president spent much less time with Admiral John Poindexter, who succeeded McFarlane as national security adviser. Within a period of time that equaled about twelve months, the amount of time Poindexter was with the president alone totaled eighty-one minutes, according to a tally by the office of the White House Counsel during the Iran-Contra congressional hearings.[137]

Edwin Meese has emphasized that Reagan made great use of group meetings, especially those involving the Cabinet. "Unlike other presidents for whom most of the decision-making was . . . within the White House, and some Cabinet members were not even consulted about things that pertained to their own department. . . . I don't think that ever happened or if it did it was an aberration during our administration."[138] However, although Reagan may have attended those meetings, it is not at all clear that he actively participated in discussions, as did Carter and Ford. Instead, he apparently agreed with options developed by others . . . and asked few questions in the meantime. Stories abound in accounts of the Reagan presidency, even those written by former aides cited in this study, of the president's lack of interest in asking questions. According to one person who helped develop the planning document for the first 100 days of his second term, " 'he was the least curious person that I ever met.' "[139]

Nevertheless, Ronald Reagan was protected, at least in his first term, by a senior staff that met regularly each morning at 8:00 and, according to Meese, communicated constantly during the day.

We communicated among ourselves all the time so that we were constantly keeping each other pretty well informed on what was going on . . . even though not all four of us . . . would necessarily be together in the meetings. I was there at almost all of them. Mr. Baker somewhat less frequently, but still most of them. Mr. Deaver at much fewer. Nevertheless, we knew what was going on and then we in turn would bring others into the meetings with the president from the top members of the White House staff and the National Security Council staff.[140]

The president lost this protection in his second term, and paid a price for the propensity to delegate decisions that had seemed to serve him well while the troika ran the White House.

REAGAN AS DECISION MAKER

In an interview with representatives of *Fortune* magazine in 1986, Ronald Reagan briefly described his approach to decision making.

I use a system in which I want to hear what everybody wants to say honestly. I want the decisions made on what is right and wrong, what is good or bad for the people of this country. I encourage all the input I can get. . . . And when I've heard all that I need to make a decision, I don't take a vote. I make the decision.[141]

Meese confirms Reagan's interest in hearing decision alternatives presented orally during his first term, indicating this preference developed during his years as California's governor, when he depended on discussions with the state's six-member Cabinet and the lieutenant governor.

We met with him at least three times a week and sometimes we would meet as often as six or eight hours at a time if it was something like the annual budget. . . . He developed this pattern of decision-making with decision memos, [and] having the matters pretty well debated by Cabinet members in front of him. And he was very much in favor of getting all the information so that even though someone might not agree with a particular point of view, if they felt there was something he ought to hear, that would be presented by somebody on the Cabinet just so that he understood the different points of view.[142]

The decision memos mentioned by Meese probably included "mini-memos," developed by William Clark when he served as Reagan's executive assistant in Sacramento. No more than 300 to 400 words long, they were comprised of four paragraphs, the first stating the issue, the second listing pertinent facts, the third providing staff analysis, and the fourth presenting a conclusion or recommendation. "On a critical policy question, Reagan [as governor] would get a stream of mini-memos, 100 or more, keeping him abreast of a changing situation. Sometimes they were accompanied by long staff studies."[143]

It is important to keep in mind that the practice of Cabinet council debate in the president's presence was a practice used mainly in Reagan's first term, at least to the extent described by Meese. It was this adviser's responsibility to organize the discussions through the Cabinet council system, which he adapted from the one used in California.

> I think I was regarded, at least by most, as an honest broker who fairly presented different points of view to the president or saw that those views were presented to him either in Cabinet sessions or other meetings in his office. A lot of people came to me, depending on me for that function. I think the president felt, as he had in California, that I would give him straightforward advice and not try to color it one way or the other.[144]

Early in the Reagan administration, Meese was criticized for appearing to act like an assistant president, apparently making decisions that seemed to be beyond his authority—such as failing to wake the president during the night when U.S. planes fought with Libyan aircraft. Additionally, Chief of Staff Baker wielded tremendous power in the shaping and execution of the president's policy-making agenda. Their behaviors, however, stemmed at least in part from the president's preference to delegate decision-making responsibilities freely, despite his comments in the *Fortune* interview. In Robert McFarlane's words:

> I suppose it's fair to say that he was not a hands-on manager. He was a delegator. . . . He relied upon his Cabinet officers to make recommendations to him. If he thought they were sound, he would get behind them and do what he was asked to do in the way of speaking, traveling, lobbying Congress, press conferences, whatever. But he was not a man given to bold initiatives on his own.[145]

As a result, Reagan sometimes was placed in the position of resolving substantive conflict between members of his Cabinet, such as secretaries Weinberger and Shultz, who were responsible for recommending options about which they sometimes disagreed. According to McFarlane, Reagan did not enjoy the role of mediator and, as a result, some decisions relating to foreign affairs "would take longer to get resolved."[146] In foreign affairs particularly, Reagan as a decision maker was only as effective as those who assumed organizational roles related to the development and execution of policy. Summarizing Reagan's characteristics as a decision maker, McFarlane refers to him as

> a man of instinct . . . not terribly sophisticated—instinctive more than analytic. He relied upon his staff to do the analysis of what in the late twentieth century was sensible and feasible and doable. . . . Only out of being challenged as responsible for leading the free world—and that, only in 1984 and 1985—did he begin to acknowledge and to accept that he had to put a lot more energy into this area.[147]

Part of the decision-making process requires that one put goals in priority, that one focus on those objectives of most importance, given the resources available to accomplish one's goals. Reagan, like Carter, found it difficult to put *specific* objectives into a priority order. Carter had a number of legislative goals he hoped to achieve during the first months of his presidency; Reagan had one ideological "vision" that he left to others to subdivide into policy areas and decision alternatives. According to McFarlane, he was unable to prompt the president to focus on a few key foreign policy issues to pursue as his presidential goals.

> I asked him for authority to really study the top twelve . . . issues that were candidates that he could choose two from to accomplish in the Reagan second term. I went outside government and asked all the experts, from the University of Texas to Harvard, to study these fairly obvious issues and came back with a nice notebook that had a huge amount of scholarship in it, and gave it to him at the ranch after the election. He studied it very hard. He got on Air Force One to come back to Washington and I very anxiously went up to hear the verdict on which two items we were going to do. He said, "Let's do them all!" That expresses Ronald Reagan. He's the heroic figure who wants to do everything. But it expresses a kind of superficial grasp of the nature of federal governments.[148]

Comparing Reagan and Ford, another president on whose staff he served, McFarlane observes: "President Ford was much more open to suggestion and to new knowledge, new information on which he could hinge a change in his point of view. He was malleable but in a constructive way. He didn't pretend to have all the answers. Reagan really does. He is very inflexible, whereas President Ford was quite flexible."[149] The inflexibility to which McFarlane refers was, in his opinion, an ideological inflexibility that had significant effects on the extent to which Reagan sought and used information. According to Meese:

> He would depend . . . on his staff . . . to take the goals and develop the action plans with objectives and milestones. . . . He would expect his staff and his Cabinet to carry out these particular projects or these particular plans. He had a very high level of trust in the people that worked for him unless . . . it was indicated that they didn't deserve that trust. It didn't happen very often that people fell down, but when they did, the consequences were serious. The . . . diversion of funds from the Iran initiative to the freedom fighters in Nicaragua being one example.[150]

The ability of Ronald Reagan to articulate a vision of America that was readily acceptable to those who supported him for two terms did not translate into strengths as an administrator and decision maker within his own organization. While Carter may have spent too much intellectual energy attempting to understand the nuances of policies and potential decisions, Larry Speakes writes that Reagan "really did have little interest in details, whether they concerned arms control or who was using the White House tennis court. . . . Nor did he choose to involve himself in many points of substance on a day-to-day basis."[151] In their study of Reagan's performance in his second term, Mayer and McManus corroborate these observations:

He seemed to have unquestioning trust in many of the small and large decisions others made for him—and when his staff could not reach a decision, he frequently made none either, unless events forced him to do so. . . . When the public began to learn of Reagan's lack of involvement in meetings, aides explained it by saying the president wanted to hide his thought process in order to avoid leaks or that he was trying to spare the feelings of those with whom he disagreed. But, as Don Regan later admitted . . . "It was a rare meeting in which he made a decision or issued an order."[152]

Indeed, these authors quote Edward Rollins, Reagan's former campaign manager, as saying that in the second term Donald Regan probably made 80 percent of the decisions in the Reagan White House—decisions that were presidential responsibilities.[153] Similarly, Bob Schieffer and Gary Gates observe that "those who worked closely with Reagan often viewed him as aloof, indifferent to those around him, and, at times, uninformed about and uninterested in his own programs."[154]

Robert McFarlane indicated in an interview with the author that Reagan was not the manager of his White House and in general delegated several, if not most, of the kinds of decisions other chief executives made during their presidencies. During the first term this tendency to delegate seemingly did little harm to the Reagan White House as an organization or to his administration in general, since the president was surrounded by competent advisers who knew him or Washington's political circles well. During the second term, however, his chief of staff was almost a stranger to him personally and a source of intraorganizational conflict professionally. Used to trusting the senior staff around him, Reagan placed trust in his former Treasury secretary, and in others who assumed organizational roles in the areas that began to be the most sensitive in the second term, particularly foreign affairs. Like many organizational leaders, Reagan accepted unquestioningly the information provided by those most accessible to him. He was not in the habit of seeking other sources of information, as Ford had been, and appeared distrustful of sources outside the White House.

According to Donald Regan, "Reagan chose his aides and then followed their advice almost without question. He trusted his lieutenants to act on his intentions, rather than on his spoken instructions, and though he sometimes asked what some of his less visible Cabinet officers were doing with their departments, he seldom spontaneously called for a detailed status report."[155] According to Mayer and McManus, "What continually amazed the staff was how seldom Reagan felt the need to become involved. To Reagan, hiring the right people to offer advice was the key to decision making."[156] However, the delegation of decision making in Reagan's White House surprised, perhaps more than pleased, his senior staff—despite the authority it gave them.

Jim Baker was stunned when . . . he presented Reagan with a legislative agenda for his first year in office, and the President promptly signed off on it without raising any questions or even discussing it in any detail. So was Don Regan when he put together a program for the second term, and received a similar response. So was Bud McFarlane when he drew up a blueprint of foreign policy goals in the hope of discovering what Reagan's priorities might be in that area, and the President blithely replied "Let's do them all!" And finally, so was John Poindexter when Reagan signed crucial Presidential findings without pondering their significance or potential consequences. The incredible thing is how lucky Reagan had been all those years before the Iran-Contra scandal. Until then, his passive approach had always worked like a charm, so it's no wonder that he himself was bewildered when his longtime habit of letting others make critical decisions for him finally led him and his presidency into deeply troubled waters.[157]

In an interview with the author, Richard Cheney, Ford's second chief of staff and secretary of defense in the Bush administration, observed that the Iran-Contra scandal would not have developed in the Ford White House, in part because "the president was intimately involved in the day-to-day running of the place," and partly because his national security adviser, Brent Scowcroft, had a "very good understanding of what constitutes presidential level decision."[158] According to Cheney, Scowcroft "wouldn't have dreamed of usurping that authority."[159] In the final analysis, however, it is the president with whom all responsibility for such scandals resides. Gerald Ford emphasized:

You cannot operate that Oval Office . . . without having yourself involved. That doesn't mean you have to get overly involved in every detail, but it does mean that you can't have a superficial knowledge of what's going on. It's not an eight-hour day and it's not a five-day week. It requires a lot of personal involvement.[160]

THE POST-WATERGATE PRESIDENTS AS DECISION MAKERS: A COMPARISON OF STYLES

Paul Light's comparisons of Ford and Carter as decision makers with some of their predecessors substantiate the observations in this chapter about those post-Watergate presidents. He observes:

Kennedy, Johnson, and Ford generally preferred to make most decisions in person. All three settled policy disputes in the presence of the interested parties; all three made domestic decisions by facing the arguments in a relatively open setting. They used policy memoranda to focus decisions, but they dealt with the major issues in person. Nixon and Carter, however, preferred to make most decisions on paper. Both chose to tackle competing demands in decision memos; both made domestic decisions in the quiet of their private study; both avoided personal confrontations.[161]

Comparing Ford and Carter as decision makers, one adviser in the Office of Management and Budget noted:

Ford and Carter were like night and day. Ford definitely wanted to meet the protagonists in a face-to-face discussion, no holds barred. If there was internal conflict, he wanted it out in the open. . . . He felt that he could mediate most differences, and wanted to hear the opposing arguments in person. Carter, on the other hand, can't stand personal confrontations. Carter has set up a system which insulates him from the conflict. He does not want to waste his time listening to people fight. He wants to read the arguments and make a choice based on the pros and cons.[162]

As a result of their preferences, the information Ford used to make decisions was richer because it was gleaned from debates and discussions that did not disguise the depth of feeling among aides about various policy alternatives. On the other hand, Carter's preference for written information and his decision-making style did not foster the use of information-rich media. Light states that "though decision memos often contain lists of assistants either for or against an idea, there is no measure of intensity."[163]

Reagan is not easily compared with his predecessors—his detachment from the day-to-day administration of the White House was so complete that he did not control, or even monitor, the system that provided him written information or arranged for meetings at which decision alternatives were presented orally. Nevertheless, Hedley Donovan observes that Reagan didn't mind listening to vigorous staff debates, but that neither he nor Carter "had anywhere near so broad and varied a circle of pre-presidential friends and connections as did Nixon, Johnson, and Eisenhower"—or for that matter, Ford—on whom they sometimes relied for information and perspectives outside the organizational influences that permeate the White House.[164]

As was seen in Chapter 3, Dwight Eisenhower was comfortable in delegating responsibilities, but not presidential authority, to his chief aides. If his was a hidden-hand presidency, as Fred Greenstein aptly suggests, "Reagan's rule bordered . . . on a no-hands presidency."[165] Indeed, as a decision maker, Ronald Reagan apparently did not just delegate his responsibilities—he sometimes abdicated them.

The "staffing system" used by Gerald Ford assisted him throughout his administration as a formalized interpersonal communication process as well as a structure for the transmission of messages. Such a system may delay the formulation of a decision for several days or weeks, depending on the complexity of an issue and the time frame in which the president is operating. However, this delay allows for the generation of information from multiple sources to uncover potential policy and political problems that might emerge after a decision is made. The chief executive may lose some time, but gain a better decision, using a structured system of information flow such as that Ford ultimately adopted. As James Connor suggests, "anywhere within that massive pile [of paper] that you would see everyday there could be some bomb ticking."[166] Ford's system was designed to uncover those "bombs"that might surprise, if not embarrass, the president. By contrast, Connor believes Jimmy Carter's system of information review did not help him focus on decision outcomes. "Carter was continually being surprised at the implications of his decisions. He would announce a policy and . . . wheels would fall off all over the place. He would be totally immersed in detail and would never understand the nature of the decision he was making."[167]

The use of a formal structure to acquire and evaluate information for all presidential decisions protects the president from himself or from those who are particularly influential around him. Keeping information and people from a president may allow for deniability, but giving him information from a variety of sources also may insure against embarrassment or a defective policy decision, and preserves the chief executive's right to make his own decisions.

The structure of information flow in Gerald Ford's White House and his use of multiple sources of information were organizational responses to the shadow that Watergate cast on the White House. They were also the effects of personal preferences and a variety of political considerations. The ways Ford sought and used information as his domestic and foreign policy decisions evolved contributed to a restoration of trust in the presidency. However, the chief executives who succeeded Ford found it difficult to attain the balance of openness and control he fashioned in their systems of information flow and decision-making processes. To those concerned about presidential involvement in information flow and staff involvement in decision making, Irangate served as a somber reminder that trust is transient, tenuous, and a delicate thread in the fabric of a presidency.

NOTES

1. Charles A. O'Reilly, Jennifer A. Chatman, and John C. Anderson, "Message Flow and Decision Making," in Fredric Jablin et al., eds., *Handbook of Organizational Communication* (Beverly Hills, CA: Sage, 1987), p. 605.

2. K. J. Arrow, *The Limits of Organization* (New York: Norton, 1973), p. 48.

3. O'Reilly et al., "Message Flow and Decision Making," p. 610.

4. Ibid.

5. Ibid., p. 612.

6. Ibid.

7. Ibid., p. 614.

8. Ibid., p. 618.

9. Ibid., p.610.

10. Theodore Sorensen, *Decision-Making in the White House* (New York: Columbia University Press, 1963), pp. 18–19.

11. See R. M. Cyert and J. G. March, *A Behavioral Theory of the Firm* (Englewood Cliffs, NJ: Prentice-Hall, 1963).

12. Paul C. Light, *The President's Agenda* (Baltimore: Johns Hopkins University Press, 1982), p. 186.

13. Alexander L. George, *Presidential Decisionmaking in Foreign Policy: The Effective Use of Information and Advice* (Boulder, CO: Westview Press, 1980), p. 98.

14. Henry Kissinger, *White House Years* (Boston: Little, Brown, 1979), p. 40.

15. Ibid., p. 100.

16. Ibid.

17. George, *Presidential Decisionmaking*, pp. 122–32.

18. Light, *The President's Agenda*, p. 201.

19. Sorensen, *Decision-Making in the White House*, p. 23.

20. Ibid., p. 39.

21. Leonard C. Hawes, "Information Overload and the Organization of 1984," *Western Speech*, Summer 1971, p. 196.

22. Sorensen, *Decision-Making in the White House*, p. 59.

23. Quoted in ibid., p. 10.

24. "Analysis of the Present White House Office," p. 3, folder, "Transition 1977—Analysis of White House Organization," box 12, Richard Cheney Files, Gerald Ford Library.

25. Ibid., p. 4.

26. James Connor, interview with the author, July 15, 1987.

27. Ibid.

28. Ibid.

29. Memo from Donald Rumsfeld, folder: "D. Rumsfeld (3)," box 17, staff files of James Connor, Gerald R. Ford Library.

30. Donald Rumsfeld, interview with the author, August 10, 1987.

31. Connor, interview with the author.

32. Ibid.

33. Ibid.

34. Richard Cheney, interview with the author, November 4, 1987.

35. Ibid.

36. Robert Hartmann, interview with the author, November 5, 1987.

37. Ibid.

38. Gerald R. Ford, *A Time to Heal* (New York: Harper & Row and The Reader's Digest Association, 1979), P. 149.

39. Connor, interview with the author.

40. Memo from James Connor, May 1, 1975, folder: "Sub-Cabinet Officials," box 19, staff files of James Connor, Gerald R. Ford Library.

41. Gerald R. Ford, interview with the author, April 21, 1987.

42. Ford, *A Time to Heal*, p. 140.

43. Ibid., p. 261.

44. Connor, interview with the author.

45. Terrence O'Donnell, interview with the author, November 4, 1987.

46. Rumsfeld, interview with the author.

47. Ford, interview with the author.

48. Ibid.

49. Ford, *A Time to Heal*, pp. 259–60.

50. Ronald Nessen, interview with the author, November 5, 1987.

51. Philip Buchen, interview with the author, November 5, 1987.

52. Cheney, interview with the author.

53. Transcript of Nelson Rockefeller interview with Trevor Arbrister, October 20, 1977, pp. 25–26, folder: "Interview with NAR by Arbrister 10/21/77," box 35, papers of James Cannon, Gerald R. Ford Library.

54. Juan Cameron, "The Management Problem in Ford's White House," *Fortune*, July 1975, p. 79.

55. O'Donnell, interview with the author.

56. Staff of the White Burkett Miller Center of Public Affairs, University of Virginia, *The Ford White House* (Lanham, MD: University Press of America, 1986), p. 11.

57. Ibid., pp. 14–15.

58. Donald Rumsfeld, ''Rumsfeld's Rules,'' mimeograph, 1980, pp. 8–9.

59. Ronald Nessen, *It Sure Looks Different from the Inside* (Chicago: Playboy Press, 1978), p. 158.

60. Ford, interview with the author.

61. David Alsobrook, interview with the author, August 17, 1988.

62. Zbigniew Brzezinski, interview with the author, June 14, 1989.

63. Memorandum from Rick Hutcheson to Bob Lipshutz, December 19, 1977, folder: ''FG 6–1–1, Hutcheson, Richard (4/16/77–1/20/81), box FG–47, White House central files, Jimmy Carter Library.

64. Jimmy Carter, *Keeping Faith* (New York: Bantam Books, 1982), p. 57.

65. Brzezinski, interview with the author.

66. ''The President's Time'' (unsigned), December 14, 1977, folder: ''White House Executive Committee,'' box 51, files of Office of Counsel—Lipshutz, Jimmy Carter Library.

67. Ibid., p. 3.

68. Carter, *Keeping Faith*, p. 56.

69. Anne Wexler, interview with the author, June 15, 1989.

70. Ibid.

71. Stuart Eizenstat, interview with the author, June 16, 1989.

72. Ibid.

73. Brzezinski, interview with the author.

74. Ibid.

75. Jack Watson, interview with the author, August 19, 1988.

76. Ibid.

77. Ibid.

78. Hans Mark, interview with the author, August 15, 1989.

79. Interview with Hamilton Jordan, ''How Carter Operates,'' *U.S. News & World Report*, February 21, 1977, p. 18.

80. Carter, *Keeping Faith*, p. 57.

81. Edward D. Feigenbaum, ''Staffing, Organization, and Decision-making in the Ford and Carter White Houses,'' *Presidential Studies Quarterly*, Summer 1980, p. 376.

82. Carter, *Keeping Faith*, p. 51.

83. Brzezinski, interview with the author.

84. Ibid.

85. Wexler, interview with the author.

86. Ibid.

87. Hedley Donovan, *Roosevelt to Reagan: A Reporter's Encounters with Nine Presidents* (New York: Harper & Row, 1985), p. 213.

88. Ibid., p. 153.

89. Robert J. Thompson, ''Juggling the President's Time: Constitutional v. Operational Roles,'' paper presented at the annual meeting of the Southern Political Science Association, Memphis, TN, November 2–4, 1989, p. 7.

90. Ibid.

91. Carter, *Keeping Faith*, p. 67.

92. Ibid., p. 68.

93. Ibid., pp. 71–72.

94. Memo from Hamilton Jordan to the president, undated but initialed, pp. 1–2, folder: "Senior Advisors with President, 1978," box 37, files of chief of staff—Jordan, Jimmy Carter Library.

95. Ibid.

96. Carter, *Keeping Faith*, p. 118.

97. Ibid., p. 59.

98. Ibid., p. 61.

99. Wexler, interview with the author.

100. Jody Powell, interview with the author, June 16, 1989.

101. Ibid.

102. Ibid.

103. Cyrus Vance, *Hard Choices* (New York: Simon and Schuster, 1983), p. 35.

104. Brzezinski, interview with the author.

105. Ibid.

106. Ibid.

107. Wexler, interview with the author.

108. Carter, *Keeping Faith*, p. 62.

109. Eizenstat, interview with the author.

110. Donovan, *Roosevelt to Reagan*, p. 235.

111. Robert McFarlane, interview with the author, June 16, 1989.

112. Edwin Meese, interview with the author, June 15, 1989.

113. Ibid.

114. Ibid.

115. Helene von Damm, *At Reagan's Side* (New York: Doubleday, 1988), p. 182.

116. Ibid.

117. Larry Speakes, *Speaking Out*, (New York: Charles Scribner's Sons, 1988), p. 111.

118. Ibid.

119. Jane Mayer and Doyle McManus, *Landslide: The Unmaking of the President* (Boston: Houghton Mifflin, 1988), p. 29.

120. Ibid., p. 28.

121. McFarlane, interview with the author.

122. Ibid.

123. Ann Reilly Dowd, "What Managers Can Learn From Manager Reagan," *Fortune*, September 15, 1986, p. 35.

124. Donald Regan, *For the Record*, (New York: St. Martin's Press, 1988), pp. 302–03.

125. George J. Church, "Is He More out of Touch Than Ever?" *Time*, January 26, 1987, p. 17.

126. Ibid.

127. McFarlane, interview with the author.

128. Ibid.

129. Speakes, *Speaking Out*, p. 78.

130. Ibid., p. 104.

131. Mayer and McManus, *Landslide*, p. 158.

132. Vicky Gordon Martin and Donald R. Martin, "The Types and Styles of Managerial Information Scanning," *Management Communication Quarterly*, 2, February 1989, p. 394.

133. Mayer and McManus, *Landslide*, p. 28.
134. Ibid., p. 29.
135. Martin and Martin, p. 397.
136. Regan, *For the Record*, p. 262.
137. Mayer and McManus, *Landslide*, p. 30.
138. Meese, interview with the author.
139. Cited in Mayer and McManus, *Landslide*, p. 90.
140. Meese, interview with the author.
141. Reagan interview with Marshall Loeb, Lee Smith, and Ann Reilly Dowd, ''Reagan on Decision-making, Planning, Gorbachev, and More,'' *Fortune*, September 5, 1986, p. 36.
142. Meese, interview with the author.
143. Hedrick Smith, *Reagan: The Man, the President* (New York: Macmillan, 1980), p. 171.
144. Meese, interview with the author.
145. McFarlane, interview with the author.
146. Ibid.
147. Ibid.
148. Ibid.
149. Ibid.
150. Meese, interview with the author.
151. Speakes, *Speaking Out*, p. 67.
152. Mayer and McManus, *Landslide*, pp. 27–28.
153. Ibid., p. 42.
154. Bob Schieffer and Gary Gates, *The Acting President* (New York: E. P. Dutton, 1989), p. 90.
155. Regan, *For the Record*, p. 299.
156. Mayer and McManus, *Landslide*, p. 95.
157. Ibid., pp. 304–05.
158. Cheney, interview with the author.
159. Ibid.
160. Ford, interview with the author.
161. Light, *The President's Agenda*, p. 170.
162. Ibid.
163. Ibid., p. 171.
164. Donovan, *From Roosevelt to Reagan*, p. 208.
165. Mayer and McManus, *Landslide*, p.27.
166. Connor, interview with the author.
167. Ibid.

Chapter 6

The President as Organizational Leader: Communication Styles in the White House, 1974–1988

In the process of developing formal and emergent structures within the White House, and in seeking, reviewing, and using information to make and implement decisions, a president communicates with his senior staff. As we have seen, some presidents, like Jimmy Carter, may prefer to communicate with even their close aides in writing. Others, like Gerald Ford, may prefer, even enjoy, face-to-face interactions with staff on a daily basis, concurrently depending on the receipt of written information for use in policy-making.

The degree to which a president communicates with his staff, the degree to which that communication can be assessed as "effective," affects the success of the White House as an information-processing, decision-making organization. As we have seen, the modern presidents have communicated with their senior aides to varying degrees, using a variety of "channels," such as meetings, memos, personal notes, and informal one-on-one sessions. The channels, or means and methods they used to speak with and/or write to their aides, have depended on their personalities, the value they place on communication in general and in the White House in particular, the political and professional backgrounds from which they entered the White House, and the situations they faced while in office that affected their commitment to intraorganizational communication. Gerald Ford, a creature of Congress, valued face-to-face discussions with senior staff; Jimmy Carter, a former state official with a science and engineering educational background, preferred interacting with aides through memos. Carter, like Richard Nixon, was personally more comfortable in his own company and did not enjoy, nor did he think he benefited from, extended discussion sessions with aides.

Communication between the president and his staff serves to discharge his functions as a manager and organizational leader, including the mediation of staff conflict and the management of internal structural and procedural change, as well as those responsibilities he assumes as the overseer of domestic and foreign policy-making. Additionally, the sets of behaviors used in his interactions with key aides, which form his communication style, transmit both intentional and unintentional cues to his staff to help them understand his expectations of their roles and responsibilities in their evolving communicative relationship. During his first few weeks in office, for instance, Jimmy Carter's propensity for communicating with senior staff thorough a flurry of handwritten notes, while using a formal, rather brusque, demeanor in meetings, signaled the communication channels he preferred to use in his interactions with them. It also established the organizational climate within which they would work—supportive yet characterized by a modicum of warmth emanating from the Oval Office. On the other hand, Gerald Ford's easygoing nature, his interest in chats with individual staff members as well as scheduled debates and discussions with several aides at once, served as an open invitation to aides during the workday. As a result, his appointment schedule often became clogged with commitments for a few minutes of his time, including moments given to his senior aides. Despite his belief in the "staffing system" discussed in Chapter 5, and the decision memos prepared and circulated by that system, Ford was a president who valued listening more than reading—and his preferences established the parameters within which a communicative relationship with his staff developed.

Since the mid-1970s, most of the studies of presidential–staff relationships have focused on three patterns of management used by chief executives, specifically those identified and discussed by Richard Tanner Johnson in his 1974 book, *Managing the White House*. According to Johnson, a president's approach to management sets the process of decision making in motion and affects the quality of decisions made, as well as how they are implemented.[1] Johnson labels the major presidential patterns or styles of management as *formalistic*, *competitive*, and *collegial*. The formalistic style, which he identifies with Dwight Eisenhower and Richard Nixon, utilizes hierarchical lines of communication in a pyramidal organizational structure. The competitive style, such as that used by Franklin Roosevelt and, to some extent, Lyndon Johnson, depends on overlapping organizational roles and a resultant competition among the president's staff engendered by an organizational structure that values generalists, not individuals responsible for functional areas within the White House. The collegial style, identified with John Kennedy, is the team-building approach to management and depends on close and continuous presidential oversight to avoid the creation of competition, and sometimes role conflict, among staff.

Richard Johnson's management styles focus on the way a president structures his White House and, as he emphasizes, "while each President may adopt a dominant pattern of management, his approach may vary from situation to situation."[2] Lyndon Johnson, for instance, may have utilized a competitive style of management, but he sometimes was collegial and a team builder. Similarly,

Kennedy fostered competition among his aides even as he seemed to facilitate their cohesiveness as a team.

Alexander George has further delineated the features of Johnson's three managerial styles, relating organizational structure to communication relationships within the White House in the course of decision making. In the competitive model, for instance, he suggests that a president fosters little communication among his key advisers, yet often requires aides "to settle differences among themselves and does not become identified with any one individual's decision alternative."[3] Over the long term, one might logically expect the communication relationships among aides to be strained, to say the least, since the major purpose for their interactions is to develop solutions while concurrently attempting to avoid conflict. With the formalistic model, George observes, "the president does not encourage his advisers to communicate with each other or to engage in joint efforts at policy analysis and problem solving"; in short, he is not a team builder.[4] However, the president does attempt to protect himself from information overload by assigning nonpresidential decisions to individual staff members and entertaining their suggested alternatives for those he must make. Finally, George suggests, the collegial approach allows senior advisers to function "as a 'debate team' that considers information and policy options from the multiple, conflicting perspectives of the group members in an effort to obtain cross-fertilization and creative problem-solving."[5] Consequently, in the collegial model of management one might expect to find a spokes-of-the-wheel organizational structure in the White House as well as informal, emergent structures used to acquire and process information and discuss decision alternatives.

Yet there is more to White House management than how the staff is organized, what system is used to bring information into the Oval Office, and what process the president prefers to use when making decisions. Indeed, the ways a president interacts with his staff give us additional clues about his management style, as well as his possible strengths as the creator of a supportive organizational climate and the leader of a communication-intensive organization. It is therefore worthwhile to consider the applicability of "communication style," as it is discussed in studies of interpersonal communication, to the communicative relationship between presidents and their senior aides, those with whom chief executives interact most on a daily basis and with whom they tend to forge the closest personal relationships inside the White House. In this chapter the communication styles of Ford, Carter, and Reagan will be analyzed after briefly reviewing the major considerations one must take into account when discussing "communication style" among modern U.S. presidents.

"COMMUNICATION STYLE" IN THE WHITE HOUSE

As is discussed in Chapter 1, "communication style" refers to the way a person communicates, "the signals that are provided to help process, interpret, filter, or understand literal meaning."[6] Styles are variable, yet sufficiently patterned to create expectations and perceptions in the minds of listeners about the style profile attributable to a given individual. Styles are not independent of each other; a person may be dominant as well as friendly; relaxed as well as contentious. (See style construct description in Chapter 1.) However, over time those with whom a communicator interacts recognize a pattern of signals that help identify him or her as dramatic, dominant, open, friendly, attentive, and so on.

To study communication style among presidents, one must rely on the perceptions of those who interacted with the chief executive. In the laboratory, scholars may observe interactions between individuals and/or study tapes of conversations. Obviously, tapes are not a research tool when studying the post-Watergate presidents; the discovery of Richard Nixon's taping system ended the use of that potential source of data! (Even evaluating the Watergate tapes would provide information about the style variables exhibited by Nixon only as he discussed that specific subject.) No researcher has sufficient access to the Oval Office to observe presidential/staff interactions and make credible determinations of a given president's style. Nevertheless, it may be argued that perceptions of a president's style by those with whom he interacts during his term in office comprise meaningful data and indeed may be the only data that matter in a discussion of communication style. For it is those perceptions which provide cues to staff on what the communication relationship between them and the president is, and will be, and perhaps on what he *intends* that relationship to be. It is also those perceptions upon which presidential–staff relationships are built. As a result, as is often true in the dynamics of human interaction, perception becomes reality for those involved in the communication relationship.

In this chapter an attempt is made to identify the communication styles of the post-Watergate presidents on the basis of comments taken from interviews with senior staff who interacted with those presidents several times a week, if not daily. Additionally, secondary source material written by or about senior aides that discuss their interactions with each president is used. As we shall see, not all those individuals interviewed observed the same style variables—but that is to be expected, since few of us communicate in the same way with every person around us. On the other hand, the communication portraits of Ford, Carter, and Reagan drawn by their senior staff reflect similar perceptions, as affected by the closeness of their relationships to their respective presidents. By studying the communication styles of these presidents, we come to understand more about them as policy-makers as well as individuals. More important, we begin to understand the significance of presidents as communicators *inside* the White House, not just as presenters of prepared texts to a national audience or as public interviewees at televised press conferences.

FORD AS ORGANIZATIONAL LEADER

The formalistic style of management used by Richard Nixon in the White House would not have been the preferred style for any of his possible successors, since that approach to management was criticized as an enabling factor in the development of the Watergate scandal. While such criticism may have been unjustified, any president succeeding Nixon most assuredly would have utilized a management style that de-emphasized a formal, pyramidal organizational structure and fostered a more open decision-making environment. Gerald Ford would have been a collegial manager in the White House regardless of his chronological placement among the modern presidents. That is the nature of the man and the result of years of accommodation and consensus-building spent in Congress as House minority leader and a member of the loyal opposition.

Those who worked as members of his senior staff describe President Ford as an honest man but a weak administrator who, like many of his predecessors, had almost no appropriate experience to prepare him for the role of organizational leader in the White House. Philip Buchen observes, ''Running a congressional office is not really very challenging and most people do it rather poorly. . . . I'm afraid that you can't give him very high marks for his administrative ability.''[7] Of course Ford, as an unelected president, was denied the time presidents-elect are afforded, during a campaign and the transition period, to forge a White House staff. He also was denied the one or two years of getting one's house in order before running for a subsequent term. Consequently, the structure of his staff and the strength or tenuousness of their relationships with each other were issues with which the president had to contend. According to Richard Cheney, Ford improved over time as the captain of his crew.

> At the beginning, he was relatively uncritical of people. He would tolerate . . . sloppy staff work, let meetings go on too long that needed to be shut off because they had done everything that they were designed to do or could conceivably do. He was willing to see virtually anybody; nondiscriminating in his use of time. That changed over time. The longer he was there, the tougher he got because he came to recognize good quality staff work and to insist upon it. He . . . constantly improved in terms of his ability to judge a quality operation and insist upon it in his own staff system. . . . It's experience, and few congressmen have that kind of experience.[8]

Ford's most significant weakness as an organizational leader was his inability to control intrastaff conflict and to fire those staff members whose participation in it was virtually constant, and sometimes public. Ford told the author, ''There were cases where there was a conflict generated primarily because of jealously of one kind or another and those types of conflict really bothered me. I never understood them because each one of the people were talented in their own right.''[9] The detrimental effect of ''turf battles'' among some members of the staff, according to Ford, was the diminution of ''a free flow of open discussion, which is what I truly felt was in the national interest . . . getting the best people I had debating pro and con what was the right solution.''[10] In his autobiography Ford admits his inability to stop or control the conflicts among some of his staff.

Throughout my political career, nothing upset me more than bickering among members of my staff. It was time-consuming, terribly distracting and unnecessary. I had told my aides that I wouldn't tolerate it. But it continued, even accelerated, when I entered the White House, and—given the ambitions and personalities of the people involved—there didn't seem to be any way to put an immediate stop to it.[11]

One of the continuing controversies among Ford's staff was the quality of the speech-writing process directed by Robert Hartmann, the president's close confidant and one aide who was continually distrustful of those staff who had worked for Richard Nixon. In describing the preparation of his 1976 State of the Union address, Ford recalls that staff disagreements over Hartmann's draft were so pronounced that separate drafts had been written and, two days before the speech was to be delivered, there was no staff agreement on a final version.

I convened a meeting in the Cabinet Room of everyone who had worked on the speech. The disagreements continued. Finally, after about three hours of this, I had heard enough. "Damn it," I said, slamming my hand on the table, "we've got to stop bickering over these little details. I want a final draft by noon tomorrow."

That was one of the few times I lost my temper during a meeting of this kind, but I was determined to avoid working over the speech right up to the last minute as had happened the year before.[12]

According to Ford, Robert Hartmann "had trouble with other people on the staff who either didn't like him or were jealous of him . . . and I had to oftentimes sort of mediate the differences between Bob's writing and the policy things that people wanted to include. But that's part of the job of being president."[13] Such mediation, however, is *not* part of the president's job. Indeed, that process took time away from presidential attention to bona fide responsibilities of the chief executive and caused Ford to appear within the organization, and sometimes in public, as a leader who was not in command of his White House staff. Ford's background as a consensus builder, and his own good-natured disposition, seemed to prevent him from solving the problem of staff conflict, as opposed to temporarily assuaging it. Comparing the handling of staff conflict in the Nixon administration with Ford's attempts, Terrence O'Donnell recalls that decisions were final in the Nixon White House, that staff might bicker temporarily with each other but there was no appeal to Haldeman or the president.

In the Ford White House there was no one with that amount of authority, that ultimate authority, other than the president, so bickering, instead of stopping with the chief of staff, sometimes went right in to the president. He really did take offense at the fact that the staff, at times senior staff members, were biting at each other's ankles and just didn't pull together. That upset him a great deal. . . . The fact that the president himself had to deal with it is significant.[14]

James Connor describes conflicts among Ford's staff as involving people "striving after authority and glory and wanting the credit for successes and trying to avoid the blame for disasters.''[15] In his opinion, Hartmann's conflicts with other staff were ''terribly injurious to Ford, and Ford did not end it. That is an administrative weakness.''[16] According to Ron Nessen, Ford was not ''tough enough'' in stopping intrastaff conflict.[17] Aside from creating organizational and individual stress, and depicting the president as a weak organizational leader, staff conflicts reflected aides' attempts to take credit for administration successes that should have gone to the president:

A lot of people in the Ford White House would . . . let on that they were the ones who wrote that speech or they were the ones who came up with that phrase or that policy in the context of putting one over on one of their staff rivals. But the effect of it was to make it look like Ford was just sitting there being manipulated like a puppet by the staff.[18]

Gerald Ford was not unlike many leaders in corporate America or academe, and certainly was one of a crowd of U.S. presidents, who have found it difficult to criticize, much less fire, their senior aides. Only major public scandals tend to force a chief executive to dismiss, or accept the resignation of, a staff member. Without significant judicial and press attention, Walter Jenkins, Sherman Adams, and Bert Lance probably would have remained in their presidents' White Houses. According to Terrence O'Donnell, even Richard Nixon ''just could not dress down anyone or could not fire anyone. . . . He just wasn't comfortable in doing that himself. He got it all done through Bob Haldeman.''[19] Gerald Ford would not delegate that authority to his chief of staff, and indeed the spokes-of-the-wheel structure made it virtually impossible to legitimately bestow that authority on Rumsfeld or Cheney. Consequently Ford was perceived, by the press and members of his own staff, to be a relatively weak administrator in the context of resolving staff conflicts. However, the very characteristics that prevented his evolution into an authoritarian organizational leader endeared him to staff as a communicator within the White House.

Those who worked most closely with Gerald Ford during his two years as president, as well as those who knew him for a number of years prior to his ascending to the presidency, describe his personal characteristics similarly.

He is a decent man. He is decent right to the core.[20]

He was much too kind to people who worked for him. Much too charitable in his evaluation of them. [When it came to keeping former Nixon employees in his White House as well as other staff who caused conflict or were the focus of it] he was too soft-hearted.[21]

He is and was a thoroughly decent man that the staff really admired and [they] worked endless hours to help him. . . . Because he was such a decent person and a friendly, personal individual . . . there was a staff dedication to helping him as well as an official necessity of helping him. . . . He engendered a great deal of support and loyalty from his staff and that's a very important leadership quality. I think he was a good leader of his staff.[22]

He wasn't mean enough to be president. He was the master of compromise, accommodation. . . . He just was not tough enough. He would hate me to say that but probably knows it down deep in his heart.[23]

Indeed, several of the personal characteristics attributed to Ford by his staff are similar to those used to describe Harry Truman (see Chapter 2). Not surprisingly, considering these assessments of Ford's personal qualities, the perceptions of his communication style when interacting with staff are that he was a friendly and relaxed communicator. Confident in the organizational structure he adopted after assuming the presidency, in the "staffing system" used to obtain information, and in his ability to make decisions based on his honest attempts to entertain multiple viewpoints from diverse sources, Ford apparently was at ease with staff in group meetings and in individual consultations. John J. Casserly, a speechwriter in the Ford White House, wrote in his diary on February 10, 1975: "My foremost impression is that Mr. Ford is remarkably calm in the job. This continues to make a deep impact on me. He exudes quiet confidence."[24] On April 25 he added this comment: "He [Ford] is candid. The man simply tells the truth when he speaks. He is good-natured, even-tempered and extraordinarily calm for a man with such responsibility."[25]

John Hersey, the author/journalist who observed interactions between Ford and his staff during a one-week period in 1975, also described an atmosphere of calmness pervading the Ford White House in a book based on his week with the president: "And the center of the calm, its essence and source, has obviously been the President. With Truman it was all nervous energy, moral intensity, emotion in harness, history clamoring for expression. Here the strongest impression . . . is of relaxation."[26] In talking with Hersey, Ford explained part of the reason his communication inside the White House appeared relaxed; it was controlled. Referring to his mother, the president emphasized: " 'She taught me that you don't respond in a wild, uncontrolled way; you just better sit back and take a hard look and try to make the best decision without letting emotions be the controlling factor.' "[27] In their interactions, according to Hersey, Ford spoke deliberately, "without emotion, sometimes pausing in midsentence to gather his thoughts, and using my first name often."[28] Additionally, Hersey observed, Ford seemed anxious to identify with each person to whom he spoke in the Oval Office, and possessed a "protean need and knack" to become the person with whom he was talking.[29]

Ford's personal interest in his staff was reflected in his tendency to encourage their contributions in policy-making discussions. Philip Buchen recalls, "I think he gave everybody a fair chance to get his point of view through and he rarely shut people off. People liked to work for him. There was no question about that."[30] Simply put, Ford enjoyed the company of other individuals; like FDR he encouraged, and was convinced he benefited from, discussions with his senior staff as well as individuals outside the White House. He learned to read and absorb information quickly but believed there was no substitute for "talking things out." He was confident in his ability to listen, and his friendly nature prompted him to talk with a variety of individuals each day, and not always just for fifteen minutes. According to O'Donnell, "Ford's schedule tended to get packed during the day, and it was very hard to keep free time for him because he would agree to see more and more people. . . . The appointment system tried to protect his time, but he sometimes was his own worst enemy in that he would add people."[31]

Even outside of formal appointments, Ford practiced the art of inclusion when it came to soliciting advice from aides. O'Donnell, who probably saw the president more frequently than any other aide during a given day, did not hold an advisory position in the White House. However, Ford sometimes asked his advice on matters. "If I were to walk back from the Residence with him or to the Residence . . . he would chat and he would ask, 'How are you doing?'; 'What do you think about this?' . . . It was very pleasant and I would give opinions."[32] Such interchanges remind one of Eisenhower seeking information from his military aides each day as they escorted him to and from the Oval Office.

Another example of Ford's attentive communication style was his approach to receiving foreign ambassadors. During the Nixon administration, on the day that foreign emissaries were invited to meet the president, each ambassador was put in a different ceremonial room in the White House so that Nixon could move from room to room and exchange only one or two minutes of pleasantries with the dignitaries. Gerald Ford, however, invited each ambassador into the Oval Office, and a ceremonial function became a substantive discussion where the emissaries "would . . . tell the president all about their countries and bilateral problems the country had with the United States."[33]

The only major departure from Ford's policy of including staff in his deliberations, in listening—often with great patience—to their ideas, was his exclusion of Jerald terHorst from the group of senior aides he convened when he informed them of his decision to pardon Richard Nixon. Although Ford may have made this decision to prevent his press secretary from having to lie to the press corps before the announcement was made, terHorst's resignation over the incident exacerbated Ford's public relations problems with the decision. The president paid a significant political price—some aides believe election to the presidency—for the pardon decision and the negative reactions to Ford it precipitated.

Nevertheless, Gerald Ford was judged by those who spoke with him the most to be a friendly, attentive, and relaxed communicator in the White House—much more effective interpersonally than as an orator. The reputation of being honest, decent, good ol' Jerry, which had ultimately persuaded Richard Nixon to select him as Spiro Agnew's replacement, continued in the White House. Despite the Nixon pardon, his private communication style ultimately was judged not to be different from his public persona. Such was not the case with his successor.

CARTER AS ORGANIZATIONAL LEADER

Just as Gerald Ford was perceived by his staff as a weak manager but a competent interpersonal communicator within his White House organization, so

Jimmy Carter impressed his staff as an attentive administrator whose public persona was much different from that displayed to staff during interactions within the Oval Office. Observing Carter shortly before his inauguration, Brzezinski recalls, "I was on the whole struck by his coolness, deliberateness, and his obvious sense of systematic planning priorities."[34] According to James Fallows, who saw Carter from the viewpoint of a speechwriter disturbed by the operation of the speechwriting unit within the White House: "The virtues of an organization man—preserving order, preventing errors—were those Carter prized; and if an attempt to produce more imaginative policies, broader sources of information, even better speech drafts, would violate these principles of order, it was not likely to prevail."[35]

This degree of commitment to organizational order was foreign to Gerald Ford, and while he might have used some of Carter's passion for order to control the internecine conflicts that sometimes plagued his White House, Carter sometimes paid a price for what seemed to be a commitment to programmatic priorities over people. Anne Wexler observed that "Carter saw himself as a manager and not a communicator. . . . He saw himself as a problem solver, but he never thought of himself as a . . . symbol or a leader."[36] However, Carter, like Ford, was a better communicator inside the White House than he was a public speaker.

> We knew what he wanted and how he wanted it. We had intensive debates as to what policy should be and how it should be implemented and what the structure should be. He knew all about it and was very much a part of it. . . . He saw himself as a problem solver, as a planner. He did not think that part of his job was selling . . . these concepts.[37]

Carter's lack of interest in "selling" his priorities was reflected in his interactions with his staff, as well as in his perceived inability to rally the public around his priority programs. As Stuart Eizenstat explains, unlike Ronald Reagan, Carter was not

> a highly ideological person—so that a lot of issues were left up for grabs because there wasn't imparted . . . to the bureaucracy nor to the White House staff a clear sense of "Here's my direction and you know what it is and you make some decisions before it gets to me. Or try to shape the process so that it comes out the way you know I want it." In that sense the broader communication sometimes was wanting.[38]

In short, Carter's perception of himself as a planner and problem solver did not include the need for team building, for mobilizing and motivating those with whom he worked daily through interpersonal interactions. It was against his personal and professional nature to be a cheerleader, though that, as Franklin Roosevelt and Lyndon Johnson well knew, is a primary requisite for an activist president—and Carter came into office intending to attain some of the most ambitious legislative program goals since those adopted by Lyndon Johnson. Carter's inability to sustain an ongoing collegial coalition of key aides to organize and prioritize his programs was one reason for his failure to meet these goals.

Jimmy Carter's senior aides perceived their president as having a dominant communication style in his interpersonal interactions with them. In general he was not judged to be friendly, like Ford, or open or self-disclosive, and certainly not relaxed. According to Robert Norton, individuals perceived as possessing a dominant style are ''enthusiastic, forceful, active, competitive, self-confident, self-assured, conceited, and business-like.''[39] Carter's senior staff have used these terms to describe their perceptions of the president.

Stuart Eizenstat observes that anyone meeting Carter in small group discussions within the White House found him ''extremely articulate, very persuasive, very focused. . . . There was a directness about his communication.''[40] To Zbigniew Brzezinski he was a paradox.

On the outside, and especially if he initiated it, he was very warm and engaging, and people . . . were always very impressed by his intelligence and also by his warmth. In fact . . . he was much colder than the image except with those with whom he was very intimate, like his wife or his daughter, and some of his close friends.[41]

In his memoirs Brzezinski recalls:

I noted in my journal that ''in personal relations he is . . . somewhat cold; but in front of groups he is warm and highly complimentary about me.'' Accordingly, I concluded . . . I had better concentrate on providing Carter with crisp briefings, frank even if irritating comments, clear memos, and effective support. Reliance and trust, rather than warmth . . . would work best in consolidating the relationship that had developed during the campaign.

Accordingly, I did not use the morning briefings, or the many other occasions when we were either traveling together or in some other one-on-one situation, to try to cultivate a personal friendship. I made it a point to be concise, businesslike, and utterly forthright.[42]

Brzezinski further emphasizes that his relationship with Carter was closer ''when things moved instinctively the way he would like to have them move,'' that is, when foreign policy decisions were popular and/or supported by Congress.[43] At other times, ''I felt some distance, even coldness.''[44] Brzezinski writes that a barrier seemed to develop between him and the president as the years of his term passed.

There were times when I felt that he was trying to puncture that barrier, to reestablish some measure of warmth and communion. Sometimes it was through a personal phone call, just to say something pleasant or funny; more often it was through an abrupt, unexpected turn in a conversation, with him mentioning—in a totally unrelated fashion—something highly personal.[45]

Additionally, he recalls, Carter's businesslike demeanor was more apt to soften on Saturday mornings, when more time was available for personal interactions. ''After the national security briefing, he would often lean back in his chair and engage me in a conversation, on any subject. We might talk about history, or religion, or speculate about politics.''[46] This account reminds one of the late afternoon discussions John Kennedy held with some of his top aides, when the pressures of the day and the appointments on his schedule had abated.

Brzezinski perceived Carter as ''very open and very frank'' in his communications with senior staff, and to boost his own staff's morale, the national security adviser sometimes invited the president to National Security Council meetings, where ''he was always very effective. If he wanted to communicate, he was very good.''[47] However, as other staff members attest, Carter did not always appear to have the interest or the ability to motivate his *senior* staff to form a collegial team. Jody Powell, who knew the president as well as anyone in the White House, explains that Carter did not spend time ''stroking'' his aides because of his own orientation to work and his personal reticence. ''He was detached in the sense of being more immune than most people I've ever known to . . . emotional swings and ups and downs. . . . Never getting too excited about the good things. Never getting depressed about the things that go wrong.''[48] His view of his job, and those of his aides, was, in Powell's words:

> ''Yeah, it's a tough job, tough life, but if you take the job, you do it the best you can, and that ought to be its own reward.'' And that's the way he approached his work and . . . he . . . pretty much expected people who worked for him to take the same approach to theirs. . . . For some others . . . probably you might have gotten more out of them if a little more back-slapping and fanny-patting would have been appropriate.[49]

In Powell's opinion, Carter expressed warmth in his communications inside the White House, in the sense that ''he inspired a tremendous . . . level of both loyalty and affection among the people that dealt with him,'' although ''he didn't spend a lot of time congratulating people on a good job.''[50] Powell's perception is not surprising, since he was an intimate confidant and friend of the president. However, other senior aides, like Brzezinski and Anne Wexler, saw the president from a greater psychosocial distance. Brzezinski, for instance, recalls that Carter ''never thanked me for anything, nor did he ever rebuke me sharply.''[51] According to Anne Wexler:

> He was quite a formal person, at least with me. We communicated a great deal with things we were working on together on a professional basis, but he was very businesslike. I have seen him often in very relaxed situations at Camp David and other places where he was very warm and very friendly and always solicitous of your family . . . but I never think of him as being extremely warm.[52]

Wexler recalls that Carter's relationship with Hamilton Jordan, Jody Powell, and Frank Moore, all Georgians, seemed more friendly than that with his other aides, mostly because they had been close personal associates since his days as Georgia's governor. ''I think that the rest of us worked with him on a truly . . . professional level. He was always very cordial. He always made his wants very clearly known. He was always extremely good with feedback.''[53] In describing the president's communication relationship with most of his staff, she emphasizes that it was not "buddy-buddy at all. . . . It was professional."[54]

Hamilton Jordan, another of Carter's closest confidants, echoed Powell's assessment of the president's communication style, and also described him as a person devoid of a temper but direct in his interactions with staff. "He wouldn't embarrass you, but he would just tell you quite frankly that he disagreed with you."[55] As was the case with most of his predecessors, however, Carter was less direct when providing negative feedback in a meeting with several individuals. According to Hedley Donovan, although his comments on paper might be "crisp," they were less so in meetings. "Along with the southern good manners, there was a distaste for face-to-face disagreement."[56] Not surprisingly, therefore, Carter listened to "head-on disagreement and even direct criticism with a tightly controlled calm" and sometimes "with visible effort."[57] With due respect to Donovan's observations, Carter's distaste for contentious discussions probably was more a function of his office than of his upbringing. As was discussed earlier, most presidents, like most organizational leaders in other sectors of American life, are uncomfortable in the presence of staff conflict and are often inept in managing it effectively.

Perhaps one reason for the perception of Carter as a rather cold, detached intraorganizational communicator was his avowed preference for communicating in writing rather than in face-to-face settings. Jack Watson, another Georgian close to the president, told the author:

> I think that he would have benefited from a somewhat more informal, more give-and-take, more personally interactive style. When he did that, he could be, he is, an extraordinarily charming man. . . . But his natural inclination, partly on grounds of efficiency . . . was to do as much as he possible could the other way [communicating in writing], because you can get more done . . . you can gather more information if you're not taking up time with personal meetings.[58]

In short, Carter didn't "chat."[59] Another reason for staff perceptions of Carter as being direct, businesslike, and not particularly warm was his personality, characterized in part by a shyness, an "inner-directedness," a "desire to be alone" such as that found in the complex of personal characteristics possessed by Richard Nixon.[60]

Carter's personality, and his preferred means of communicating, resulted in a dominant communicator style that sometimes sent conflicting cues to his staff as well as to other individuals in his administration. According to Brzezinski, the president used several phrases in his interactions that meant the opposite of what he actually said. "I understand" meant "I don't want to argue with you any more, but I don't agree with you"—an attempt by Carter to pacify the person. "I will stand firm" meant he might change his position. "This doesn't bother me at all" meant he might indeed be deeply troubled.[61] Obviously it was important for staff to understand the intended meanings behind the president's words, and Brzezinski indicates that misunderstandings were often created among staff when the president used these phrases.

Finally, a nonverbal component of Carter's communication style was his smile, although Brzezinski has noted that the president exhibited different smiles depending on whether he was communicating in public or private settings.

Carter was famous for his smile. I soon learned that he in fact had several smiles. There was first of all the genial smile for public consumption. I was initially deceived by it because it seemed so warm and so forthcoming, and yet once you got to know him you knew that this was an outward smile, one with little individual affection in it. . . . Then there was the smile which he used to mask anger. More often than not, when angry, he would smile even while expressing displeasure, but only if one knew him well did one sense that behind the mask was unadulterated fury. Then there was a shy, relaxed smile, the expression of the individual at ease, which Carter revealed only occasionally to his intimates.[62]

Direct, forthcoming, businesslike—these are the words used to describe Jimmy Carter's communication style by those with whom he interacted the most. Yet these words do not describe Carter as a public communicator, famous for the big smile, the compassionate public demeanor. It is clear from speaking with several of the president's senior aides that his public persona was not reflected in his private communication style. His interest in working alone and in communicating in writing rather than orally is not usually associated with dominance in interpersonal exchanges. And yet, in his interactions with staff Carter communicated in ways reflecting the dominant style: directly, self-confidently, forcefully, businesslike. His was a style shaped by his personality and his past—but it was not a style conducive to mobilizing a team or creating an organizational climate supportive of an activist presidency. Jimmy Carter's public persona masked his private one, and his communication style inside inside the White House did not facilitate the accomplishment of his goals outside its walls.

A DIFFERENT LOOK AT THE GREAT COMMUNICATOR: RONALD REAGAN AS ORGANIZATIONAL LEADER

The manager of the White House in Ronald Reagan's presidency was not Ronald Reagan, as is discussed in Chapter 5, and as a result, the formalistic style of management described by Richard Tanner Johnson does not adequately account for the type of presidential detachment from the management of the White House that characterized the Reagan administration. After all, the Eisenhower model, based on informed and involved, albeit hidden-hand, control is synonymous with the formalistic style. The style of management used in Reagan's organization, however, *was* the formalistic approach, where decisions and lines of communication reached the president in a hierarchically structured, pyramidal organizational arrangement. In the first term the "manager" of the White House was the troika of individuals in charge of conducting its daily operations, developing and implementing a legislative agenda, and conducting an effective public relations campaign about Reagan and his presidency. In the second term the manager was Donald Regan, and for a short time Howard Baker. In short, the management style exhibited in the Reagan White House was formalistic, but the degree of presidential attention to management was much different from that characteristic of Eisenhower's style.

Reagan's strength was not in managing the functions of his staff inside the White House but in articulating his general goals for the country to public audiences. Hans Mark, who served both Carter and Reagan as secretary of the Air Force, describes the latter's leadership ability as being able to communicate "a very clear vision about where the country should go and what he was going to do. In a certain sense, he was almost the reverse of Carter. That is, he clearly had the capacity to see into the future and he had an agenda when he became president."[63] Reagan's priorities, according to Mark, were to reduce the federal government's control over individuals' lives and to improve the nation's position as an international power.

> He really made those two things his big priorities. It was simple. People could understand that. And the interesting thing was that this was not only something that he said in public, but in the meetings I sat through. . . . It was something that his close associates probably got tired of hearing, but it really was there. I think he understood that his job really was to formulate large ideas in simple terms and then talk to people about it.[64]

Agreeing with Brzezinski's perception of Carter's public and private personas, Mark attributes Reagan's ability to communicate his priorities, both to the public and to his own staff, to an "integrated" personality. "Carter felt he had to act out when he was talking to the public. The real Jimmy Carter was the guy you saw in the Cabinet Room, not the guy you saw on television."[65] Ronald Reagan's public persona, to a great degree, was a manifestation of his private self.

One of the characteristics of this private self was an easygoing temperament, according to Hedley Donovan, that was more open than that of Carter, Nixon, or Johnson, and that prevented Reagan from feeling threatened by senior staff who questioned his views.[66] Of course part of Reagan's "openness" may have been due to the president's understanding that he was a delegating chief executive who had little choice but to listen to those to whom he had assigned specific responsibilities. However, it was also due in part to the nature of the man—a successful politician confident about his view of the world as it was and as it should be. If he was not the manager of the White House organization, he was certainly its head cheerleader. Edwin Meese recalls:

> I think there probably are very few leaders who projected or instilled the sense of loyalty and enthusiasm that he did. If he walked down the halls, as he did, and poked his head in offices and talked to people, this was a tremendous stimulus to everybody from Cabinet members . . . to secretaries, janitors, and everybody else. He was a person that people liked to be with. He was a person that was able to bring out the best in people.[67]

Interestingly, in their discussion of Reagan's second term Jane Mayer and Doyle McManus paint a contradictory picture of Reagan as the White House's spiritual leader. "He . . . seemed unsure about the location of most of his aides' offices, and he only visited his chief of staff, who worked a few yards down the hall, two or three times a year on special occasions, like birthdays. Likewise, White House officials rarely wandered into the Oval Office except on official, prescribed business."[68] However, Robert McFarlane, who certainly was not the Reagan friend and loyalist that Edwin Meese was during the president's terms, describes the president as being

> always warm and solicitous, more than gentlemanly caring. That was both in daily dialogue and in his consideration of things beyond our formal agenda—my family, my welfare, my children's welfare and little things which expressed a genuine warmth and a caring attitude. . . . He was a good guy, a hail-fellow-well-met, a man given to humor and to kind of performing, but a very nice person—genuinely caring about people who worked for him.[69]

According to Helene von Damm, the president's personal secretary, Reagan was informal and warm in manner, possessed an even disposition and an impish and self-deprecating sense of humor, and never said anything unkind about anyone.[70]

If Jimmy Carter's personality was complex, Reagan's was equally so. Despite the above descriptions of his personal characteristics by those who know him well, other staff relate different perceptions of the man. Larry Speakes, Reagan's press secretary for most of his administration, suggests that privately Reagan tended "to be a loner, content to spend most of his time with his wife and no one else," who almost never revealed his emotions to anyone but his wife.[71] Similarly, Mayer and McManus found Reagan a paradox in relating to his staff. "Members of the White House staff often marveled at the President's demeanor: all genial smiles on the surface, yet always maintaining a certain distance and avoiding any real intimacy."[72] Indeed, they emphasize that "just as the star on a movie set would tend to be oblivious of members of the crew who did not directly interact with him or his performances, Reagan evinced almost no curiosity about officials on his team who were not among his inner circle. Beneath the friendly facade was a relentless indifference."[73] Even von Damm admits in her memoirs: "He did it when we nudged him, but it was not natural for him to express gratitude or admiration for a job well done."[74]

Two additional observations are relevant to a discussion of Ronald Reagan's approach to White House management. First, Reagan, like his predecessors, detested confrontations. Robert McFarlane observed "A president, to communicate, must be willing to tolerate conflict, and President Reagan didn't like conflict very much."[75] Indeed, Donald Regan has written that Reagan disliked confrontations "more than any man I have ever known."[76] In fact, Reagan's description of the conversation between him and the president when the decision was made for Regan to leave his position as chief of staff portrays Reagan as sad, not angry or combative. David Stockman's version of the conversation he had with the president after his critical assessment of the Reagan administration's economic policies was published in *The Atlantic* also depicts Reagan as a sorrowful grandfather, wronged by a family member. The president's distaste for confrontations, even those which did not directly involve him, probably accounted for his inability to fire members of his staff—a managerial weakness shared by Carter, Ford, and most of the modern presidents. According to Edward Rollins, who ran Reagan's political office in the White House during the first term and helped conduct the 1984 campaign, Reagan " 'just couldn't bring himself to fire anyone. If he had fired some of the people who created some of the early problems, we wouldn't have had a lot of the others that came along later.' "[77] One strength of an organization's leader is his ability to remove detrimental members from its midst, as well as to select and cultivate the contributions of its loyal workers. Yet several presidents, including Harry Truman, Richard Nixon, and Jimmy Carter, suffered the consequences of waiting too long to sever the bond between the White House and a staff member.

Second, Reagan, like many decision makers, judged the quality of the information he received by the depth of his trust in the one communicating that information to him. According to Bob Schieffer and Gary Gates: "If Reagan trusted a staffer, he seldom questioned his recommendations. The problem was that once he placed his faith in someone, he seemed unable to revise his judgment about him."[78] Such trust was one reason that Reagan fell victim to the Iran-Contra scandal, if indeed he was a victim. The president refused to believe that those he trusted would deceive him or give him bad advice. Moreover, he was sufficiently detached from the management of the White House to be in no position to determine the credibility of the people around him or of the information they provided him. He had structured his White House so as to manage by delegation, and he was caught in the trap he himself had lain. The ways presidents manage their staffs sometimes help disentangle them from such traps, or prevent them in the first place. Reagan's approach was little help in this regard.

As was discussed in Chapter 5, Ronald Reagan was an "oral" president, preferring to listen to opinions from his staff, to discuss specific ideas in the context of his overarching presidential goals. He understood the relative richness of information presented face-to-face, perhaps because of his sensitivity to nonverbal language acquired during years as an actor. According to sources cited by Schieffer and Gates, "he did seem to possess an uncanny ability during discussion to read body language and to sense concerns among staff members even when they were unspoken."[79] Additionally, Reagan "felt that memoranda by themselves were so inanimate that you couldn't get a real clash of ideas or a meeting of minds."[80] Consequently he preferred face-to-face discussions with aides to the presentation of ideas in writing, and had done so since his years in California's statehouse. Meese stated in 1980:

> He likes to sit down and listen to the arguments. . . . He feels that in the adversary situation, in the contest of ideas, you get the best possible ideas, the widest scope and variety of

action. If you're just reading, it's only two-dimensional. But orally, it allows him to question the participants. One idea sparks another. Having a meeting creates a focal point for decision-making. You get the key policy advisers and after they've had an input, it builds teamwork.[81]

These discussions with aides, particularly during the first term, therefore resulted not only in richer information for the president's use in decision making but also in the establishment of networks among presidential aides that cemented their relationships as part of the president's White House team.

In describing Reagan's communication style, his aides portray someone exhibiting a dramatic style, generally because of his use of stories in conversations inside the Oval Office. According to Meese,

Usually he did that to put people at ease. But he would often open meetings and occasionally close meetings [with stories], particularly if they had been intense meetings, because he wanted people to leave in a relaxed frame of mind. It was a device that he's used all of his life. . . . Sometimes he would use it to make a point. . . . And other times he had just heard a story and thought it was funny and he wanted to share it with people.[82]

Donald Regan recalls that "Reagan started nearly every meeting with a story . . . ; he thought that laughter brought people closer together and dispelled the anxiety that they feel in the presence of the mighty."[83] Accordingly, "Deaver had a new joke or bit of amusing gossip for him every morning as the first order of business—a practice I carried on with support from the Vice President."[84]

Reagan also was perceived as an animated communicator—when interacting with staff and other aides he knew well. Regan calls him a "talented conversationalist with a gift for listening," a chief executive who was animated in Cabinet meetings because "he loved the give-and-take of policy discussions in the Cabinet councils, when he had a chance to pronounce on the broad general principles that primarily interested him."[85] Mayer and McManus write that in Cabinet and staff meetings, Reagan was "a wonderful raconteur . . . as well as a good listener. But he rarely made substantive points. A staff member who . . . also served in the Ford White House said, 'Ford led the discussion; Reagan followed it.' "[86] In meetings with people he did not know well, Reagan is described as being shy and passive. In such situations, according to Regan, "jokes were usually omitted and the President would listen intently but seldom speak."[87] Additionally, his former chief of staff recalls, Reagan would be especially passive in esoteric discussions when experts on the subject were present. When asked why he was relatively uncommunicative in those situations, the president told Regan "that he hesitated to ask questions because he did not wish to seem uninformed in the presence of people he did not know well."[88]

With people he did know well, however, the president was more comfortable communicating in Oval Office discussions—in large part because of the ability of senior staff to tailor their messages to the president's communication style. According to Larry Speakes, James Baker purposively "spoke in short sentences, used anecdotes to illustrate his points, and repeated what he said'' to communicate his views to the president.[89] Similarly, the president's personal secretary recalls that Reagan's first national security adviser, William Clark, and Edwin Meese ''cultivated very direct styles of speaking. No circumlocution. They got straight to the point, and they'd maintain eye contact with him as they spoke. As soon as his eyes wandered, they'd try another approach.''[90] According to von Damm, Robert McFarlane's rate of speaking at times was too slow, his style too dull to maintain Reagan's attention. On the other hand, the close personal and professional relationship shared by Reagan and Meese contributed to an ease in communication between them that seemed to rely on body language.

> During Cabinet meetings, Ed was always busily scribbling on a yellow legal pad and only every now and then—just when the President was shooting him a glance—would Ed look up. Their eyes would meet and they'd seem to understand each other. Only at the end of the meeting would Ed speak. He'd sit back in his chair and summarize everything that had been said. . . . And as he spoke, Ronald Reagan would nod vigorously. . . . I'd seen them do this for years, first in California and then in Washington.[91]

Attentive in staff discussions, passive in meetings with several strangers, a storyteller in a number of circumstances—these are the perceptions of Reagan as a communicator inside the White House. Unlike many of his predecessors, he apparently was slow to anger and almost never expressed that anger. Even Donald Regan emphasizes that he never heard the president lose his temper or ''utter a rude or unkind word.''[92] During telephone conversations with congressmen when he sought their support, he ''never bullied, never threatened, never cajoled''; he spoke in even tones, explained his position, and made meticulous notes as he listened to the party on the other end of the line.[93]

Edwin Meese also describes Reagan as a *friendly* communicator in the White House, and one whose private and public personas were similar. Other aides describe the president as attentive, yet detached to varying degrees from his staff or from the discussions among them in which he participated. Mayer and McManus provide more critical assessments of the president as a communicator than do former members of his senior staff:

> The Great Communicator, it turned out, was frequently uncommunicative with those closest at hand. In critical policy decisions, Reagan often kept his thoughts to himself, leaving his aides to interpret his ambiguous signals as they pleased. He exuded manly bonhomie at a distance, yet seemed wooden and remote to those who worked with him. Magnetic in public and sometimes inspirational on the stump, behind the scenes he was both amiable and friendless, ill informed and incurious, trusting and careless, stubborn and passive, larger than life yet less than imagined.[94]

These authors also have described Reagan as a president for whom most meetings, conferences, and consultations were scripted, that he studied note cards each evening in preparation for comments he was expected to deliver the following morning. According to Meese:

> I think that sometimes some people did tend to go overboard on that. It was more a mannerism of the people who were writing those kinds of memos. I never did, and the people who worked for me never did. I think some of them did tend to get overly detailed in terms of trying to get out a script, talking points as they are known, in more detail than was necessary. My view was that . . . talking points and the . . . outline . . . were better than trying to do something in script form.[95]

However, Meese recalls that Reagan would sometimes ''make a couple of notes on a card to make sure that he remembered the points himself.''[96]

Taking into account the perceptions of his friends as well as of his detractors, those senior aides who understood him and those who simply attempted to serve him, it appears that an assessment of Ronald Reagan as a communicator within the White House should depend on who his audience was at a given time. He was an enigma as an organizational leader, able to motivate individuals toward the accomplishment of his presidential goals yet unable and/or unwilling to oversee, even in the broadest sense, the efforts of those upon whose work those accomplishments depended. Reagan, or his designates, practiced a formalistic style of management, using hierarchical lines of communication and responsibility to delegate work and to make decisions. The president was an enigma as an interpersonal communicator—his style can be characterized as attentive, relaxed, animated, and dramatic, yet at times he exhibited none of the behaviors associated with these style constructs. He could also be passive, disinterested, and inattentive.

It is interesting to note that the observations of Mayer and McManus are based on assessments of Reagan in the second term, when the troika of his closest associates was not surrounding him daily. It was then that decisions seemed to be made around him, not by him, as had been the case when he was a participant in the Meese–Deaver–Baker discussions that had characterized Oval Office communication in the first term. It was in the second term that individuals outside the senior staff began to conduct and oversee some of the responsibilities of senior staff, as was done in Nixon's second term, when the president's detachment allowed individuals other than his senior aides to make decisions that would later haunt him, such as the evolution of the Watergate cover-up. Reagan, to some degree, found the same situation in his second term, when his only link with the White House organization—and Cabinet officers, for that matter—was his chief of staff.

Under these circumstances the Iran-Contra operation began, developed, and eventually erupted into a major political scandal and an organizational embarrassment. The president who cared little about learning from his predecessors' mistakes was doomed to repeat some of them, including a preference for delegation and detachment, even the abdication of his executive responsibilities. The

White House is an organization, and though a chief of staff may oversee its daily operation, the responsibility for its products, its decisions and policies, and its integrity reside solely with the chief executive. As a result, the ways a president communicates with his senior staff, his communication style, and the way he directs the work of that staff, his management style, are inextricably linked and crucial to the success of the White House as the source and sustenance of presidential policies.

THE SIGNIFICANCE OF COMMUNICATION STYLE IN THE WHITE HOUSE

The management styles of Gerald Ford and Jimmy Carter were adopted, in part, because of the perceived deleterious effects of the Watergate scandal on public trust in the presidency and in the White House as an organization. Their communication styles, however, were composites of behaviors based on personal characteristics, their professional backgrounds, and the communication experiences they brought to the Oval Office that had served them well in previous leadership positions. By the time Ronald Reagan reached the White House, the shadow of Watergate over it had faded, and his management style was one with which he was comfortable and one that seemingly had been successful for him as a state governor. It also was a style that contrasted with that of his predecessor. He well knew the criticism Carter had engendered for appearing to be too attentive to detail, too unwilling to delegate nonpresidential tasks to subordinates.

Consequently, although Reagan's formalistic approach to management was already his favored approach, it did not hurt his presidential image to distance himself from a managerial style that seemed to create disorganization in the Carter White House and inordinate attention by the president to staff tasks. Reagan's communication style with his staff, presidentially passive during formal discussions but personally animated in less formal interactions, was a by-product of his detached approach to White House management. It was also a style based, at least to some degree, on his experiences as an actor, where communication is scripted, rehearsed, recorded, and then, at least for a time, forgotten.

Gerald Ford was more effective than either Carter or Reagan as a communicator inside the White House. After his first few weeks in office he adopted an organizational structure that facilitated order among his staff *and* accessibility to the president. He was an excellent listener, a relaxed, friendly communicator with his staff. His collegial management style helped create an environment conducive to the search for and use of information from multiple sources. His communication style engendered trust and loyalty in subordinates, and fostered a supportive organizational climate in which they felt encouraged to provide ideas and recommendations that were sometimes at odds with the president's opinions. Nevertheless, Ford's public image did not depict the competencies seen in private settings. Despite the supposed good quality of the information he received, it did not emerge as a package of well-defined presidential proposals that precipitated congressional or public support. His strengths as a communicator inside the White House did not translate into an image of strong leadership ability outside its walls.

Jimmy Carter had laudable aspirations for his presidency and emphasized his value as a trustworthy Washington outsider—an alternative to the Nixon/Ford years. Unfortunately for the president, he could not, or would not, spend the time it takes to mold an organizational team that could cohesively and coherently plan and execute the myriad policies he wished to initiate. His style of management was less collegial than it was cooperative. Senior aides from Georgia may have felt close to the president as a result of his communications with them—such was not the case with other members of his senior staff. Carter spent considerable time honing his ability to read and assimilate information; he spent little time, until assessing the state of his presidency in the summer of 1979, reflecting on how he might change the ways he related to, and interacted with, the members of his staff, his Cabinet, and the leaders of Congress.

During the last year of his term, the president spend much time and energy following the daily events in Iran and the ongoing fate of U.S. hostages there; he was and is a humanitarian of the first class. However, his inability to organize his White House early in his presidency and to put his presidential goals into a priority order affected his credibility in Congress and ultimately within the nation in general. Moreover, the personal detachment, even coldness, that he apparently communicated during interactions with several of his senior staff reflected a presidential inability to sustain a group of energetic enthusiasts throughout his first three years in office. The strengths of Carter as planner and problem solver, as administrator, arc not necessarily traits of organizational leadership either in or outside the White House.

Despite the competencies Ford and Carter exhibited within the White House, both were rejected—although the 1976 election was a close one—for return to the presidency. On the other hand, Ronald Reagan, who received approbation as a public communicator, captured the support of the voting public and became the first two-term president since Dwight Eisenhower. However, as the initiator of structure, the seeker of information, the manager and leader of staff, he was the weakest of the post-Watergate presidents. The degree of his involvement in the Iran-Contra scandal is still to be determined as of this writing, but assuming he knew nothing of the plan to trade arms for hostages and divert some of the monetary proceeds of the deal to Contra forces in Nicaragua, such ignorance is perhaps more damning than if he had been aware of the operation. Staff may protect their president to provide him "deniability"—but ignorance of the magnitude suggested in the Iran-Contra congressional hearings, and even admitted by Reagan himself, is quite another matter.

Gerald Ford remarked in an interview with the author, "General Scowcroft [Ford's national security adviser] never in the first place had anybody in his NSC undertaking such things [as the Iran-Contra operation]. Secondly, if we did do something of that nature, he would personally supervise it and would see to it that I knew about it and supervised it. And that is another problem that caused our more recent difficulties."[97] The president was referring to Mr. Reagan's penchant for delegation, resulting in a detachment from, and an ignorance of, the activities in which his senior aides were engaged.

To date, Reagan's detachment from the management of his White House, as well as from substantive communication relationships with more than one to three members of his senior staff, has not affected an apparent public perception that his was a successful presidency. His popularity ratings were high as he left office, and a number of programs and policies derived from his vision of what the United States should be is his legacy. His weaknesses as a manager and communicator inside the White House perhaps seem inconsequential because his was indeed a public presidency—based on personal image, not professional competence. Mayer and McManus write:

> His was a rhetorical presidency, capable at its best of uniting the country behind a common vision. . . . But the Iran-contra affair revealed his rhetoric to be disconnected from his actions, and his actions to be disconnected from his policies. Ronald Reagan's talents had hidden his flaws too well; inevitably his unmasking was his unmaking.[98]

The ability to unite people behind a vision, however, is indeed a characteristic of an organizational, as well as a public, leader. It is no small feat, and Reagan deserves credit for that accomplishment, although his conservative agenda was not popular with some segments of society. The Iran-Contra scandal may become a scrape on the "Teflon presidency"—but it should be the managerial and communication incompetence behind that scandal, not the operation itself, that should cause historians to take more critical looks at Ronald Reagan's White House.

Do managerial and communication skills exhibited inside the White House make any difference to the success of a presidency? Is there a balance that presidents may achieve to lead both senior staffs and the public competently? What have the post-Watergate presidents taught us about the importance of structures and behaviors that encourage, rather than impede, the communication between a president and his senior staff? What communication competencies should presidents and their key aides possess to assist the development and execution of the policies that represent a president's goals or his national agenda? These are the questions that deserve attention in the final chapter.

NOTES

1. Richard Tanner Johnson, *Managing the White House* (New York: Harper & Row, 1974), p. 239.
2. Ibid., p. 3.
3. Alexander L. George, *Presidential Decisionmaking in Foreign Policy: The Effective Use of Information and Advice* (Boulder, CO: Westview Press, 1980), p. 150.
4. Ibid., p. 152.

5. Ibid., p. 158.
6. Robert Norton, *Communicator Style* (Beverly Hills, CA: Sage, 1983), p. 47.
7. Philip Buchen, interview with the author, November 5, 1987.
8. Richard Cheney, interview with the author, November 4, 1987.
9. Gerald R. Ford, interview with the author, April 21, 1987.
10. Ibid.
11. Gerald R. Ford, *A Time to Heal* (New York: Harper & Row and The Reader's Digest Association, 1979), pp. 184–85.
12. Ibid., p. 350.
13. Ford, interview with the author.
14. Terrence O'Donnell, interview with the author, November 4, 1987.
15. James Connor, interview with the author, July 15, 1987.
16. Ibid.
17. Ronald Nessen, interview with the author, November 5, 1987.
18. Ibid.
19. O'Donnell, interview with the author.
20. Donald Rumsfeld, interview with the author, August 10, 1987.
21. Buchen, interview with the author.
22. O'Donnell, interview with the author.
23. Robert Hartmann, interview with the author, November 5, 1987.
24. John J. Casserly, *The Ford White House* (Boulder, CO: Associated University Press, 1977), p. 39.
25. Ibid., p. 81.
26. John Hersey, *The President* (New York: Alfred A. Knopf, 1975), pp. 21–22.
27. Ibid., p. 86.
28. Ibid.
29. Ibid., p. 102.
30. Buchen, interview with the author.
31. O'Donnell, interview with the author.
32. Ibid.
33. Ibid.
34. Zbigniew Brzezinski, *Power and Principle* (New York: Farrar, Straus, Giroux, 1983), p. 14.
35. James Fallows, ''The Passionless Presidency II,'' *The Atlantic*, June 1980, p. 78.
36. Anne Wexler, interview with the author, June 15, 1989.
37. Ibid.
38. Stuart Eizenstat, interview with the author, June 16, 1989.
39. Norton, *Communicator Style*, p. 65.
40. Eizenstat, interview with the author.
41. Zbigniew Brzezinski, interview with the author, June 14, 1989.
42. Brzezinski, *Power and Principle*, p. 18.
43. Brzezinski, interview with the author.
44. Brzezinski, *Power and Principle*, p. 22.
45. Ibid., p. 19.
46. Ibid.
47. Brzezinski, interview with the author.
48. Jody Powell, interview with the author, June 16, 1989.
49. Ibid.

50. Ibid.
51. Brzezinski, *Power and Principle*, p. 18.
52. Wexler, interview with the author.
53. Ibid.
54. Ibid.
55. "How Carter Operates," an interview with Hamilton Jordan, *U.S. News & World Report*, February 21, 1977, p. 18.
56. Hedley Donovan, *From Roosevelt to Reagan* (New York: Harper & Row, 1985), p. 239.
57. Ibid., p. 209.
58. Jack Watson, interview with the author, August 19, 1988.
59. Ibid.
60. Joseph A. Califano, Jr., *Governing America* (New York: Simon and Schuster, 1981), p. 89.
61. Brzezinski, *Power and Principle*, p. 22.
62. Ibid, pp. 21–22.
63. Hans Mark, interview with the author, August 15, 1989.
64. Ibid.
65. Ibid.
66. Donovan, *From Roosevelt to Reagan*, p. 209.
67. Edwin Meese, interview with the author, June 15, 1989.
68. Jane Mayer and Doyle McManus, *Landslide* (Boston: Houghton Mifflin, 1988), p. 29.
69. Robert McFarlane, interview with the author, June 16, 1989.
70. Helene von Damm, *At Reagan's Side* (New York: Doubleday, 1988), p. 184.
71. Larry Speakes, *Speaking Out* (New York: Charles Scribner's Sons, 1988), p. 92.
72. Mayer and McManus, *Landslide*, p. 169.
73. Ibid.
74. Von Damm, *At Reagan's Side*, p. 319.
75. McFarlane, interview with the author.
76. Donald Regan, *For the Record* (New York: St. Martin's Press, 1988), p. 109.
77. Quoted in Bob Schieffer and Gary Gates, *The Acting President* (New York: E. P. Dutton, 1989), p. 95.
78. Ibid.
79. Ibid., p. 94.
80. Meese, interview with the author.
81. Quoted by Hedrick Smith in *Reagan: The Man, The President* (New York: Macmillan, 1980), p. 171.
82. Meese, interview with the author.
83. Regan, *For the Record*, p. 278.
84. Ibid., p. 279.
85. Ibid., pp. 278, 305.
86. Mayer and McManus, *Landslide*, p. 28.
87. Regan, *For the Record*, p. 305.
88. Ibid.
89. Speakes, *Speaking Out*, p. 305.
90. Von Damm, *At Reagan's Side*, p. 320.
91. Ibid., p. 198.

92. Regan, *For the Record*, p. 299.
93. Ibid., p. 309.
94. Mayer and McManus, *Landslide*, p. 393.
95. Meese, interview with the author.
96. Ibid.
97. Ford, interview with the author.
98. Mayer and McManus, *Landslide*, p. 394.

Chapter 7

Lessons from the Past, Suggestions for the Future

As is the case with all organizations, the "White House" has undergone changes since its inception in the 1930s. As more individuals were assigned to provide assistance to the president, role specializations evolved, functional areas of responsibility developed, and hierarchical levels emerged. Over time, more attention focused on the development of structures, both formal and emergent, as well as on systems of information flow. A variety of factors affected each White House organization, including the president's personality, his working and social relationships with staff, and his managerial and communication styles. These factors were interactive influences on the functions for which a president and his staff are responsible from one administration to another. In the White House, as in other organizations, its structure(s), both formal and informal, and its systems of information flow are developed and utilized by the president and his key aides. These structures and systems, along with the president's decision-making, management, and communication styles, interrelate in the conduct of the organization's daily business.

This study's emphasis on the White House as an organization and the special role of the president's inner circle in that organization is a result of the senior staff's evolution as a significant influence on the chief executive since the 1930s. In the 1980 edition of *Presidential Power*, Richard Neustadt admits that the lack of attention paid to presidential staffs in the 1960 version of his book was a mistake: "A President's associates can so contribute to his personal destruction that the staffing of the Presidency ought to be discussed in its own terms."[1] Additionally, more recent studies of the presidency by political scientists show evidence of their increasing awareness of the relevance of organizational theory to the study of the presidency, and the importance of the staff, particularly the senior staff, in the conduct of the presidency.

In Stephen Hess's first edition of *Organizing the Presidency*, for instance, he emphasizes that the book's chief conclusion is that "effective presidential leadership in the immediate future is likely to result only from creating more nearly collegial administrations in which Presidents rely on their Cabinet officers as the principal sources of advice."[2] In the second edition of his book, Hess discusses the need for a "more functional" presidency (eliminating mention of a collegial one) in which the chief executive must determine "what a cabinet can and ought to do, what a staff can and ought to do."[3] In most of the modern presidencies, emphasis has been placed on what the *staff* can do; organizational structures have been developed to purposively assign increasing responsibility to, and therefore invest greater power in, the president's personal aides. And, as this study illustrates, the choices a chief executive makes to develop structure, create systems of information flow, and communicate with key and close aides are often reactions to the choices made by his predecessor(s).

Harry Truman's concern about Franklin Roosevelt's competitive management style affected the ways he directed and communicated with his staff. Dwight Eisenhower's concerns about the lack of administrative efficiency in the Democrat presidencies he succeeded prompted his adoption of a hierarchical, pyramidal formal organizational structure. Kennedy and Johnson, convinced that formal structures did not enhance idea generation and policy development, preferred to initiate less formal, more fluid structures in their White Houses. Gerald Ford and Jimmy Carter, in reaction to what they perceived as structural, as well as managerial, deficiencies in Nixon's administration, initially decided to become hubs of information-receiving wheels in order to avoid the isolation from information they attributed to Nixon. Jack Watson, former senior staff member in the Carter administration, described the Ford–Carter reaction to the perceived problems in the Nixon White House as follows:

> The fallout from Watergate and the Nixon imperial presidency and 'the palace guard'; the authoritarian doorkeeper chief of staff; the 'us and them' mentality between the president and his men and women and his Cabinet, all those negative connotations to the Nixon presidency had profound effects on the ways both Ford and Carter conducted their presidencies.[4]

Colin Campbell, who has studied White House management in the Carter and Reagan presidencies, has written that since the Nixon administration, "incumbents have wrestled with the rehabilitation of the presidency. . . . As well, they have had to take pains to avoid even the appearance of a Nixon-style White House."[5] According to Michael Medved, Nixon's abandonment of his self-imposed isolation would not have prevented the Watergate scandal because the Nixon presidency was doomed by the personal characteristics of the man interacting with a set of circumstances that seemed to seal his fate: "There is absolutely no evidence to suggest that even the most unlimited communication between this particular President and all of his chosen aides could have rescued him from his self-destructive course."[6]

Ironically, Nixon's formal organizational structure, with its use of a strong chief of staff, initially did not prevent information flow into the Oval Office. Had the president continued to use the structure he instituted, borrowed from the man he served as vice president, it might have protected him from the isolation with which he eventually surrounded himself. Gradually, and as the Watergate cover-up evolved, the president's lack of communication with most of his senior aides contributed to his personal and political demise. By mid-1974, Nixon's White House, specifically the cadre of senior aides he had chosen as his personal staff, was no longer a team, a work force he once tried to mold, manage, and motivate as an extension of himself.

In 1981, when Ronald Reagan was inaugurated, the scandal known as Watergate had dimmed in the public memory and other sets of problems and issues, such as the nation's economic slump and its weakened image as an international military power, had captured the interest and/or concern of voters in the 1980 election. For a time the choices Reagan made to structure and manage the White House served him well—until he forgot some of the lessons in organizational leadership that Ford and Carter had learned. In his second term, Reagan failed to remember some of the mistakes made by his fellow Californian as the Watergate scandal evolved, including a propensity for detachment from close aides, the avoidance of multiple viewpoints from other sources of information, and an ambivalence about presidential management of, and communication with, his senior aides. As a result, he was doomed to repeat these mistakes, and the result was a scratch on the "Teflon presidency": the Iran-Contra debacle.

Hess emphasizes that there are no easy answers to the question of how best to organize and manage the presidency, and that though organizational design, or a lack thereof, may help or hinder a president in reaching his goals, the mettle of the president remains the decisive factor in assessing his ability to attain success.[7] While the author agrees with this statement, too few scholars, particularly in the field of communication, have studied the implications of organizational design for the White House, including the ways that structure, both formal and informal, may limit or increase the flow of information to the president, as well as the sources from which that information comes, and the influences of structure on the communicative relationships among participants in the decision-making process. Scandals such as Watergate do result for a time in the alteration of hierarchical structures and systems of information flow in the White House, and they prompt isolated scholarly assessments of the relationship among structures, staffs, and a president's personal characteristics. But between scandals little is done to recommend ways that presidents can design structures to fit functions and improve policy-making interactions between a chief executive and his staff.

With the understanding that structure is only one, albeit one very important, element of the White House as an organization, what is the optimal structure that a president can create and use to organize and implement the work of the White House? Ronald Reagan's return to a formal, pyramidal structure and an accompanying philosophy of detachment from White House management may be an anomaly among post-Watergate presidents in the foreseeable future. Some of the problems Nixon faced emerged under similar organizational conditions in the Reagan White House in the form of the Iran-Contra scandal. George Bush appears to have returned, despite his appointment of a strong chief of staff, to an organizational structure and system of information flow using multiple sources that is reminiscent of Gerald Ford. A president's choice of organizational structure is a reflection of his personality, his past experience, his work habits, and, to some extent, his presidential goals. Such was certainly the case with Dwight Eisenhower, and Greenstein has suggested that aspects of Ike's informal, "hidden-hand" leadership within the formal structure he created may be useful to future presidents. Would Eisenhower's style be effective in a political climate different from that in which he found himself? Would his structure be suitable to a chief executive with a different background, a different personality?

Although Hess has observed that "imaginative people prefer to work within systems of least constraint," presidents who view themselves as policymakers and not administrators would do well to remember that formal structure need not undermine policy generation; it does provide a framework that may offer a difference between creativity and chaos, a lesson learned by staff in the Carter administration.[8] Accordingly, the author agrees with Colin Campbell that "a mix of the hierarchical and spokes-in-a-wheel models . . . best serves the president in pursuing the often conflicting goals of executive branch harmony and access to the Oval Office."[9] He observes that an "excessively hierarchical White House" may collapse under its own weight or, perhaps more to the point, the sole use of hierarchical lines of responsibility and communication to generate ideas, solutions, and programs may strangle such attempts.[10] A total lack of structure, however, leaves the doors of the White House open to anyone wishing to wield power and authority in the name of the president, without the permission of the president—to build coalitions within the organization that may serve personal, not presidential, ends.

The combination of a hierarchical formal structure and a spokes-of-the-wheel communication system between president and staff is a workable design for the modern presidency. Such a design should include a chief of staff, not as a guard but as a guide to both the president and other members of the White House's senior staff. Samuel Kernell has discussed the White House as an organization of transients who need someone, a chief of staff, to assume authority and responsibility among a president's staff. While one may disagree with this characterization of the White House, especially since a number of senior staff in one White House may reappear one or two administrations later in similar organizational roles, one can agree with his observation that internal coordination breaks down in the absence of authority within the organization, and that it may become unresponsive if no one is in a position of authority to override procedures occasionally.[11]

Therein lies a lesson learned, albeit too late, by the post-Watergate presidents: that there is a middle ground between openness and accessibility in the White

House and the structural control needed to maintain order and organizational discipline, especially among senior staff, and facilitate the accomplishment of organizational goals. As an organizational leader, a president cannot exhibit a completely democratic or a completely autocratic, a totally participative or a totally directive, style as he interacts with the people who serve him. Gerald Ford's organizational structure was conducive to a relatively free flow of communication between him and his aides, yet it could not prevent, and perhaps facilitated, intrastaff conflict.

Jimmy Carter's spokes-of-the-wheel structure, made more unwieldy by the lack of a designated staff coordinator or chief of staff until late in his presidency, could not prioritize and adequately monitor the development of his programmatic ideas. His open administration became synonymous with an inadequately managed organization, a view fostered by the president's management and communication styles. Ironically, the president apparently put great stock in the linking role he asked Jack Watson to assume, that of being a liaison between the White House and state and local governments. Had Carter invested more time and attention in the creation of organizational linkages between his White House and Congress, as well as other groups external to the Executive Branch, he might have improved his relationships with a variety of constituencies outside the White House.

Ronald Reagan's pyramidal organizational structure fostered organizational control but little creativity—a result in large part of the president's detached management style that eschewed a personal reliance on information and ideas from multiple sources that might have challenged the ideological bases for programs and policies created in his White House. The Iran-Contra scandal illustrated that presidents must not equate delegation with abdication of their responsibility to seek and use information from sources outside their inner circle in the decision-making process. Moreover, as the preceding pages reveal, presidents must understand the importance of using information-rich media to assess the depth and breadth of staff knowledge of, and commitment to, proposed programs and policies. Face-to-face interactions, whether in small groups or individual consultations, and the use of candid memoranda have no equal as means of communicating one's perceptions and suggestions within the White House.

Organizational structures and processes of information flow are not, of course, the only elements essential for the development and maintenance of the White House organization—and the creation and motivation of the president's senior staff. The ways he communicates with staff are related to the formal and informal structures within which the work of the White House is conducted, his preferred means of seeking and receiving information, and especially the personal preferences for communicating with other human beings he brings with him to the Oval Office. In Chapter 6 the communication styles of former presidents are discussed on the basis of observations from senior staff who interacted frequently with them. While communication styles generally are reflections of personal characteristics, it may be beneficial to future presidents to suggest communication competencies that presidents and their key aides should possess and/or develop to assist the development and execution of the policies that represent a president's goals—his national agenda.

Medved has suggested that character, "rather than specialized skill or a record of accomplishment, is the key criterion for a successful Presidential aide. His effectiveness will be determined by the personal chemistry between two human beings."[12] Yet that personal chemistry is achieved and nurtured through the communicative relationship that develops between the president and a member of his staff. In their discussions with the author, former White House senior staff suggested a variety of communication skills or competencies that White House aides should possess to assist each other and the president in the attainment of organizational goals.

The ability to speak and write clearly and succinctly was the competency mentioned by senior aides from all three post-Watergate presidencies as being particularly important in White House interactions between the chief executive and his aides. Terrence O'Donnell suggested the need for force and clarity in memoranda not only to communicate information and advice adequately but also to recognize the demands on the president's time. Zbigniew Brzezinski, who served a president who relied on written communications as a primary source of information, confirmed the need for this ability among senior staff. Similarly, Jack Watson, another senior member of the Carter staff, emphasized:

> You've got to be able to write. You've got to be able to express thoughts, opinions, analyses on paper clearly, succinctly, and cogently. And if you can't do that, you're not going to be successful. It is not enough to be able to speak clearly and to communicate clearly in an oral way. That's terribly important, but in order to really be at the highest level of effectiveness, you've got to have the capacity for the other—written communication.[13]

Edwin Meese, apparently unlike Robert McFarlane, was adept at developing a communication style that captured the attention and interest of President Reagan. He observed that the "ability to organize thoughts and express them concisely and comprehensively" is a critical communication competency within the White House.[14] McFarlane confirmed the importance of brevity and clarity when communicating with the president. In his words, comments to the president, particularly delivered orally, "had to be brief."[15] According to McFarlane, aides should "think through their central points and present them as succinctly as they can and not blabber on forever."[16]

A second communication competency mentioned by former senior staff interviewed for this study is the ability to listen. Indeed, according to Jody Powell, "the best and most important communication skill is the ability to listen."[17] To be an effective listener, Donald Rumsfeld observes, "You have to have energy because it takes time to deal with human beings—above you, below you. And it takes a good deal of patience.''[18] Rumsfeld also emphasizes the importance of team building as a competency needed by staff members, suggesting that it is important for individuals in the White House, as in other organizations, to ''feel that they're a part of something.''[19] This skill not only assists in task accomplishment but may help staff members avoid intraorganizational conflict if they relate to one another as members of a team rather than a loose-knit coalition of individuals whose self-interests override their commitment to the president and his agenda.

Anne Wexler suggests that effective communicators in the White House ''don't hold power to themselves but share power. I think people have to have enough sense of themselves to be able to deal with the kind of power that comes with working in the White House, to be able to share it without worrying about it.''[20] If team building *within* the White House is a valued communication skill, so is the ability to mediate differences of opinion and conflicting information brought to staff from *outside* the White House. According to Stuart Eizenstat, the White House is a place where conflicts concerning significant issues with important consequences for groups and individuals are brought for resolution.

> Therefore, the people who bring those conflicts to the White House . . . bring them with a sense of passion, a sense of mission, and a sense of urgency which creates every day a sense of semi-crisis because the people involved in the process feel so passionate about the positions that they are taking. You've got to be able to, at one and the same time, understand those passions and understand those conflicts and . . . get to the real facts, knowing that you're going to get conflicting facts as well as conflicting recommendations, and present the president with all the ammunition and all the information he needs to make a coherent judgment, and to try to fit that decision into what you think to be his broader goals.[21]

A related requisite skill needed by White House staff is the ability to negotiate with colleagues, representatives of constituencies outside the White House, including the federal departments, and sometimes the president. Indeed, in the early months of an administration negotiation is an important skill as the White House is being organized; in subsequent months it becomes important when developing and promoting policy recommendations as one communicates with other members of the staff, the president, and then a variety of external constituencies, including members of Congress and special interest groups.

Consequently, the ability to *persuade* one's peers, as well as the president, becomes an important communication competency in the White House and may be exhibited in a variety of ways. For instance, James Connor recalls the persuasive ability possessed by Alan Greenspan in the Ford White House. His authority within that administration

> grew, and grew not because Alan is the most dynamic, powerful speaker in the world. He is not a table-pounding person, but day in and day out Alan Greenspan said sensible things. . . . And as the administration evolved, I think Alan's role and advice became

more and more important. And Alan managed to do it in a way that ultimately did not become terribly threatening.[22]

Concurrently, Connor notes the importance of establishing credibility among one's peers inside the White House by honoring an internal "code of ethics." In the Ford administration Connor observed that those staff not known to leak information to the press or other individuals outside the White House were listened to more carefully than those recognized as organizational sieves.

When you know somebody doesn't play the game in the press, then you are likely to bring them in on more things; you are more likely to be more candid in your judgments or reservations or hesitations about a thing. You are likely to be more honest in your discourse with them than with somebody . . . you have to be guarded with.[23]

Based on the comments of staff interviewed for this study, the ability to communicate effectively in small groups emerges as a significant communication skill inside the White House, one that Alexander Haig, Donald Regan, and H. R. Haldeman, to name three senior staff in different administrations, did not appear to possess. Yet Donald Rumsfeld and James Baker, two crucial components of the communication process in their White Houses, understood the importance of regularly discussing issues and information among the senior staff, and were adept at structuring discussions as well as involving all, or most, members of their senior staffs in such settings.

The abilities to write and speak clearly, to listen, to manage conflicts through mediation, to develop a team approach to task accomplishment, and to persuasively communicate one's opinion to peers and the president are necessary communication competencies needed by senior staff in the White House, according to former presidential aides. Zbigniew Brzezinski valued several of these skills, as is evidenced by the following description he gave the author of ways he communicated with members of his own staff in the National Security Council to facilitate task accomplishment and improve morale.

I had a weekly meeting in which I would in some length tell them about my meetings with the president, including little items of personal gossip. . . . I could give them the feeling vicariously that they were working for the president by sharing these things with them, and never once in the four years did I have an indiscretion. Yet I gave them a lot of feeling that they were involved. At the same time, I would also insist on a thorough reporting of everything they do at the end of each day. No staffer was permitted to leave for home until he filed with my office a minimum one-page, maximum two-page, report of everything he did that day that was of consequence and I should know about, in his judgment. That was his responsibility to make sure that I knew what I ought to know. And that included any decisions taken in interagency meetings, any position taken by him on my behalf at an interagency meeting, any contacts with foreign diplomats, any contacts with the press, any significant cable traffic that should be brought to my attention, and anything else they felt I ought to know.

I would get at the end of the day a book of about fifty pages in a black folder. And before I went home, I would read the damn thing and I would write in the margins my responses or comments, such as "good" or . . . "come and see me" or "provide more detail," etc. And that would go back to the staffer first thing in the morning. And then the entire book, minus some sensitive sections which were indicated by them or by me, would be available for the entire staff to see, so that every staffer would know what others are doing.

That procedure was abandoned after I left office by my successors. And I am convinced that part of the Irangate problem wouldn't have arisen if they had had such a procedure, because you wouldn't have had that whole section of the staff running foreign policy on its own. That gave each staffer a sense that he was very valuable. Secondly, I had the principle that any staffer could see me anytime he wanted. . . . Not every national security officer has done that. In fact, I know that most of them have not. Again, that was important to the staff. So I used these techniques essentially to give them the feeling of involvement, that they were engaged in a very special enterprise.[24]

The coordinated written and oral communications with his staff that Brzezinski developed attempted to fashion a balance between accessibility and control that chief executives often find difficult to attain in their interactions with senior staff. He used rich sources of information, such as small group meetings, to share data as well as to increase staff morale. Additionally, he used written materials to maintain ongoing documentation of highly sensitive data. In so doing he satisfied the information needs of his own organization as well as the social needs of its members. To be effective communicators within the White House, presidents must satisfy these same needs, and to do so requires a number of communication competencies.

One such skill is the ability to initiate structure in the White House, including the creation of a formal system of reporting relationships, the use of structuration (such as rules, procedures, and regularly scheduled meetings), and the oversight of informal, emergent structures, such as work teams in specific policy areas. Some presidents are more experienced than others as the creators and managers of structure. However, all must have an understanding of the implications for a White House where structure does not fit the president's information needs and/or is not clearly understood by those whose work is organized and monitored in accordance with their place in the organization's formal structure and their participation in its emergent networks.

Among the post-Watergate presidents, Jimmy Carter misunderstood the worth of formal, hierarchical structure in the White House, and as a result senior staff were forced to develop a number of time-consuming processes to organize the White House and its work. Gerald Ford, reacting to the Watergate scandal, almost made the same mistake until he personally observed the chaos caused by the absence of a chief of staff or staff coordinator. Ronald Reagan initiated the same type of structure in his White House that he used in California's statehouse, forgetting that the success of a hierarchical, pyramidal organizational structure depends on the abilities and capabilities of those who are granted authority at the top of such structures. In his first term he was well served by this structure; in the second term he was not. However, it was the fault of the staff, not the structure, that caused organizational and political problems for the president.

Future presidents would do well to learn from this lesson—any organizational structure is as good as the people who comprise it. And a president is ultimately responsible for the structure he chooses to use in the White House and for communicating the expectations he has for what that structure is designed to accomplish, including effective intrastaff working relationships *and* the development and implementation of policies and programs.

A second communication competency needed by chief executives, as identified by several former White House staff interviewed for this study, is the ability to provide clear directions to staff about a president's expectations, either orally or in writing. Stuart Eizenstat, Carter's chief of domestic policy, observes that

> Just as a chief executive of a corporation has got to impart to the corporation, to the vice presidents and the line managers and the shareholders and the investors and the Wall Street community a sense of where the company is going, so, too, a chief executive has to do more than make decisions. He's got to be able to put those decisions into a broader context or under a broader umbrella . . . the decisions have to have a common thread. They have to hold together so people have a sense of what it is you're trying to do.[25]

More specifically, Edwin Meese suggests, a president must have the ability to "communicate his wishes and his aspirations, his visions of what ought to be done so that somebody doesn't go quite a ways down the line and then find that he's on the wrong track as far as what the president wants."[26] Hans Mark, secretary of the air force in both the Carter and Reagan administrations mused:

> You can burn all the position papers and all the leather-covered reports and all the rest of the stuff that the think tank turns out. In the end the president is the one who has to wrap the country around himself and then distill from that a few things—two or three things that are important—and then go on from there.[27]

This distillation process is equally important for communication with staff, as Robert McFarlane emphasized in a discussion with the author, so that staff can understand the president's two or three major priorities in a given policy area, such as foreign affairs. To lead a staff, much less a country, a president must know where he is going. If he knows but is not able to communicate the directions to his staff, he will not arrive at his preferred destination.

When communicating with his staff about his goals and the priorities among them, a president would do well to understand the importance of team building in the White House. This, too, is a communication competency—the ability to forge a coalition of staff around him in order to stifle temptations for individuals to pursue their individual political agendas, minimize intrastaff conflict, and facilitate task accomplishment. The passion seen in public oratory is no less important inside the White House—leaders cannot mobilize followers, and presidents cannot mold teams and motivate them, without emphasizing the need for intrastaff cooperation and group commitment to the organization's, the president's, goals. Few of the modern presidents have been competent team builders inside the White House, even though several knew how to harness the support of external constituent groups to win elections. Some, like Nixon, were uncomfortable in groups because of the nature of their personalities. Others were simply unable to motivate their staffs, because the sets of experiences that prepared them for the presidency did not prepare them to be organizational leaders, or even leaders of a small group of senior staff.

Additionally, some presidents have found it difficult to translate their passion for public issues into motivational communication strategies within the White House. Anne Wexler, who emphasizes that Jimmy Carter was a better communicator inside the White House than he was in public settings, observes: "I don't think he was a passionless president. He just couldn't express passion. I think he was a very passionate president about a lot of things, but he never was publicly passionate. They couldn't write passionate words for him because he didn't know how to say it."[28] Moreover, Carter's penchant for receiving and sending written communication in the White House further distanced him from staff as a team builder.

On the other hand, Ronald Reagan apparently was passionate about one or two major issues or themes around which his administration built a legislative agenda. In private, as well as in public, Reagan repeatedly and forcefully articulated these themes to staff, and as a result, at least in his first term, the senior staff was more of a team, a cohesive working group, than was the case in previous administrations.

Two additional communication competencies that presidents would do well to possess were identified as interview transcripts, archival materials, and secondary sources were reviewed for this study. Presidents must become more adept at confronting and managing conflict among their staffs. Such conflict affects both the personal and the professional relationships of those involved and may undermine policy-making as well as the president's position as organizational leader. Additionally, the president should understand the importance of feedback, communicated orally and/or in writing, as a mechanism to assure his policy is being implemented, as well as to praise and critique staff work. Robert McFarlane emphasizes that "The president basically should be able to . . . set goals and criteria and from then on . . . criticize the ideas and programs that are sent back to him for achieving those goals."[29]

Lyndon Johnson, though intemperate at times in both praise and "punishment," understood the worth of responding frequently to staff work. A president's verbal reactions to staff work may also assist in conflict management and in the process of team building, as was the case in the White House of Harry Truman. George Christian, press secretary to Johnson, doubts that "we'll ever have a system again where you have the opportunity [as a staff member] to discuss things in depth with the president."[30] He anticipates that oral communication between president and staff will become increasingly difficult due to the time demands on the chief executive. One would hope that such does not become the case. As is indicated throughout these pages, senior staff who have served in recent administrations feel a strong, existing need for presidents and their staffs to possess several communication competencies, both oral and written, in order to organize and conduct the work of the White House. In an era where corporations as well as nonprofit organizations are emphasizing the need for personnel with a variety of communication skills, the White House, the Oval Office, should be no exception.

This study is based on the premise that we may pay too much attention to public posturing by a president and insufficiently acknowledge that the products of his administration are results of the reading, listening, debating and persuading that is the daily regimen of "private" presidential activity. The degree to which a president is an effective communicator within the White House may not be publicly seen or rewarded. That does not mean it is unimportant. Indeed, as the previous chapters illustrate, the White House is a communication-intensive organization where every function, every task, depends on the flow and exchange of oral or written information. Information processing is an important activity in the birth stage of any organization so as to reduce equivocality. In the White House it is part and parcel of every stage within a president's term, even the transition from an outgoing administration to an incoming one. Effective communication between president and staff—that which provides for the sharing of information that is cogent and clear and outlines a president's alternatives and the ramifications of each alternative, that which fosters an environment of interpersonal trust between the chief executive and his staff and among staff, that which creates a system that provides for accessibility to the president as well as the delegation of nonpresidential responsibilities—affects a president's success as a decision maker and a creator of public policy.

Do managerial and communication skills exhibited inside the White House make any difference to the success of a presidency? Ronald Reagan was neither an effective manager nor an effective communicator within his White House. Yet if success is measured by popularity ratings and election results, he was indeed a successful president. When Reagan's detachment from his organization, which was very different from Eisenhower's hidden-hand leadership style, is analyzed by historians in the context of policies made and decisions executed, when the glow of the "shining city on the hill" is gone, the "success" of the Reagan administration may be seriously questioned. Greenstein has written that Eisenhower was a much more effective leader than most scholars and many citizens have realized, but he was not an adept politician. Therefore his management style and the methods of intraorganizational communication he used may be his greatest legacy, not his use of them.[31] A similar argument can be made for Gerald Ford, whose presidency is still under the historian's microscope.

Communication within the White House is the process through which presidential decisions are made and executed, and the quality of those decisions depends in large part on the effectiveness of communication between the president and his senior aides. Presidential–staff interaction is therefore not an insignificant dynamic in the conduct and the study of the presidency. Moreover, despite the relative success of Reagan's Cabinet councils, and the suggestions that Cabinet government is the more appropriate form of presidential government, the White House staff have been, and for a long time to come will continue to be, those who in reality, not theoretically, have the trust and the ear of the president. Ann Whitman, personal secretary to Eisenhower, wrote in a letter to the president of the *Nashville Banner* on March 10, 1955:

> First of all—the White House is a human organization composed of men and women, who do get tired; who do lose their tempers; who do occasionally rub people against the grain; who sometimes, because an instant decision is required, may have to make up their minds before they have all the facts.
>
> Of course, in all their relations with the public, they must do everything they can to further the purposes of any person or group honestly and intelligently concerned with the betterment of the country. But the staff's first objective must always be such service to the President that he may most easily and wisely make decisions for himself. His peace of mind, for instance, must come first before the maintenance of the staff's own friendly relations with any individual or organization. That is true, too, of his schedule, the conservation of his energy, and scores of other factors that may affect his effectiveness.[32]

In discussing the White House senior staff as an organization with those interviewed for this study, it is clear that the White House staff is not a family. James Connor muses: "Families have idiot sons and paterfamilias . . . long-suffering aunts and that ain't what a president's staff should be."[33] It is a group of individuals assuming organizational roles, usually with defined or semi-defined responsibilities in functional areas. It is a working organization whose members often do not socialize outside the work environment because there is not sufficient time in their lives and because, like members of other organizations, their friends are not necessarily their colleagues. However, as is the case with other organizational leaders, the president must recognize, from the moment he realizes he will be a successor to Washington, Lincoln, and the Roosevelts, that he must endeavor to listen to them, to talk with them, to create an organizational environment that will be mutually beneficial as they attempt to serve him. They must understand what he expects in the form of information and advice; he must assure them he will listen to the products of their labors.

A president need not, and should not, agree with every bit of information, every piece of advice, his senior staff provides. Yet he must know how to ask for and evaluate that information and advice. He must develop an organizational structure that ensures staff access to him and *his* access to information, with the understanding that a chief of staff need not be an impediment to, but a facilitator of, those processes. He must understand that communication inside the White House is no less important than that which he directs to press and public. It is less visible, but just as critical, to the exercise of his duties as chief executive, commander in chief, and head of state.

In an era of American history in which corporate executives are realizing the worth of intraorganizational communication to create supportive climates for employees and to maximize the productivity of their organizations, future U.S. presidents would do well to remember that productivity and morale are interrelated and interdependent. They would do well to remember that the chosen few who literally and figuratively surround a president inside the White House are those to whom he has entrusted much of his future, a future that will depend in large part on the communicative relationships that evolve within its walls.

NOTES

1. Richard E. Neustadt, *Presidential Power: The Politics of Leadership from FDR to Carter* (New York: John Wiley & Sons, 1980), p. 193.
2. Stephen Hess, *Organizing the Presidency* (Washington, DC: The Brookings Institution, 1976), p. 154.
3. Stephen Hess, *Organizing the Presidency*, 2d ed. (Washington, DC: The Brookings Institution, 1988), p. 232.
4. Jack Watson, interview with the author, April 12, 1989.
5. Colin Campbell, S.J., *Managing the Presidency: Carter, Reagan and the Search for Executive Harmony* (Pittsburgh: University of Pittsburgh Press, 1986), p. 263.
6. Michael Medved, *The Shadow Presidents* (New York: Times Books, 1979), p. 364.
7. Hess, p. 233.
8. Hess, p. 73.
9. Campbell, *Managing the Presidency*, p. 111.
10. Ibid.
11. Samuel Kernell and Samuel Popkin, *Chief of Staff* (Berkeley: University of California Press, 1986), p. 224.
12. Medved, *The Shadow Presidents*, p. 365.
13. Jack Watson, interview with the author, August 19, 1988.
14. Edwin Meese, interview with the author, June 15, 1989.
15. Robert McFarlane, interview with the author, June 16, 1989.
16. Ibid.
17. Jody Powell, interview with the author, June 16, 1989.
18. Donald Rumsfeld, interview with the author, August 10, 1987.
19. Ibid.
20. Anne Wexler, interview with the author, June 15, 1989.
21. Stuart Eizenstat, interview with the author, June 16, 1989.
22. James Connor, interview with the author, July 15, 1987.
23. Ibid.
24. Zbigniew Brzezinski, interview with the author, June 14, 1989.
25. Eizenstat, interview with the author.
26. Meese, interview with the author.
27. Hans Mark, interview with the author, August 15, 1989.
28. Wexler, interview with the author.

29. McFarlane, interview with the author.

30. George Christian, interview with the author, August 1, 1989.

31. Fred I. Greenstein, *The Hidden-Hand Presidency: Eisenhower as Leader* (New York: Basic Books, 1982), p. 248.

32. Quoted in Robert J. Donovan, *Confidential Secretary: Ann Whitman's Twenty Years with Eisenhower and Rockfeller* (New York: E. P. Dutton, 1988), p. 84.

33. Connor, interview with the author.

Selected Bibliography

Adams, Sherman. *Firsthand Report*. New York: Harper & Brothers, 1961.

Ambrose, Stephen E. *Eisenhower. Vol. 2: The President*. New York: Simon and Schuster, 1983.

Bonafede, Dom. "White House Staffing: The Nixon-Ford Era." In Thomas E. Cronin and Rexford G. Tugwell, *The Presidency Reappraised*, 2d ed. New York: Praeger, 1977.

Brzezinski, Zbigniew. *Power and Principle*. New York: Farrar, Straus, Giroux, 1983.

Campbell, Colin, S.J. *Managing the Presidency: Carter, Reagan and the Search for Executive Harmony*. Pittsburgh: University of Pittsburgh Press, 1986.

Carter, Jimmy. *Keeping Faith*. New York: Bantam Books, 1982.

Cyert, R. M., and J. G. March. *A Behavioral Theory of the Firm*. Englewood Cliffs, NJ: Prentice-Hall, 1963.

Daft, Richard L., and Robert H. Lengel. "Organizational Information Requirements, Media Richness and Structural Design," *Management Science*, 32, no. 5, May 1986, pp. 554–71.

———. "Information Richness: A New Approach to Managerial Behavior and Organization Design." In Larry L. Cummings and Barry N. Staw, eds., *Research in Organizational Behavior*, Vol. 6. Greenwich, CT: JAI Press, 1984.

Donovan, Robert J. *Confidential Secretary: Ann Whitman's Twenty Years with Eisenhower and Rockefeller*. New York: E. P. Dutton, 1988.

Ehrlichman, John. *Witness to Power: The Nixon Years*. New York: Simon and Schuster, 1982.

Eisenhower, Dwight D. *The White House Years: Mandate for Change, 1953–1956*. Garden City, NY: Doubleday, 1963.

Feigenbaum, Edward D. "Staffing, Organization, and Decision-making in the Ford and Carter White Houses." *Presidential Studies Quarterly*, Summer 1980, pp. 364–77.

Ford, Gerald R. *A Time to Heal*. New York: Harper & Row and The Reader's Digest Association, 1979.

George, Alexander L. *Presidential Decisionmaking in Foreign Policy: The Effective Use of Information and Advice*. Boulder, CO: Westview Press, 1980.

Graff, Henry F. *The Tuesday Cabinet: Deliberation and Decision on Peace and War Under Lyndon B. Johnson*. Englewood Cliffs, NJ: Prentice-Hall, 1970.

Greenstein, Fred I. *The Hidden-Hand Presidency: Eisenhower as Leader*. New York: Basic Books, 1982.

Haldeman, H. R., with Joseph DiMona. *The Ends of Power*. New York: New York Times Books, 1978.

Heller, Francis H., ed. *The Truman White House: The Administration of the Presidency, 1945–1953*. Lawrence: Regents Press of Kansas, 1980.

Henderson, Phillip G. *Managing the Presidency*. Boulder, CO: Westview Press, 1988.

Hess, Stephen. *Organizing the Presidency*, 2d ed. Washington, DC: The Brookings Institution, 1988.

The Hoover Commission Report on Organization of the Executive Branch of the Government. New York: McGraw-Hill, 1949.

Jablin, Fredric M. "Formal Organization Structure." In Fredric M. Jablin, Linda L. Putnam, Karlene H. Roberts, and Lyman W. Porter, eds., *Handbook of Organizational Communication*. Beverly Hills, CA: Sage, 1987.

Kernell, Samuel, and Samuel Popkin. *Chief of Staff*. Berkeley: University of California Press, 1986.

Kissinger, Henry. *White House Years*. Boston: Little, Brown, 1979.

Light, Paul C. *The President's Agenda: Domestic Policy Choice from Kennedy to Carter*. Baltimore: Johns Hopkins University Press, 1982.

Lincoln, Evelyn. *My Twelve Years with John F. Kennedy*. New York: David McKay, 1965.

Mayer, Jane, and Doyle McManus. *Landslide: The Unmaking of the President, 1984–1988*. Boston: Houghton Mifflin, 1988.

McPhee, Robert D. "Formal Structures and Organizational Communication." In Robert D. McPhee and Phillip K. Tompkins, eds., *Organizational Communication: Traditional Themes and New Directions*. Beverly Hills, CA: Sage, 1985.

Medved, Michael. *The Shadow Presidents*. New York: Times Books, 1979.

Miller, Danny, and Peter H. Friesen. "A Longitudinal Study of the Corporate Life Cycle." *Management Science*, 10, 1984, pp. 1161–83.

Monge, Peter R., and Eric M. Eisenberg. "Emergent Communication Networks." In Fredic M. Jablin et al., eds., *Handbook of Organizational Communication*. Beverly Hills, CA: Sage, 1987.

Nathan, Richard P. *The Plot That Failed: Nixon and the Administrative Presidency*. New York: John Wiley & Sons, 1975.

Nixon, Richard M. *The Memoirs of Richard Nixon*. New York: Grosset & Dunlap, 1978.

Norton, Robert. *Communicator Style*. Beverly Hills, CA: Sage, 1983.

O'Reilly, Charles A., Jennifer A. Chatman, and John C. Anderson. "Message Flow and Decision Making." in Fredric M. Jablin et al., eds., *Handbook of Organizational Communication*. Beverly Hills, CA: Sage, 1987.

Ott, J. Steven. *The Organizational Culture Perspective*. Chicago: Dorsey Press, 1989.

Paper, Lewis, J. *The Promise and the Performance: The Leadership of John F. Kennedy*. New York: Crown, 1975.

Patterson, Bradley H., Jr. *The Ring of Power: The White House Staff and Its Expanding Role in Government*. New York: Basic Books, 1988.

Pfiffner, James P. "White House Staff Versus the Cabinet: Centripetal and Centrifugal Roles." *Presidential Studies Quarterly*, 16, no. 4, Fall 1986, pp. 666–90.

Poole, Marshall Scott, David R. Seibold, and Robert D. McPhee. "Group Decision-making as a Structurational Process." *Quarterly Journal of Speech*, 71, 1985, pp. 74–102.

Porter, L. W., and K. H. Roberts. "Communication in Organizations." In M. Dunnette, ed., *Handbook of Industrial and Organizational Psychology*. Chicago: Rand McNally, 1976.

Redford, Emmette S., and Richard T. McCulley. *White House Operations: The Johnson Presidency*. Austin: University of Texas Press, 1986.

Regan, Donald T. *For the Record*. New York: St. Martin's Press, 1988.

Riley, Patricia. "A Structurationist Account of Political Culture." *Administrative Science Quarterly*, 28, 1983, pp. 414–37.

Rollins, Alfred B. *Roosevelt and Howe*. New York: Alfred A. Knopf, 1962.

Salinger, Pierre. *With Kennedy*. Garden City, NY: Doubleday, 1966.

Sherwood, Robert E. *Roosevelt and Hopkins, an Intimate History*. New York: Harper & Brothers, 1948.

Sorenson, Theodore C. *Kennedy*. New York: Harper & Row, 1965.

———. *Decision-Making in the White House*. New York: Columbia University Press, 1963.

Spragens, William C. "White House Staffs, 1789–1974." in Bradley D. Nash, with Milton S. Eisenhower, Gordon R. Hoxie, and William C. Spragens, eds. *Organizing and Staffing the Presidency*. New York: Center for the Study of the Presidency, 1980.

Staff of the White Burkett Miller Center of Public Affairs, University of Virginia. *The Ford White House*. Lanham, MD: University Press of America, 1986.

Tetlock, Phillip E. "Accountability: The Neglected Social Context of Judgment and Choice." In Barry N. Staw and Larry L. Cummings, eds., *Research in Organizational Behavior*, Vol. 7. Greenwich, CT: JAI Press, 1985.

Thompson, Kenneth W., ed. *The Nixon Presidency*. New York: University Press of America, 1987.

Tower, John, Edmund Muskie, and Brent Scowcroft. *The Tower Commission Report*. New York: Bantam Books and Times Books, 1987.

Tully, Grace. *F.D.R. My Boss*. New York: Charles Scribner's Sons, 1949.

Wann, A. J. *The President as Chief Administrator: A Study of Franklin D. Roosevelt*. Washington, DC: Public Affairs Press, 1968.

Weick, Karl E. *The Social Psychology of Organizing*, 2d ed. Reading, MA: Addison-Wesley, 1979.

Index

ABOUT THE AUTHOR

PATRICIA DENNIS WITHERSPOON is associate dean of the College of Communication at the University of Texas and a faculty member in its Department of Speech Communication. Prior to joining U.T. Austin in 1985 she was Assistant to the Executive Vice Chancellor for Academic Affairs in the University of Texas System Administration. She holds an M.A. in Communication Arts from the University of Wisconsin and a Ph.D. in Communication from The University of Texas at Austin.

Dr. Witherspoon teaches in the area of organizational communication and currently offers a course on organizational leadership. She serves as a consultant to various professional organizations, conducting workshops related to different aspects of organizational communication. Her research interests are in organizational and political communication. She has published articles and book chapters, in addition to *Within These Walls*, in these areas of study.

Dr. Witherspoon has served on the board of directors of several community organizations, and chairs, or is a member of, numerous University and College of Communication committees. She has been listed in *Who's Who in American Women*, and has received the Eyes of Texas Award, given for excellence in service to the University of Texas.